NEVER BEFORE IN HISTORY
AMERICA'S INSPIRED BIRTH

BY GARY AMOS AND
RICHARD GARDINER

WILLIAM DEMBSKI
ACADEMIC EDITOR

*There are rare times and places, in the long human story, when
outbursts of human genius supply human civilization with the supreme wonders
of human greatness. It is the contemplation of these that raises the mass
of mankind to levels not unworthy of the divine image in which we were created.
Such moments of supreme achievement are to be found in Periclean Athens,
in the Florence of the Medecis, and in the London of Elizabeth—and Shakespeare.
However, never before—or since—has political genius burst in such profusion
on the human scene, as in the British colonies in America, in the latter part of the
eighteenth century. The period of the American Founding, from the Revolution
to the Framing, Ratification, and Inauguration of the Constitution, saw political
thought and action in the service of human freedom, of a wisdom and power
unsurpassed even by the glory of Greece or the grandeur of Rome. Every human
good we enjoy today is, directly or indirectly, a legacy from what the
Founders wrought, and Lincoln preserved.*

Harry V. Jaffa

PANDAS PUBLICATIONS: A SERIES ABOUT CENTRAL QUESTIONS
FROM HAUGHTON PUBLISHING COMPANY · DALLAS, TEXAS

*This publication was made possible
by a grant from the Hillcrest Foundation,
founded by Mrs. W.W. Caruth, Sr.*

ii

Book design: Buell Design

Printed in the United States of America

ISBN 0-914513-51-6
Library of Congress Catalog Card Number: 98-072936

The present book, *Never Before in History*, is a stirring call to re-evaluate the Founding of the United States. Its primary task is to teach us about the decisive role that Christianity played in the American Founding. It rightly recalls that many of the leading political theorists admired by the Founders were professed Christians. It rightly points out that the New England Puritans were already devoted to democratic government, long before independence in 1776. It rightly argues that the Founding principles are fully compatible with Christianity. It rightly asserts that the "separation of church and state" spoken of by Jefferson did not mean that government should not promote sound religious opinions among the people. Above all, this book demonstrates that if religion is banned from the public life of the nation, America's history and traditions are unintelligible.

There is no doubt that America is a Christian nation in the sense that the large majority of American citizens are and always have been Christians. But this book is careful to remind us that it is not true that America's principles are Christian in the sense that one must be a Christian to discover or believe in them. On the contrary: The Declaration of Independence, the Constitution, and the other Founding documents of our nation all make it clear that one does not have to be a Christian to be an American.

Scholars from America's most prestigious universities have long been telling us that we live under a "Godless Constitution."[1] It is not surprising that those hostile to religion would believe in a "Godless Constitution." Such people pretend to believe in government neutrality between religion and irreligion. But it is almost always religion that loses out when the neutrality principle is applied in practice.

Under the guise of the neutrality principle, the Supreme Court has ruled that children in public schools must be taught that human beings have evolved through a mindless, materialistic process from which the Creator is excluded. The same Court forbids the teaching not only of the Biblical account of creation, but even of any scientific evidence that points toward creation. The absurdity of this ruling is obvious on a moment's reflection. Creation is taught by our original Founding document, the Declaration of Independence: human beings are "endowed by their *Creator*" with the rights to life, liberty, and the pursuit of happiness. The Supreme Court has ruled, in effect, that it is unconstitutional to teach in public schools that the Declaration of Independence is true![2]

What is odd is that many Christians and traditionalists also accept the view that America's principles are hostile to Christianity. *Never Before in History* rightly contests that claim. What we need to understand today is that there are two great truths about America's original relation to Christianity. On the one hand, Christian theology, as it was understood in the English Whig tradition, strongly supports the basic ideas of the American Revolution. But the "sacred rights of mankind" are not knowable solely through the Christian tradition. Human reason, observing and reflecting on the basic facts of human nature, also affirms the "self-evident" truths of the Declaration without an appeal to Biblical revelation. The Founders considered both of these sources—Christian revelation and natural law—divine in origin and compatible with one another.

In 1780, before an audience including the governor, Senate, and House of Representatives of Massachusetts, the Reverend Samuel Cooper said:

> We want not, indeed, a special revelation from heaven to teach us that men are born equal and free.... These are the plain dictates of that reason and common sense with which the common parent of men has informed the human bosom. It is, however, a satisfaction to observe such everlasting maxims of equity confirmed...by the instructions, precepts, and examples given us in the sacred oracles [i.e., the Bible];...that they come from him "who hath made of one blood all nations to dwell upon the face of the earth."[3]

For Cooper, reason and revelation agree on the truth of human equality, the first principle of political justice.

Alexander Hamilton once wrote, "The sacred rights of mankind are not to be rummaged for among old parchments or musty records. They are written, as with a sunbeam, in the whole volume of human nature, by the hand of the divinity itself; and can never be erased or obscured by mortal power."[4] One does not have to read the Bible to understand this luminous truth.

Christian faith and human reason both teach the same lesson: all men are created equal. In this respect, *and in this respect alone*, the fundamental principles of the American Founding may rightly be said to be the principles of Christianity. *Never Before in History* shows, convincingly, that Christian writers before, during, and after the Reformation supported many of the ideas that led to the American Founding. However, this does not permit us to conclude that human reason, unassisted by faith, had nothing to do with the American Founding. This is perhaps the cardinal weakness of *Never Before in History*.

In its effort to remind us of the role of Christianity in the Founding, it does not discuss the philosophical, Enlightenment foundations of America in the depth that they merit. Nevertheless, this book is a welcome ally in the battle to reclaim the noble heritage that our Founders have bequeathed to us. That heritage has been covered over, denied, and denounced for too long. *Never Before in History* shows, without a doubt, that the authentic legacy of the Founding deserves our full and unhesitating loyalty.

Thomas G. West, Author of *Vindicating the Founders*

P R E F A C E

American History is a required course for high school students throughout the United States. Perhaps more than any other factor, this course shapes our understanding of American history and expresses who we are as a nation. Since America has become increasingly diverse in its cultural, ethnic, and religious makeup, many American history teachers and textbook authors now adapt their presentation of American history to this cultural shift. Consequently, early American history is increasingly taught as the history of diversity.

There is no question that many different cultural factors contributed to the development of the United States. Historians have done an excellent job highlighting their contributions. But this emphasis on being inclusive has led to a tremendous amount of historical revision, and in some cases to a disregard for historical accuracy. Nowhere has the revision of historical data been more severe than with the place of religion in early America.[1] A century ago, early American History was widely seen as inseparable from the history of Christianity in America.[2] Students in the past were taught that Christianity was pivotal in the formation of their republic.

It is now widely assumed that religion played a minimal role in forming America's Founding ideals. America's Founders, it is said, consciously rejected religious principles and borrowed their best ideas about law and politics from the ancient Greeks and Romans in addition to Renaissance and Enlightenment philosophers. This view is common throughout most history textbooks today. Although Greek, Roman, Renaissance, and Enlightenment sources were important, their influence has been overemphasized and misstated, while the Christian influence has been seriously understated and even misrepresented.

It is an overstatement to say that American history is synonymous with the history of Christianity in America. But it is a more serious understatement to say that Christianity was simply one of a multitude of equal influences upon our Founding. Christianity was a central and pervasive force in the early development of America, and the political principles enshrined in our Founding documents can be directly traced to the Christian context of the Founders. Indeed, the aim of this book is to show that connection.

If Christianity was so important to American history, why is it neglected in American history courses? The main reason is the widespread suspicion against mixing public education with religion, a suspicion so deep that it controls the way American history is presented. Teachers and school officials feel uncomfortable acknowledging the explicitly Christian character of American history. What will students who are not Christians think? What will their parents think? Will we get complaints? Furthermore, many educators are under pressure to affirm the disenfranchised groups within society.

Although the impulse to include as many factors as possible in the Founding of the United States is commendable, its effect has been to distort history. As a result most high school students leave their American history course with the sense that Christianity had only a peripheral influence upon our Founding. Once, however, we put aside the political and social pressures that lead us to neglect our religious roots, it becomes clear that Christianity pervades our nation's past, both its splendor and its horror.

This is not to say that current textbooks are silent about the influence of Christianity on the early development of America. Most textbooks acknowledge that the Pilgrims and Puritans were devout believers in God. Most acknowledge that there was a religious revival in the 1740s across the colonies called the Great Awakening. Many acknowledge some role of Christianity within education. Many textbooks concede that the colonists and Founders were members of Protestant churches. But then they claim that the political ideas the Founders embraced came primarily from non-Christian sources like the ancient Greeks or Renaissance philosophers.

This text will challenge those claims by arguing that the key principles and ideals in the Founding of this nation were Christian. America's most important ideals, like the separation of church and state, inalienable rights, and equality of all persons, derive from Christian sources. That said, this text will not argue that to be an American one must be a Christian. Any such claim utterly contradicts what the Founders had in mind. This text will show that the liberties we enjoy in this land—including religious freedom—are the result of Christian teachings. Freedom of religion is the offspring of religion.

Another reason American history courses ignore our religious roots is that during the last two generations, scholars have begun to define Christianity quite narrowly. Christianity is nowadays identified with a purely personal faith that is incompatible with reason and science. The term for this flawed conception of Christianity is *fideism* (pronounced *FEE-day-ism*), from the Latin word *fides* for faith. Fideism separates reason from faith and insists that reason, logic, and science have no place in genuine Christianity. True Christianity, it is said, focuses on a person's inner life and leaves the world to itself.[3]

From this flawed conception of Christianity it follows that Christianity cannot possibly have anything significant to say about justice, politics, social order, science, psychology, rights, law, reason, and so forth. As a result, scholars draw the obvious conclusion: Christianity cannot possibly have had any significant influence on the ideas that shaped our nation. Such ideas must have come from philosophers, not theologians.

Christianity is thus eliminated apart from any examination of evidence. According to this flawed conception of Christianity, any element of reason, logic, or critical thinking must have non-Christian roots, and any Christian who engages in philosophy must be embracing reason at the expense of Christianity. In the American colonies, however, religion permeated every aspect of life. Christianity impacted the colonists' educational philosophy, their love for science, and their understanding of law and rights.

The Christian roots of our nation are historically evident, logically compelling, and easily researchable. Christianity was central, pervasive, and indispensable in the Founding of our nation. This is not to suggest that non-Christian influences played no role. But it is to suggest that Christianity wasn't just one more vendor in the marketplace of ideas. Christianity underlies the principles and ideals that most Americans, Christian or not, continue to hold dear. Historical accuracy, not religious bias, demands that American history courses make this point clearly. The aim of this textbook is to show how Christianity pervaded the political, social, theological, and philosophical context of America's Founding.

TABLE OF CONTENTS

viii

The birth of America is one of the most pronounced examples in all of history

that ideas have consequences. Here is the record that certain ideas about

religious freedom, freedom of conscience and right government, hammered

George Washington's letter case is symbolic of this

out on the anvil of European and especially British history, set in motion

central truth...that certain ideas, once discovered and

human forces; habits of worship, convictions of polity, voluntary associations,

then deemed worthy as ideals, would set their

declarations of renunciation and independence, and yes, armies who would

carriers in motion until history is born of those ideals

deny themselves and their families, to offer the ultimate sacrifice, if necessary. ☆

and the courage and sacrifices they spawned. ☆

THE POLITICAL AND RELIGIOUS

The American Revolution might thus be said to have started, in a sense, when Martin

BACKDROP OF THE FOUNDING

Luther nailed his 95 theses to the church door at Wittenberg. It received a substantial

OF THE UNITED STATES

part of its theological and philosophical underpinnings from John Calvin's <u>Institutes</u>

<u>of the Christian Religion</u> and much of its social theory from the Puritan Revolution

of 1640–1660, and, perhaps less obviously, from the Glorious Revolution of 1689.

Put another way, the American Revolution is inconceivable in the absence of the con-

text of ideas which have constituted Christianity. The leaders of the Revolution in

every colony were imbued with the precepts of the Reformed faith. ☆

- Page Smith

THE REFORMATION'S ROLE IN ADVANCING POLITICAL AND RELIGIOUS LIBERTY

1.1 MARTIN LUTHER'S PROTEST

The founding of the United States and the principles on which it was established belong to the ongoing human quest for political and religious liberty. That quest is ancient and has been a central theme of Western civilization. During both the Græco-Roman era and the Middle Ages, governments legislated not only proper social conduct, but also what a person could and could not believe. In Western Europe throughout the early Middle Ages, even though Roman Catholicism was the official state religion, kings and their political associates were only too eager to limit and interfere with the civil and religious liberties of their subjects.

In 1075, however, Pope Gregory VII instituted sweeping reforms to free the Roman Catholic Church from the control of European political rulers. By denying political rulers the right to control church affairs, Gregory VII redefined the limits of state power as well as the extent of individual rights.[1] Over a century later these reforms would lead the English to draft a document called the Magna Carta (Great Charter), which protected not only the rights of the church, but also the rights of English citizens generally.[2]

These events profoundly affected the political values and commitments of the English people in the centuries leading up to the founding of the United States. A crucial step along the way was the religious and political reforms initiated in Germany in the early sixteenth century. This movement, known as the Protestant Reformation, provided the socio-political context in which the United States was established.

The Protestant Reformation began in 1517 in Germany when a Catholic priest named Martin Luther (1483–1546) publicly challenged his own Roman Catholic Church. On the door of the church in Wittenberg, Luther posted a list of ninety-five theses—objections to abuses in the Catholic church. One abuse Luther cited was the Catholic practice of indulgences, namely, buying forgiveness from God by paying money to the church. When Luther posted his ninety-five theses, he had no intention of leaving the Catholic church. Luther held that sincere religious beliefs come from the heart and cannot be forced or bought.

The pope expelled Luther from the Roman Catholic Church on January 3, 1521. A trial was set for

Martin Luther posting 95 theses on Wittenberg door

Martin Luther's trial

that March in which Luther was to defend his religious beliefs. If convicted, he would be burned at the stake. When Luther stood before the court and told the authorities that it was wrong for anyone to act against his or her conscience in religious matters, a seed was planted for a future society based on *liberty of conscience*. That society would emerge over the next three centuries and culminate in the founding of the United States. Luther's call for religious freedom unleashed the forces responsible for that new nation.

Liberty of conscience is the principle that people should be free to believe whatever religious ideas they hold true. Luther was convinced that Jesus himself embraced this principle.[3] Through the Protestant Reformation, liberty of conscience would become a fundamental principle of the American nation. Indeed, our most cherished American freedoms can ultimately be traced to Christian thinkers like Luther.

Luther was a monk, a priest, a college professor, and a town preacher. His sermons and writings marked a turning point in European history. Although Luther is widely recognized as an important figure in religious reform, he is just as important for his political views. That importance is not as widely recognized today. Luther's sermons and pamphlets challenged much more than the existing religious order. He insisted that the civil government had no authority to force people to believe any religious doctrine. He also insisted that it is always illegitimate to use coercion, torture, or any other physical punishment to force people's beliefs.

For Luther, God alone had authority over peoples' consciences. Drawing from the classic Christian teaching on the creator-redeemer distinc-

Martin Luther

tion, Luther argued that a person's life is divided into two spheres. One sphere deals with a person's physical life in society as he or she interacts with other human beings and the world at large. This part of a person's life relates to God as *creator*, who has made universal laws for ordering the world and our place in it. The other sphere deals with a person's spiritual life as someone made in God's image and needing redemption. This part of a person's life relates to God as *redeemer*, who through Christ brings salvation from sin.

God governs both spheres differently. God governs one sphere through the law of

7

creation, the other through the law of redemption. The law of creation, or what is sometimes called the *law of nature* or *natural law*, denotes how God created the universe and intends it to operate. It includes not only physical laws (like the laws of physics and chemistry), but also moral laws. For instance, within politics God's law of creation requires rulers to protect the people and not to exploit them. The law of redemption, on the other hand, specifies how people come to salvation. It is sometimes called the *ordo salutis* (the order of salvation).

Christianity's new approach to social order meant that all people, Christians and non-Christians, were obligated to obey God as creator. Since all people are creatures of God, all people must govern their daily lives in society in obedience to God's moral law. But since Christians also embrace God as redeemer, they are additionally called to follow God's law of redemption. The state, however, has no authority where the law of redemption is concerned. Redemption is outside the state's jurisdiction.

Luther described the creator-redeemer distinction this way: "God has ordained the two governments: the *spiritual*, which by the Holy Spirit under Christ makes Christians and pious people; and the *secular*, which restrains the unchristian and wicked so that they are obliged to *keep the peace outwardly*."[4] For Luther, the creator-redeemer distinction meant that there was a clear difference between the role of the church and the role of the state. Because church and state are separate institutions, the government's role has to be restricted:

> *The laws of worldly government extend no farther than to life and property and what is external upon earth. For over the soul God can and will let no one rule but himself. Therefore, where temporal power presumes to prescribe laws for the soul, it encroaches upon God's government and only misleads and destroys souls. We desire to make this so clear that every one shall grasp it, and that the princes and bishops may see what fools they are when they seek to coerce the people with their laws and commandments into believing one thing or another.*[5]

The civil government's job is simply to keep *civil peace* in society. It can only use the force that is necessary to cause people to behave in a civilized way so that they don't harm their neighbors.

> *We are to be subject to governmental power and do what it bids, as long as it does not bind our conscience but legislates only concerning outward matters.... But if it invades the spiritual domain and constrains the conscience, over which God only must preside and rule, we should not obey it at all but rather lose our necks. Temporal authority and government extend no further than to matters which are external and corporeal.*[6]

Luther lamented that the creator-redeemer distinction was poorly understood by the people of his day. He observed:

> *Few people make the proper distinction. This is what commonly happens: The temporal lords want to rule the church, and, conversely, the theologians want to play the lord in the town hall. Under the papacy mixing the two was considered ruling well, and it is still so considered. But in reality this is ruling very badly.... Noblemen and young lords want to rule consciences and issue commands in the church. And someday, when the theologians*

get back on their feet, they will again take the sword from the temporal authorities, as happened under the papacy.[7]

Addressing whether the state should allow its citizens to believe religious views that are unpopular, Luther said, "Heresy can never be prevented by force…. Heresy is a spiritual matter which no iron can strike, no fire burn, no water drown."[8] For Luther it was folly to legislate and enforce correct religious beliefs. He called for both the government and the church to permit liberty of conscience.

Wartburg Castle

To prevent him from being killed, Luther's friends kidnapped him and hid him in Wartburg castle. In May 1521, the emperor signed an imperial ban on Luther. Had Luther been captured within the emperor's territory, he would have been executed. That never happened. Instead of being burned at the stake, Luther went on to become the leader of the newly organized Protestant movement.

Although Luther's theological views were more readily accepted than his political views, the German political scene of the 1500s prevented Luther's views on government from being taken seriously. No European political entities were prepared to implement the Lutheran principle of liberty of conscience. It would take another century for that to happen, and another two centuries before a nation dedicated to liberty of conscience was established in the New World.

9

HOW FAR SECULAR AUTHORITY EXTENDS

From Secular Authority: To What Extent it Should be Obeyed
January 1, 1523

MARTIN LUTHER

The first point to be noted is that the two classes into which the children of Adam are divided, the one the kingdom of God under Christ, the other the kingdom of the world under the State, have each their own kind of law. Everyday experience sufficiently shows us that every kingdom must have its own laws and that no kingdom or government can survive without law. Secular government has laws that extend no further than the body, goods and outward, earthly matters.

But where the soul is concerned, God neither can nor will allow anyone but himself to rule. And so, where secular authority takes it upon itself to legislate for the soul, it trespasses on God's government, and merely seduces and ruins souls. I intend to make this so unambiguously clear that no one can fail to grasp it, in order that our lords the princes and bishops may see the folly of trying to compel belief in this or that by means of laws and commands…

[S]ecular authority drives souls to eternal damnation with such blasphemous commands. For this is to compel people to believe that something is certain to please God, when it is not certain at all; on the contrary, it is certain that it displeases God, since there is no clear Word of God to warrant it.…

Another important point is this. However stupid they are, they [the civil government] must admit that they have no power over the soul. For no human being can kill the soul or bring it to life, or lead it to heaven or to hell. And if they will not believe us, then Christ will show it clearly enough when he says in Matthew 10[28]: "Do not be afraid of those that kill the body and after that can do nothing more. Fear rather him who, after he kills the body, has the power to condemn to hell." Surely that is clear enough: the soul is taken out of the hands of any human being whatsoever, and is placed exclusively under the power of God.

Now tell me this: would anyone in his right mind give orders where he has no authority? You might as well command the moon to shine at your behest. What sense would there be in it, if the

people of Leipzig were to lay down laws for us here in Wittenberg, or vice versa? Anyone who tried it, would be sent a dose of hellebore by way of thanks, to clear their heads and cure their cold. But this is just what our Emperor and our prudent princes are doing; they let the Pope, the bishops and the sophists lead them, the blind leading the blind, commanding their subjects to believe as they see fit, without God's Word. And then they still want to retain the title of "Christian Princes," which God forbid.…

[I]t is impossible and futile to command or coerce someone to believe this or that. A different skill is needed here; force will not do. I am surprised at these lunatics, seeing that they themselves have a saying: *De occultis non iudicat ecclesia*; the Church does not judge in secret matters. Now, if the Church, the spiritual government, only rules over matters that are public and open, by what right does secular authority, in its folly, presume to judge a thing as secret, spiritual, hidden as faith?

Each must decide at his own peril what he is to believe, and must see to it that he believes rightly. Other people cannot go to heaven or hell on my behalf, or open or close for me. And just as little can they believe or not believe on my behalf, or force my faith or unbelief. How he believes is a matter for each individual's conscience, and this does not diminish secular governments. They ought therefore to content themselves with attending to their own business, and allow people to believe what they can, and what they want, and they must use no coercion in this matter against anyone. Faith is free and no one can be compelled to believe. More precisely, so far from being something secular authority ought to create and enforce, faith is something that God works in the spirit. Hence that common saying which also occurs in Augustine: "no one can or ought to be forced to believe anything against his will."

Those blind and wretched people do not realize what a pointless and impossible thing they are attempting. However strict their orders, and however much they rage, they cannot force people to do more than obey by word and deed; they cannot compel the heart, even if they were to tear themselves apart try-ing. There is truth in the saying: Thought is free. What is the effect of their trying to force people to believe in their hearts! All they achieve is to force people with weak consciences to lie, to perjure themselves, saying one thing while in their hearts they believe another. And in this way load on themselves the horrifying sins done by others, because all the lies and perjuries such weak consciences utter, when they are spoken under compulsion, fall back on the one who compels their being done. It would be much easier, although it may mean allowing their subjects to fall into error, just to let them err, rather than to force them to lie and profess what they do not believe in their hearts. And it is not right to prevent one evil by doing another, even worse, one.

1.2 CALVIN AND THE PRESBYTERIANS

After Luther, the next significant Protestant movement occurred in Geneva, Switzerland. Here a society of Christians, often called Presbyterians, struggled to establish a community under the leadership of John Calvin (1509–64). Calvin shared many of Luther's concerns about liberating Europe from church and state oppression.

Calvin wrote a famous set of volumes called the *Institutes of the Christian Religion*.[9] Calvin's *Institutes* exerted a tremendous influence on the Founders of the United States.[10] Many of them acquired their worldview from the Bible in one hand and Calvin's *Institutes* in the other. Calvin's theology profoundly affected John Witherspoon, John Hancock, Benjamin Rush, Samuel Adams, John Adams, Benjamin Franklin, Roger Sherman, John Trumbull, Paul Revere, Alexander Hamilton, and James Madison.[11] Calvin's theology also had a profound impact on the key political thinkers who influenced America's Founders, like Johannes Althusius, Hugo Grotius, Samuel Pufendorf, Algernon Sidney, Samuel Rutherford, and John Locke.[12] Through their political writings, Calvin's ideas shaped the Founders' political views.[13]

John Calvin

Calvin's views on the creator-redeemer distinction agreed with Luther's. For Calvin, the creator-redeemer distinction meant that the spiritual kingdom of Christ and the civil jurisdiction of the state "have a completely different nature."[14] The kingdom of Christ deals with people's minds, hearts, and beliefs. These are off-limits to civil government. Christ's kingdom is an internal kingdom, situated in the heart. Civil government, on the other hand, deals with people's physical existence and with their outward conduct toward others.

There is a twofold government in man: one is spiritual, whereby the conscience is instructed in piety and in reverencing God; the second is political, whereby man is educated for the duties of humanity and citizenship that must be maintained among men.... The one we may call the spiritual kingdom, the other, the political kingdom.[15]

Since Calvin strongly believed that humans are sinners, he assumed they would often act badly toward others in society. In this part of human life, the creator had wisely provided that there should be civil government to deal with such bad conduct. Civil government was there to restrain people so that their conduct did not harm others. Concerning the need for laws instituted by civil government, Calvin writes,

We see that some form of organization is necessary in all human society to foster the common peace and maintain accord. We further see that in human transactions some procedure is always in effect, which is to be respected in the interests of public decency, and even of humanity itself.... Since such diversity exists in the customs of men, such variety in their minds, such conflicts in their judgments and dispositions, no organization is sufficiently strong unless constituted with definite laws.[16]

Calvin's concern here is with civil conduct, or with how one acts toward others as a member of society. The power of civil government, Calvin explains, "pertains only to civil justice and *outward* morality...."[17] [Emphasis added] Those who reject morality in civil law and insist that only what harms another is wrong should consider that even the criterion of harm to another came from the law of creation. But concerning the need for liberty of conscience, Calvin is also clear:

If God is the sole lawgiver, men are not permitted to usurp this honor.... We should be able with ease to distinguish what human constitutions are contrary to the Lord's Word. All of these are the sort that pretend to relate to the true worship of God, and that consciences are bound to keep, as if their observance was compulsory.[18]

The role of the state is limited to secular things. People's minds and opinions are exempt from civil government's control. Government only deals with the physical and the temporal. Calvin argued that the civil authorities have no right to make laws regarding the beliefs which a person conscientiously holds: "Now let us return to human laws. If they are passed to lay scruples on us, as if the observance of these laws were necessary, we say that something unlawful is laid upon conscience. For our consciences do not have to do with men but with God alone."[19] Calvin insisted that government can only regulate external conduct. He called it a "vanity" to think that the government can control the church. For instance, he held that first century Jews misused the Old Testament when they had Jesus executed for blasphemy.[20]

1.3 CALVIN'S RESISTANCE THEORY

The final pages of Calvin's *Institutes* are extremely important for America's birth. They address the limits of royal authority. The final paragraphs discuss whether in religious matters a person ought to obey one's conscience or the dictates of the political authorities. Citing the example of Daniel's disobedience to the Persian king's edict,[21] Calvin says humans *must* disobey ungodly magistrates: "If they [political authorities] command anything against him [God], let it go unesteemed. And here let us not be concerned about all the dignity which the magistrates possess."[22]

If a king requires any behavior offensive to God, resistance is not only permitted, it is demanded. By citing the example of Daniel, Calvin implies that a subject may disobey any king who mandates a religious practice which the subject does not conscientiously believe. As for authorities who abuse their subjects, Calvin writes: "They dishonestly betray the freedom of the people, of which they know that they have been appointed protectors by God's ordinance."[23]

Calvin's writings on the role and limit of civil government sparked a long debate and spawned an enormous amount of literature throughout the next two centuries leading up to the founding of the United States. There is a direct link between this Calvinist resistance literature and the establishment of the United States.[24] Calvin's successor in Geneva, Theodore Beza, authored *The Right of Magistrates*, in which he explicitly justified armed resistance against tyrants.[25]

Another work titled *Vindiciae Contra Tyrannos* [*The Legal Claim Against Tyrants*] appeared in 1579 among French Calvinists (Huguenots) and used Calvin's theory to support resistance against corrupt monarchs. President John Adams indicated that this document was extremely significant to America's birth.[26] The *Vindiciae* set forth an idea which was to become the bedrock of American political theory, namely, the social contract: "There is ever, and in all places, a mutual and reciprocal obligation between the people and the prince.... If the prince fail in his promise, the people are exempt from obedience, the contract is made void, the rights of obligation of no force."[27] Few contemporary historians identify the religious roots of the social contract theory.[28]

Other Christian thinkers elaborated Calvin's political views. John Knox, a disciple of Calvin who founded the Scottish Presbyterian Church, argued on Christian principles for rebellion against, overthrow of, and execution of an unrighteous monarch.[29] Calvin's views inspired John Ponet, a bishop of the Church of England in the 1550s, to write a document titled

John Milton

A Shorte Treatise of Politike Power.[30] This text justified, on Christian grounds, the right of resistance to tyrannical kings. According to President John Adams, Ponet's work contained "all the essential principles of liberty, which were afterward dilated by Sidney and Locke."[31]

In 1558 Christopher Goodman followed up with a book called *How Superior Powers Ought to be Obeyed*, which straightforwardly defended the right of revolution.[32] In 1618 the Dutch Calvinist Johannes Althusius echoed Calvin and the *Vindiciae* when he wrote on "Tyranny and Its Remedies."[33] John Milton, the prominent Puritan poet, defended the execution of Charles I, King of England.[34] The Westminster Confession (1646), the central creed of English Calvinists known as Puritans, affirmed a Christian's right to "wage war upon just and necessary occasions."[35]

In the 1640s Samuel Rutherford, the Scottish Presbyterian theologian, adopted Calvin's resistance theory to defend the people's rejection of King Charles I. In the 1680s, appealing to Rutherford and other Christian scholars, Algernon Sidney and John Locke in turn defended the people's rejection of King James II. From there we find Sidney and Locke influencing Thomas Jefferson and his colleagues as they defended the American people's rejection of King George III in 1776. The American Revolution has clear roots in Calvin's resistance theory.

1.4 THE TUDOR FAMILY AND THE ENGLISH REFORMATION

Roman Catholicism was the religion of western Europe throughout the medieval era. When Henry VII, the first English king from the Tudor family, died in 1509, England was still officially a Roman Catholic nation. His son, Henry VIII, changed that. After becoming king, Henry VIII entered a fierce controversy with

King Henry VIII

14

Rome regarding divorce. Henry wanted to divorce his wife, Catherine of Aragon, because she did not provide him with a male heir. The Pope, however, would not allow the divorce. As a result, Henry VIII renounced England's attachment to Rome and in 1534 established the Church of England with himself as head.[36] At first the only difference between the Roman Catholic Church and the Church of England was the supreme human authority. But with the Protestant Reformation underway throughout Europe, Henry VIII's separation from Rome was the first step toward a full-scale English Reformation.

After Henry VIII died in 1547, his son Edward VI was enthroned. Young Edward was a friend to Reformation-minded Christians. Edward's closest advisor was Arch-

King Edward VI

bishop Cranmer, himself a supporter of Luther and Calvin. During Edward's reign, the Reformation cause greatly advanced in England.[37] Especially significant during this era was the movement among professors and students at the universities of Cambridge and Oxford to reform the English church. These professors and students were dubbed "Puritans" because they argued that the English Reformation under Henry VIII did not go far enough in purging the English church from Roman Catholic abuses. They therefore sought to "purify" the church further—hence the name "Puritan."

Edward died very young and thereby enabled his sister, Mary I, to assume leadership. Mary, daughter of a Spanish queen, was completely at odds with her brother's theological views. She was dedicated to bringing all of England back into the Roman Catholic Church and ridding the country of Protestants.[38] To accomplish this, she had many Protestants executed—hence her nickname "Bloody Mary." To save their lives, many English Protestants fled to the continent of Europe, especially to Geneva where John Calvin was active. There they translated the Bible into English (the Geneva Bible) and became more committed than ever to Calvin's ideas of theological and political reform.

Mary died in 1558, and her Protestant sister, Elizabeth I, ascended the throne. Gradually these Puritan exiles began to return to their homeland. Filled with zeal for the Protestant cause, they hoped to complete the reforms

Queen Mary I

Queen Elizabeth I

1.5 THE STUART FAMILY AND THE DIVINE RIGHT OF KINGS

begun under Edward.[39] During Elizabeth's reign, the Puritans continued to grow in number, but neither she nor her successors, the Stuart kings, would be friendly to their efforts at reform. The tension between the English monarchy and the Puritans would reach a breaking point in the early seventeenth century, causing some of them to venture to the New World.

Elizabeth, "the virgin queen," left no heir and thus ended the reign of the Tudor family. Her closest relative was James VI of the Stuart family in Scotland, who was crowned James I of England in 1603. James was not nearly as well liked by the people as Elizabeth. Whereas Elizabeth traveled throughout the countryside and stopped at various estates for tea, James was distant from, and at times even surly to, his subjects.[40]

James I and the Stuart family that succeeded him were firm believers in the Græco-Roman theory of "Divine Right of Kings." The ancient Græco-Roman political philosophy maintained that the king was divinely appointed and therefore could dictate and enforce not just civil behavior, but also religious beliefs. Because God, rather than the people, had selected him as king, everything the king required should be honored by the people as God's will. And since he answered only

King James I

to God, the king could not be restrained or punished by earthly law—even if he acted criminally. Kings could only be punished by God in the next life.

Divine right theory holds that kings have authority to compel obedience and submission because they are God's direct representatives on earth. The divine right theory concentrates total power in the state. The state has power to control people's hearts and minds, as well as their outward conduct. The government can punish people not only for what they do, but also for what they believe. Under the divine right theory, governments can use force, imprisonment, torture, and even the death penalty to control people's religious beliefs and practices. James personally authored an essay, "The True Lawe of Free Monarchs," defending this "absolutist" position.[41] It was a position which the Puritans rejected.

In his religious sentiments, James was sympathetic to Roman Catholicism and antagonistic to Puritanism.[42] James therefore did not approve of the Puritans' Geneva Bible. Instead, he commissioned a government-authorized version of the Bible in 1611. This Bible became known as the King James Version or the Authorized Version. It holds the record as the best-selling book in world history.

James's son, Charles I, came to power in 1620. Charles adhered to the divine right theory, and was even more friendly to Rome than his father. Not only did Charles marry a French Catholic bride, but he also appointed William Laud as Archbishop of Canterbury. Laud reinstituted many Roman Catholic practices. He also despised the Puritans, having many of them tortured.

At the same time that Charles was promoting the absolutism of his father, Parliament was becoming increasingly filled with Puritans. In 1628 they

King Charles I

17

forced Charles to acknowledge that the Magna Carta and the English Common Law placed the king under the rule of the law of nature.[43] Parliament presented Charles with a document called the Petition of Right. The Petition of Right asserted that the people possess basic human rights of *due process* which the king is bound to honor.

EXCERPT FROM THE PETITION OF RIGHT

Addressed to King Charles I by Parliament

The petition exhibited to his majesty by the lords spiritual and temporal, and commons in this present parliament assembled, concerning divers rights and liberties of the subjects…by the statute called the Great Charter [Magna Carta] of the Liberties of England, it is declared and enacted that no freeman may be taken or imprisoned, or be disseised of his freehold or liberties or his free customs, or be outlawed or exiled or in any manner destroyed, but by the lawful judgment of his peers or by the law of the land; and in the eight-and-twentieth year of the reign of King Edward III it was declared and enacted by authority of parliament that no man, of what estate or condition that he be, should be put out of his land or tenements, nor taken, nor imprisoned, nor disinherited, nor put to death, without being brought to answer by due process of law: nevertheless, against the tenor of the said statutes and other the good laws and statutes of your realm to that end provided, divers of your subjects have of late been imprisoned without any cause showed; and when for their deliverance they were brought before your justices by your majesty's writs of habeas corpus, there to undergo and receive as the court should order, and their keepers commanded to certify the causes of their detainer, no cause was certified, but that they were detained by your majesty's special command, signified by the lords of your privy council; and yet were returned back to several prisons without being charged with anything to which they might make answer according to the law.

Charles I did not take Parliament's grievances seriously. In the resulting conflict, Charles, by royal prerogative, shut down Parliament and attempted to impose his religious views on his subjects. The people had two options: *fight* or *flight*. They did both. The next two chapters will examine both responses. Some of the Puritans stayed in England and eventually waged war against Charles I. Others looked to *Mundus Novus*—the New World—as God's provision for them to escape persecution and establish a nation founded on liberty of conscience.

The Shock of the English Army Halts the Scots at Verdem. — Falkirk, 1297

TWO REVOLUTIONS IN ENGLAND SET THE STAGE FOR AMERICA'S BIRTH

Two revolutions took place in England in the 1600s: the English Civil War of 1641 and the Glorious Revolution of 1688. These two seventeenth-century revolutions prefigured the American Revolution of 1776.[1] To adequately grasp America's founding, we need to understand these earlier revolutions and the ideas that set them in motion. Samuel Rutherford and John Locke gave particularly apt expression to the ideas responsible for these revolutions. Their views complemented each other and were crucial in the birth of the United States of America.

The English Civil War

During the reign of Charles I, a terrible civil war took place in England (1641–49). On one side were those loyal to the king and the old way of doing things. They were called Cavaliers. On the other side were the dissenters, many of them English Puritans and Scottish Presbyterians (the difference between Puritans and Presbyterians is mainly one of geography—Puritans were English Calvinists; Presbyterians were Scottish Calvinists). For decades they had felt mistreated both by the king and by the Church of England. Now finally they had reached a breaking point. They were called Roundheads, and their primary concern was to remain true to their Protestant beliefs.

The civil war was triggered when Charles I began to impose his religious views throughout his kingdom, including Scotland. In the previous century, under the leadership of John Knox, the people of Scotland had rejected Roman Catholicism and embraced Calvin's ideas of theological and political reform. In the spring of 1637 Charles I, through his deputy Archbishop Laud, insisted that his Scottish subjects begin using the English worship book, which required them to worship in ways they found offensive.[2] For the Scottish people this was like imposing Roman Catholicism on them.[3] Their reaction was quick and deliberate. The ministers of Scotland met and drew up a National Covenant, reclaiming their ecclesiastical and civil liberties, and reasserting their Presbyterianism.

In response, Charles I called a meeting of Parliament to organize a military campaign against the defiant Scots. Charles had not called Parliament into session since 1628. When it reconvened in 1640, the members of Parliament had their own agenda. They proposed radical changes, none of which the king had in mind. They also refused to let the king dismiss them, which is why the session is called the Long Parliament, lasting from 1640–60. Charles I's decision to call this session of Parliament ultimately resulted in his downfall.[4]

During this period the British social order was severely tested. On the one hand, the Puritans and Presbyterians insisted that all people shared fundamental rights which even the king was not permitted to take away. Charles disagreed and used every means at his disposal to stop this challenge to his authority. He controlled the national treasury. He had enormous control over newspapers, book publishers, and every other channel of communication. He outlawed books with which he disagreed, especially those written by Puritans, and he paid people to write books supporting his own ideas and policies.

Just prior to 1644, a clergyman named John Maxwell wrote a very influential book claiming that the English kings ruled by "Divine Right," completely apart from any legal restraint. Maxwell was on the king's payroll. In response, the Puritans and Presbyterians wrote many books and pamphlets refuting Maxwell. Perhaps the most famous of these books was written by a Scottish Presbyterian named Samuel Rutherford.

In 1644, Rutherford published *Lex Rex* at Westminster in London (the title is usually translated as *The Law and the Prince*; a more literal translation would be *The Law Is King*). Rutherford's book reflected the theological and political ideas of Calvin as they were transmitted through the French Huguenots to the Scottish Presbyterians and English Puritans. Rutherford's book was organized into sixty-four questions. Each question was the topic of a chapter. For each question, Rutherford gave the divine right argument and then refuted it with the Puritan/Presbyterian argument.

Whereas the king claimed to rule entirely by God's grace, and therefore was not accountable to the law of nature or subject to any legal restrictions, Rutherford countered that the king was indeed subject to God's law of nature. When the people made someone king, they did not give up their rights by doing so.[5] If the king violated the law of nature, he was a criminal and could be punished as a criminal. He could also be deposed and lose his throne.

Rutherford wrote *Lex Rex* at Westminster Abbey in London only a few years before John Locke, a philosopher who profoundly influenced the founding of the United States, was a high school student there. Locke's father was a member of the Puritan forces that fought against King Charles I. What's more, his father was a personal acquaintance of Rutherford. The Locke family knew Rutherford's thinking intimately, and it is reasonable to suppose that Rutherford's ideas were planted in young Locke's psyche and became the seed for his political theories.[6]

Although Rutherford wrote with great force and precision, his actual arguments and conclusions were not unique. He was one voice among many. He expressed views that were well known in Puritan and Presbyterian circles—not only in England, but in America as well. It should come as no surprise, therefore, that language similar to Rutherford's appears in the constitutions of some New England states. That is where the Puritan and Presbyterian influence was strongest.

Even so, Rutherford's arguments were not merely Puritan or Presbyterian. His arguments derived not only from Protestant sources, but also from Catholic sources. Rutherford saw himself as speaking for Christianity as a whole and not just for a narrow brand of Protestantism. Throughout his book Rutherford cited earlier Christian leaders and scholars. His sources ranged from Jerome in the fourth century (who translated the Bible into Latin) to Aquinas in the thirteenth century (who to this day remains the premier Catholic theologian) to Suarez in the seventeenth century (who was a Jesuit).

Rutherford's arguments and conclusions were compelling not because they were so original, but because they were so mainstream. That is why his views on law and rights seem so familiar. They were drawn from a time when Catholicism was the dominant form of European Christianity. Rutherford drew on a heritage shared by both Catholics and Protestants.

The ideas in *Lex Rex* were immediately embraced by Puritans and Presbyterians in the American colonies, as was the Westminster Confession which Rutherford also helped author.[7] *Lex Rex* dealt with political theory, the Westminster Confession with religious doctrine. For the Puritans and Presbyterians, political theory and religious doctrine went hand in hand.

At the beginning of the Long Parliament, Parliamentary forces desired to call a convention of English clergymen to address the proper "Government and Liturgy for the Church of England." They proposed this convention time and again, but, to no surprise, King Charles I would not give his assent. On June 12, 1643, the convention was called without the king's permission. In defiance of the king, the Westminster Assembly convened at Westminster Abbey on July 1, 1643, and elected William Twisse as its moderator.[8]

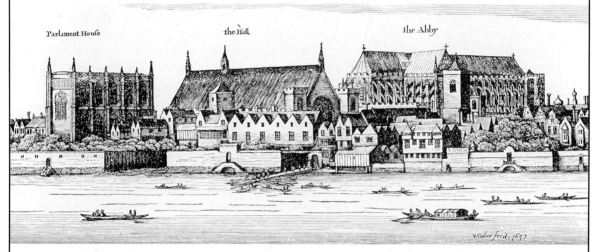

Westminster Abbey in the 17th century

In August 1643, the political conflict between the king and Parliament became fierce. The Roundheads, who sided with Parliament, were losing. To strengthen their military position, commissioners from Parliament ventured to Edinburgh, Scotland, to seek aid from the Scots. The Scots agreed to help if they were given a say at the Westminster Assembly. This agreement between the Roundheads and the Scots is known as the Solemn League and Covenant. As a result of this covenant, Scotland sent representatives to Westminster. Among them was Samuel Rutherford, the author of *Lex Rex*.

The Puritans and Presbyterians at Westminster authored a classic statement of the Protestant Reformation known as the Westminster Confession. It affirms the Protestant commitment to the Bible as the ultimate authority. Beginning in chapters 19 and 20, the confession discusses the relationship between church and state. The confession reaffirms the Protestant resistance theories of the previous century. Chapter 20, titled "Of Christian Liberty and Liberty of Conscience," stresses the need for voluntary assent in religious faith:

God alone is Lord of the conscience, and hath left it free from the doctrines and commandments of men which are in any thing contrary to His Word, or beside it in matters of faith

24

or worship. So that to believe such doctrines, or to obey such commands out of conscience, is to betray true liberty of conscience; and the requiring of an implicit faith, and an absolute and blind obedience, is to destroy liberty of conscience, and reason also.[9]

A century later this position became firmly implanted in the mind of James Madison. As a divinity student at Princeton, he studied the Westminster Confession closely.[10] Madison was the chief architect of the United States Constitution, including the First Amendment, which states that our government shall not establish or prohibit the exercise of religion. The Westminster Confession contains and illuminates many of the ideals upon which our nation was established. Its influence during the formative years of our nation was vast.

Second only to the Bible, the Shorter Catechism of the Westminster Confession was the most widely published piece of literature in the pre–Revolutionary era in America. It is estimated that some five million copies were available in the colonies.[11] With a total population of only four million people in America at the time of the Revolution—and only two million of European descent—that number is staggering. The Westminster Catechism was a central part of colonial education. In New England learning it *was required by law*.[12] Each town employed an officer to visit homes and hear children recite the catechism.[13] The primary schoolbook for children, the *New England Primer*, included the catechism.

Assent to the Westminster Confession was an admission requirement at Harvard, Yale, and Princeton.[14] Daily recitations of it were required at these schools. Their curriculum included memorization of the Westminster Confession and the Westminster Larger Catechism.[15] There was not a person at Independence Hall in 1776 who had not been exposed to the Westminster Confession

Westminster Assembly

and its two catechisms—the Westminster Larger Catechism and the Westminster Shorter Catechism. Most of them had the Shorter Catechism memorized by the time they were ten. The Shorter Catechism itself runs over ten ordinary sized pages, numbers more than a hundred questions, and includes the Lord's Prayer, the Ten Commandments, and the Apostle's Creed.

In its first fifty years, the Westminster Confession went through forty separate printed editions, including translations into Latin and German. Its impact was immense. The Princeton scholar Benjamin Warfield wrote: "It was impossible for any body of Christians in the [British] Kingdoms to avoid attending to it."[16] Benjamin Franklin, who became very wealthy through his printing press, owed much of his success to the sale of his 1745 edition of the Confession. Franklin urged one young admirer, "Don't forget your catechism."[17]

Massachusetts and Connecticut adopted the Westminster Confession as their official statement of faith. Although slightly altered and called by different names, it became the basic statement of faith for Congregationalist, Baptist, and Presbyterian churches throughout the English-speaking world.[18]

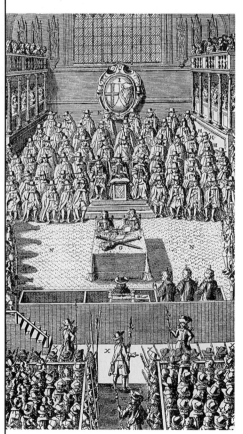

Trial of Charles I

The Westminster Assembly, unapproved by the king, became the working model for the unapproved assemblies held throughout the colonies in the eighteenth century. The Continental Congress in particular followed its pattern. Even the format of many colonial positions statements, including the United States Constitution, resembles the Westminster Confession's organization into chapters and articles.

2.3 THE DEFEAT OF CHARLES I AND THE PROTECTORATE OF OLIVER CROMWELL

In the English Civil War, the Puritans were ultimately victorious over the armies of King Charles I. Consequently, in 1649 he was put on trial for treason and tyranny. At his trial Charles invoked the divine right of kings:

Remember I am your king, your lawful king, and what sins you bring upon your heads, and the judgment of God upon this land. Think well upon it.... I have a trust committed to me by God, by old and lawful descent. I will not betray it to answer to a new unlawful authority.[19]

The Puritan leaders responded by citing the *social contract* theory of the *Vindiciae* and Rutherford:

This we learn, the end [purpose] of having kings or

any other governors, is for the enjoying of justice.... For there is a contract and a bargain made between the king and his people, and your oath is taken, and certainly sir the bond is reciprocal.... Sir if this bond be broken—farewell sovereignty.[20]

American colonists appealed to the same political theory 130 years later. Many of the patriots who founded the United States looked to the Puritans of the English Civil War as their forerunners (see chapter 3).

During the English Civil War, the leader of the Puritan armies was Oliver Cromwell. As a young man Cromwell wished to come to America with his Puritan friends to settle in Boston.[21] He was detained in England. Thus, instead of avoiding persecution by means of *flight*, he was compelled to *fight*.

After their victory over Charles, the Puritans took steps to turn England into an independent democratic republic, or what is known as a *commonwealth*. In this way the Puritans reformed the English government and rejected monarchy. In 1653, Cromwell was made

Oliver Cromwell installed as Lord Protector

"Lord Protector" of England. He thus became the title chief executive but did not assume the title "king." As Lord Protector he refused to make either Puritanism or Presbyterianism the official religion of state.[22] It is certain that Cromwell knew of the early Protestant reformers' emphasis on the creator-redeemer distinction. He held opinions very similar to Luther's. Cromwell and his supporters rejected the view that governments have the power to dictate people's beliefs.

On December 16, 1653, Cromwell introduced a written constitution called the Instrument of Government.[23] It provided for complete religious freedom for everyone as long as their religious beliefs did not require the overthrow of the government. Religious freedom therefore extended to everyone except Catholics. At the time, Rome required Catholics in England, Scotland, and Ireland to overthrow Protestant governments and set up Catholic governments in their place. As long as each Catholic was a potential revolutionary and terrorist, Cromwell would not grant them religious liberty.

Cromwell limited the government's use of force to dealing with outward acts that harm others. It was not government's place to punish belief or worship. For Cromwell, government could only punish conduct that caused civil injury or a breach of the public peace. He therefore wrote,

> *That such as profess faith in God by Jesus Christ (though differing in judgment from the doctrine, worship or discipline publicly held forth) shall not be restrained from, but shall be protected in, the profession of faith and the exercise of their religion; so as they abuse not this liberty to the civil injury of others and to the actual disturbance of the public peace on their parts.*[24]

After Cromwell died in 1658, the people yearned to restore the monarchy. Cromwell's commitment to the creator-redeemer distinction resulted in widespread religious liberty throughout England, but was an idea still ahead of its

Oliver Cromwell

time.[25] His Puritan vision of a constitutional government combining democracy and republicanism would have to await another time and place.

King Charles II

In 1660 Charles II was crowned king of England. This event is referred to as "The Restoration." Charles II was able to regain the confidence of those who had executed his father by pledging to maintain and protect Protestantism as the religion of the realm.

Charles was interested in America and initiated several new colonies there. Pennsylvania, Delaware, and New Jersey are sometimes called Restoration Colonies. In addition, Charles annexed New Amsterdam from the Dutch and gave control of it to his brother, James, the Duke of York. It was fittingly renamed "New York."[26]

But Charles's favorite project in America was settling a colony named after himself: Charleston. Because the Latin form of Charles is *Carolus*, the region surrounding Charleston was named *Carolina*. Charles's advisor, Lord Shaftesbury, was given the task of drafting a constitution for the new colony. Shaftesbury turned to his colleague, John Locke (1632–1704), for assistance.

Locke was the son of a Puritan who had fought with Oliver Cromwell in the 1640s.[27] Locke's views on church/state relations followed those of Martin Luther. His language in the Carolina Constitution about religion is reminiscent of the Westminster Confession. Locke insisted on liberty of conscience and the creator-redeemer distinction.

The Carolina Constitution was a remarkably progressive document: "No other colony, English or foreign, was ever started with guarantees for 'liberty of conscience.' "[28] This constitution was written more than twenty years before the Salem witch trials. It granted religious rights to Jews, Native Americans, "heathens, and other dissenters."[29] Besides granting legal privileges to all sects, it also prohibited anyone from harassing a person on religious grounds: "No person whatsoever shall disturb, molest, or persecute another for his speculative opinions in religion or his way of worship."[30]

There were only two exceptions: (1) A religious sect had to have a membership of seven or more persons, and (2) they had to worship a deity. In other words, the document does insist that all persons worship a creator: "No person above seventeen years of age shall have any benefit or protection of the law…who is not a member of some church or profession."[31] The role of government is to promote and establish God as the *creator*, but in *redemptive* matters the heart cannot and should not be coerced.

John Locke

Although Locke may not have been an orthodox Puritan like his father, there is no question that he was a sincere Christian.[32] Locke believed that the Bible was "infallibly true." He explicitly relied on the Bible as the authority and basis for his political theories:

> *The holy Scripture is to me, and always will be, the constant guide of my assent; and I shall always hearken to it, as containing the infallible truth relating to things of the highest concernment…. And I shall immediately condemn and quit any opinion of mine, as soon as I am shown that it is contrary to any revelation in the holy Scripture.*[33]

Locke embraced all the essential doctrines of the Christian faith. He affirmed that belief in Jesus Christ was necessary for salvation.[34] He accepted the doctrine of original sin, agreeing that all men are corrupt by nature.[35] He defended miracles, answers to prayer, and the resurrection of Jesus Christ.[36] He devoted much energy to defending "the reasonableness of Christianity." Later in life, he considered his most important work to be his commentaries on the New Testament.[37]

Why, then, did Locke require the citizens of Carolina only to believe in God, but not in Christ? Why did Locke want the government to allow for a marketplace of religious doctrines? Locke's view was that of the Puritan John Milton: "Let [Truth] and Falsehood grapple; who ever knew Truth put to the worse in free and open encounter? She needs no policies, nor stratagems, nor licensings to make her victorious…. Give her but room."[38]

Locke held that Christianity was true. Hence, when religions were placed on a level playing field, Christianity would prevail. On the other hand, when Christians forced their religion upon others, they committed a "great offense to Almighty God and great scandal to the true religion we profess." For Locke, only an uncoerced religious commitment could be sincere. Religious toleration was the best way for non-Christians to "be won over to embrace and unfeignedly receive the truth [of the gospel]."[39]

Locke's famous *Letters Concerning Toleration* were extremely influential in England and America. Locke's thesis in these letters was that if all views are given equal opportunity, the truth would prevail. In Locke's view, Christians had nothing to fear, for the truth of the gospel had its own force and authority. Only false religions needed to rely for their protection on the "force and helps of men."[40] This libertarian approach, which was adopted by the American Founders,[41] flowed directly from Locke's understanding of Christianity, which in turn flowed from the Puritanism of Milton and Rutherford, to whom he was exposed in his youth.[42] For Locke and the Founders, religious liberty was the only way to guarantee genuine Christian faith among the people.

THE RELIGIOUS CLAUSES IN THE FUNDAMENTAL CONSTITUTIONS OF CAROLINA

JOHN LOCKE

90. In the terms of Communion of every church or profession, these following shall be three [beliefs], without which no agreement or assembly of men upon pretence of Religion shall be accounted a Church or Profession within these Rules:
  1. That there is a God.
  2. That God is publicly to be worshipped.
  3. That it is lawful, and the duty of every man, being thereunto called by those that Govern, to bear witness to truth; and that every church or profession shall, in their Terms of Communion, Set down the External way whereby they witness a truth as in the presence of God, whether it be by laying hands on and Kissing the Gospel, as in the Protestant and Papist Churches, or by holding up the hand, or any other Sensible way.

91. No person above seventeen years of Age shall have any benefit or protection of the law, or be capable of any place of profit or honor, who is not a member of Some church or profession, having his name recorded in Some one, and but one Religion Record at once.

92. The Religious Record of every church or profession shall be kept by the public Register of the Precinct where they reside.

93. No man of any other Church or profession shall disturb or molest any Religious Assembly.

94. No person whatsoever shall speak any thing in their Religious assembly Irreverently or Seditiously of the Government or Governors or States matters.

95. Any person Subscribing the terms of Communion of any church or profession in the Record of the said church before the Precinct Register and any one member of the church or profession shall be

thereby made a member of the Said church or profession.

96. Any person striking out his own name out of any Record, or his name being struck out by any officer thereunto Authorized by any church or profession, shall cease to be a member of that Church or profession.

97. No person shall use any reproachful, Reviling, or abusive language against the Religion of any Church or Profession, that being the certain way of disturbing the public peace, and of hindering the conversion of any to the truth, by engaging them in Quarrels and animosities, to the hatred of the professors and that profession, which otherwise they might be brought to assent to.

98. Since Charity obliges us to wish well to the Souls of all men, and Religion ought to alter nothing in any man's civil Estate or Right, It shall be lawful for Slaves, as all others, to enter them selves and be of what church any of them shall think best, and thereof be as fully members as any freemen. But yet, no Slave shall hereby be exempted from that civil dominion his Master has over him, but be in all other things in the same State and condition he was in before.

99. Assemblies, upon what pretence soever of Religion, not observing and performing the above said Rules shall not be Esteemed as churches, but unlawful meetings, and be punished as other Riots.

100. No person whatsoever shall disturb, molest, or persecute another for his speculative opinions in Religion or his way of worship.

2.5 EXCURSION: THE ENLIGHTENMENT

The Enlightenment denotes an intellectual movement that spanned the seventeenth and eighteenth centuries. Enlightenment thinkers stressed the role of scientific and philosophical inquiry as a means for attaining truth. Although there is no official beginning to the Enlightenment, it is generally traced to the scientific revolution of Copernicus, Galileo, and Newton.

Not all Enlightenment thinkers embraced reason at the expense of biblical authority and tradition. This may have been the case in France, but frequently the connection between the Enlightenment and Christianity was close and friendly.[43] The chief representatives of the Enlightenment in England, for instance, were Francis Bacon, Isaac Newton, and John Locke. Each of them defended the Bible—including its miracle stories.[44] George Berkeley succeeded Locke as the premier Enlightenment philosopher of England. He was a bishop in the Anglican Church and his most important philosophical work, *The Three Dialogues*, was written to prove the existence of God.

René Descartes and Blaise Pascal were forerunners of the French Enlightenment. They combined love for philosophy and reason with love for their Roman Catholic heritage.

René Descartes

Blaise Pascal

Samuel Pufendorf and Gottfried Leibniz were among the top German intellectuals of the late seventeenth century: Pufendorf was a political theorist and Leibniz a philosopher and mathematician. Both were Christians, and openly so. Pufendorf developed Calvin's political theory further and was embraced by Calvinists in Europe as well as America.[45] One of Leibniz's best-known texts, the *Theodicy*, counters the skeptics who claim that evil disproves the existence of a good God.

Nonetheless, in the eighteenth century, particularly in France, the Enlightenment turned anti-Christian. Voltaire led the way. Voltaire's target included Leibniz and the Catholic philosophical tradition known as scholasticism. The French Enlightenment's radical swing against Christianity ultimately resulted in the violent overthrow of the Roman Catholic Church and King Louis XVI in that country. Instead of ushering in a new golden age, however, the French Revolution quickly led to a reign of terror in which people suspected of disloyalty were routinely guillotined. Unlike the American Revolution, the French Revolution failed quickly and radically. Its ideals of liberty, equality, and fraternity quickly disintegrated under Napoleon Bonaparte's dictatorship.[46]

In America, the Enlightenment flourished at the Ivy League schools, whose first priority was theological education.[47] Indeed, the aim of schools like Harvard, Yale, and Princeton was to produce and maintain an educated clergy. Jonathan Edwards, a Yale graduate and the first president of the College of New Jersey (later renamed Princeton University), was a leader of

French Revolution

the American Enlightenment. Not only was Edwards a towering intellectual, but he was also a fervent preacher. Indeed, he is best remembered for his role in the religious revival known as the Great Awakening (see section 3.5). In America the Enlightenment combined a love for scholarship with a love for spiritual renewal, an unusual combination by today's standards.

Toward the end of the eighteenth century, however, the Enlightenment veered away from orthodox Christianity, substituting in its place Unitarianism and deism. Unitarians rejected formal creeds and instead made reason and conscience the criteria for religious belief and practice. Benjamin Franklin summarized Unitarianism as follows:

The most acceptable service of God was the doing good to man; that our souls are immortal; and that all crime will be punished, and virtue rewarded, either here or hereafter. These I esteem'd the essentials of every religion; and being found in all the religions we had in our country, I respected them all, tho' with different degrees of respect, as I found them more or less mix'd with other articles, which, without and tendency to inspire, promote, or confirm morality, serv'd principally to divide us, and make us unfriendly to one another.[48]

Unitarianism attempted to strip Christianity down to what is common to all religions. In the process Unitarianism threw out much of what was distinctive about Christianity.

Some Unitarians like Thomas Jefferson were also deists. According to deism, a supreme being created the universe but no longer intervenes in it. The deistic universe is a giant clock that once it is wound up continues on its own. Although a handful of America's Founders were Unitarians or deists (like Franklin and Jefferson), the majority were orthodox Christians who accepted the Bible as a whole and not a stripped-down version of it.[49]

2.6 THE WHIGS AND ALGERNON SIDNEY

In the late 1670s it became apparent to Parliament that Charles II was getting old, and that according to the rule of royal succession his brother would soon inherit the throne.

His brother was James, Duke of York. James married a Roman Catholic princess and in 1672 announced that he himself had become a Roman Catholic. This frightened many Puritan leaders who, as veterans of the Civil War, feared that England would soon face another civil war if James were permitted to become king.

They did everything in their power to prevent it. They spread the rumor that there was a "Popish plot" to assassinate Charles and to convert all of Britain to Catholicism. They attempted to pass legislation that would forbid James from becoming king.[50] Instead of Charles's brother, they wanted Charles's Protestant son, James, Duke of Monmouth. Their efforts to exclude Charles's brother from the throne led the king to dissolve Parliament in 1681, never to call it back. Charles remained committed to his brother. Not only were they good friends, but Charles had a high regard for the tradition of royal succession.[51] He was not about to let political hotheads undo the monarchy again.

Algernon Sidney

The most outspoken representative of the Puritan cause at this time was Algernon Sidney (1623–83). Sidney had fought with the Roundheads in the English Civil War and been a member of the Long Parliament. By the 1670s he had become a seasoned political philosopher. Responding to a treatise defending the divine right of kings (Robert Filmer's *Patriarcha*), Sidney wrote his best-known book, *Discourses Concerning Government*. This book reiterated many of the arguments and conclusions of Rutherford's *Lex Rex*. Sidney developed the resistance theory of the earlier Puritans and carefully presented the social contract theory of government.

According to Sidney, a government's legitimacy derives from the consent of the people; moreover, both the law of God (in the Bible) and the law of nature (in creation) permit, and even demand, resistance to a government that betrays the people's consent. Sidney was a thorough-going Protestant who in his *Discourses* used the Bible extensively to defend the theory of social contract. Sidney's discourses emphasize the covenant theology of the Old Testament and especially the legal codes of Deuteronomy.[52]

Although Locke remains the key figure who shaped the Founders' political thought, Sidney's writings were extremely influential. The Founders actually quoted Sidney more often than Locke.[53] Sidney's *Discourses Concerning Government* has been called the "textbook for the American Revolution."[54] During a visit to the University of Copenhagen, Sidney wrote in the visitor's book,

> *Manus haec inimica tyrannis*
> *Ense petit placidam cum liberate quietem.*
> (This hand, enemy to tyrants,
> By the sword seeks calm peacefulness with liberty.)

This was printed beneath the frontispiece of early editions of the *Discourses* and to this day remains the official motto of the Commonwealth of Massachusetts.

In 1775 when Presbyterians in Virginia were deciding what name to bestow on their first college in that colony, they chose two Puritan leaders of the previous century: John

Hampden, who died fighting in the Puritan Revolution in 1643, and Algernon Sidney.[55] The college exists to this day: Hampden-Sydney College ("Sidney" and "Sydney" are alternate spellings). Late in life, Jefferson wrote a letter saying that the ideas in the Declaration of Independence were really not new, and he cited Sidney as one of the writers he paraphrased.[56] When the Founders of our nation were asked what political writers were most important, they would answer Locke *and* Sidney in the same breath.

In 1683, Sidney conferred with Charles II's son about a plan to take the throne by force once Charles was dead and thereby to prevent Charles's Roman Catholic brother from becoming king. When Charles discovered this conspiracy, known as the "Rye House Plot," Sidney was put on trial for treason.[57] His *Discourses Concerning Government* was used as evidence against him. When he was executed, he took satisfaction that he was being martyred for the Protestant cause in which he had enlisted as a young man.[58] Locke was likewise accused but went into hiding, and thus avoided execution.[59]

Sidney and his political allies had ties to the earlier Roundheads, who had made a pact with the Scottish Presbyterians in the English Civil War. That association earned them the designation "Whigs"—a slang term commonly used for Scottish thugs. Sidney and his allies embraced the insult, claiming that the letters W H I G stood for "We Hope In God." In response, they labeled the supporters of the Duke of York "Tories"—a slang term used for Irish Catholic hoodlums. The insults stuck, and this ideological conflict set the stage for the famous party divisions in America in the eighteenth century.[60] Those who adopted Sidney's position, which included the Founders and patriots of the United States, called themselves Whigs; those who remained loyal to the king called themselves Tories.

2.7 THE GLORIOUS REVOLUTION

When Charles II died in 1685, his brother James II ascended the throne. James revived his grandfather's views about the divine right of kings. Committed to Roman Catholicism, James revoked the protections that Protestants had enjoyed, especially liberty of conscience. In America, James refused to recognize the colonies of New England (Massachusetts, Connecticut, Rhode Island, New Hampshire, and New York) and combined them into one government under one royal governor. These combined colonies were called the Dominion of New England.

Neither Parliament nor America was happy with James. In 1688 Parliament forced James from the throne without violence. This event is called the Glorious Revolution, or sometimes the Bloodless Revolution. In a move that satisfied both monarchists and Puritans, Parliament offered the throne to James's daughter Mary, who was married to William, a Calvinist prince in the Netherlands.[61] William and Mary quickly became the most beloved monarchs in England and America since Elizabeth I. It is therefore no surprise that the second college in America was named after them—the College of William and Mary. This

King James II

The Coronation of William III

college was located in a colonial capital city named for Prince William—Williamsburg. Williamsburg in turn was located in a colony named after the virgin queen Elizabeth—Virginia.[62]

Making William and Mary monarchs, however, raised a problem: There was no way to justify their claim to the throne on the basis of royal succession. Such a drastic change in political procedure had to be justified and defended. What right did the English have simply to terminate the reign of a king? John Locke gave the required justification. Locke wrote *Two Treatises of Government* in 1688 and 1689 during the Glorious Revolution. Along with Sidney's *Discourses*, these treatises were later quoted, cited, and plagiarized throughout America. Jefferson and the Founders made extensive use of them. It is important, therefore, to understand Locke's political philosophy.

2.8 JOHN LOCKE'S POLITICAL PHILOSOPHY

The essence of John Locke's political theory is that people set up civil governments to protect their rights of life, liberty, and property. Any government that does not serve these aims is tyrannical, and the people have the right to overthrow it.

Was this theory original with Locke? Hardly. Locke was simply articulating the views of his Roundhead and Whig colleagues. Most of Locke's political ideas are found, at least in seminal form, in Rutherford's *Lex Rex*. Locke's arguments in chapter 1 against the divine right of kings came directly from *Lex Rex*. His ideas about the scope of political power, the "state of nature," the place of reason in the law, the right of property, equality, and liberty are also found in *Lex Rex*.

Although Locke did extend Rutherford's ideas, the overlap between Locke's *Second Treatise* and Rutherford's *Lex Rex* is striking. The core of the compact theory of government is identical in both. They contain identical views on the laws of nature, human rights, property, and the authority of government. A careful study of Locke's phraseology shows that he borrowed the language of other Puritans.[63] Locke distilled concepts that were the common coin of Puritan political theory.[64]

Even Locke's distinction between natural law and divine law derives from earlier Puritan sources. Locke spoke of the "moral law" or the "law of nature" which is evident in the creation and the "law of God" which is the law given in the Bible. This distinction is taken directly from the writings of Puritans and can be found in the Westminster Confession, which speaks of the law of nature and law of the word. For his views on the law of nature, Locke frequently cited the apostle Paul's first two chapters in the epistle to the Romans.

Locke's political theory helped to inspire America's founding. Locke developed the Protestant resistance theories and gave them their final form. The English Civil War of 1641 and the Glorious Revolution of 1688 can be traced directly to the political ideas of the Protestant Reformation. The English revolutions of the seventeenth century foreshadowed the American Revolution, which looked to the same Protestant resistance theories.[65] Consequently, the royal forces in England called the American Revolution "the Presbyterian Rebellion" (see chapter 8).

THE FLIGHT OF THE REFORMATION TO AMERICA

In the decades preceding 1600, the English became interested in settling the New World, but their attempts failed. Roanoke, "the lost colony," was settled in the 1580s but mysteriously disappeared by the 1590s. The first permanent English settlement was at Jamestown, Virginia, in 1607. Thirteen years later a small group of persecuted English Protestants turned their sights on the New World as the providential answer to their quest for liberty and refuge. Those Protestants, known as the Pilgrims, sailed for the New World on August 5, 1620.

As fear and discontentment with the absolutism of Charles I accelerated, a much larger group of English Puritans would soon follow the Pilgrims so that they too could enjoy "the liberty and exercise of their own persuasions."[1] They believed that their faith could best be nurtured in a new land, away from persecution by the king and the Church of England. Cotton Mather, the most notable historian of colonial New England, was very clear: "Thus was the settlement of New England brought about...to express and pursue the Protestant Reformation."[2]

Pilgrims Landing at Plymouth Rock

When the Pilgrims arrived off the coast of Cape Cod, they quickly realized that they were about to set foot in a territory where the king's horsemen would not be available to restrain lawlessness. No existing government "had the power to command them."[3] How, then, would they be governed? Who would keep law and order? To address this problem, they gathered aboard the Mayflower and prepared a provisional social agreement, which in Latin was called a *pactus*, but in the English of those days was called a *covenant* or a *compact*. They drew up a document, now called the Mayflower Compact, which pledged their mutual submission to each other and to fair laws.

In the years that followed, as more and more Protestant communities relocated to America, more compacts and covenants were prepared throughout the colonies. For these Protestants, the essence and foundation of government is the "voluntary submission"[4] and "mutual covenant"[5] of the people. From the signing of the Mayflower Compact and throughout the settling of New England, Puritans were unanimous on this point. As early as 1640, Thomas Hooker, the founder of Connecticut, claimed that to have a legitimate government, "there must of necessity be a mutuall ingagement, each of the other, by their free consent."[6] John Winthrop, the founder of Boston, concurred: "the essentiall forme of a common weale or body politic.... I conceive to be this—The consent of a certaine companie of people, to cohabite together, under one government for their mutual safety and welfare."[7] In writing these words, Winthrop claimed to be expounding the New Testament (Romans 14:5).

For the Puritans, not only did government have its foundation in the consent of the governed, but this was a *Christian* ideal. Perry Miller, the celebrated twentieth century historian of the Puritans, states the case plainly:

> *The Puritans maintained that government originated in the consent of the people...because they did not believe that any society, civil or ecclesiastical, into which men did not enter of themselves was worthy of the name. Consequently, the social theory of Puritanism, based upon the law of God, was posited also upon the voluntary submission of the citizens.*[8]

The Puritan commitment to "free consent of the governed" played a crucial role in America's founding. Indeed, the United States was explicitly founded on this principle. Although Enlightenment thinkers adopted this principle, they hardly originated it. The Puritans had embraced it before Locke or the French philosopher Rousseau ever picked up a pen. Stanton Evans rightly observes: "The chronological factor is decisive; the evidence cited here not only predates the *Second Treatise*, most of it predates the existence of Locke himself."[9]

THE MAYFLOWER COMPACT

Composed November 1620

In the Name of God, AMEN. We whose names are underwritten, the loyal subjects of our dread Sovereign Lord King James,[10] by the Grace of God of Great Britain, France, and Ireland, King, Defender of the Faith, etc.,

Having undertaken, for the glory of God and advancement of the Christian faith and Honour of our King and Country, a Voyage to plant the first colony in the Northern parts of Virginia, do by these presents solemnly and mutually in the presence of God and one of another, Covenant and Combine ourselves together into a Civil Body Politic, for our better ordering and preservation and furtherance of the ends aforesaid; and by virtue hereof enact, constitute and frame such just and equal Laws, Ordinances, Acts, Constitutions and Offices, from time to time, as shall be though most meet and convenient for the general good of the Colony, unto which we promise all due submission and obedience. In witness hereof we have hereunder subscribed our names at Cape Cod, the 11th of November, in the year of the reign of our Sovereign Lord King James, of England, France and Ireland the eighteenth, and of Scotland the fifty-fourth. *Anno Domini* 1620.

Mr. John Carver, Mr. William Bradford, Mr. Edward Winslow, Mr. William Brewster, Isaac Allerton, Myles Standish, John Alden, John Turner, Francis Eaton, James Chilton, John Craxton, John Billington, Joses Fletcher, John Goodman, Mr. Samuel Fuller, Mr. Christopher Martin, Mr. William Mullins, Mr. William White, Mr. Richard Warren, John Howland, Mr. Steven Hopkins, Digery Priest, Thomas Williams, Gilbert Winslow, Edmund Margesson, Peter Brown, Richard Britteridge, George Soule, Edward Tilly, John Tilly, Francis Cooke, Thomas Rogers, Thomas Tinker, John Ridgdale, Edward Fuller, Richard Clark, Richard Gardiner, Mr. John Allerton, Thomas English, Edward Doten, Edward Liester

Signing of the Mayflower Compact

3.2 A GOVERNMENT OF LAWS, AND NOT OF MEN

Having experienced persecution and tyranny back in their homeland, the Puritans made sure they would not again be subjected to an absolute human ruler. The Puritans viewed their settlement in New England as a *theocracy*, that is, a government where God was their king. This, however, raised a question. Since God wasn't physically present among them, how was he to reign? The Puritans answered this question without hesitation: through the Bible. The Puritans regarded the Bible as the Word of God. Though not present physically, God could exercise his kingship through the Bible.

Public Worship at Plymouth by Pilgrims

The Bible was consulted in all church and civil matters. Although human leaders could be capricious, the Word of God was seen as eternal, unchanging, reliable, and true. Moreover, God himself was seen as merciful and just. God was the perfect king and the Bible was the perfect expression of his will. As a result, the Puritans advocated a government in which written words, not human beings, were sovereign.[11]

This, however, raised another problem. The Bible is not a systematic book of laws. It is not organized as a comprehensive set of legal statutes designed to cover every eventuality. To make the Bible's teachings more systematic, the Puritans therefore organized them into a series of covenants. The word *covenant* occurs nearly 400 times in the Old Testament and thirty-three times in the New Testament.

To the Puritans, all of God's dealings with humanity occurred through covenants. The first covenant was God's covenant with nature, reaching back to the beginning of time at the start of the human race. The Puritans viewed a covenant as a contract or agreement in which each participant was expected to do certain things. Those expectations had the force of law and, if broken, entailed certain consequences. A covenant created a binding relationship between the contracting parties that passed from generation to generation. If your parents made a covenant with someone, then you had a covenant with that person as well.

The early New England constitutions were covenants. These covenants clearly foreshadowed the United States Constitution. The first such American covenant was the Mayflower Compact discussed earlier. The second historic covenant in America, drawn up by the settlers at Salem, began with this preamble:

> We Covenant with the Lord and one with another; and doe bynd our selves in the presence of God, to walke together in all his waies, accordingly as he is pleased to reveale himself unto us in his Blessed word of truth.

Unfortunately, early Massachusetts did not honor the creator-redeemer distinction in its covenants. As a result, it was the colony most plagued with church-state conflicts, the Salem witch trials being the most notorious example.

In 1638 Thomas Hooker and several of his fellow Puritans became uneasy with Massachusetts politics. Hooker was particularly troubled because one had to be a church member to vote in civil matters. He firmly believed in the creator-redeemer distinction and the

Thomas Hooker and friends reach the Connecticut

43

Protestant doctrine of liberty of conscience. Hooker therefore envisioned a more democratic civil arrangement where one could participate in the political process without first having to join a church. He believed this would ultimately help protect the church since otherwise someone might join the church insincerely, simply for political gain. Hooker and his friends also believed strongly in a government "by the people." In this respect, Hooker was a forerunner to later Founders of the United States like Jefferson and Madison.[12]

Hooker's vision became reality when he and fellow Puritans settled the Connecticut River valley. There they founded Connecticut. In 1639 Hooker and his colleagues drafted the Fundamental Orders of Connecticut. It clearly prefigured the United States Constitution. The Fundamental Orders of Connecticut was America's first run at a constitution. Whereas the Mayflower Compact spoke in general terms about majority rule and the common welfare, the Fundamental Orders specified a detailed form for government. This document set the standard for other American constitutions.

The Fundamental Orders of Connecticut guaranteed people a voice in government regardless of church membership. What's more, this document made absolutely no mention of the king's authority.[13] Connecticut thus became "a government of laws, and not of men." John Adams later used this phrase to describe the government of the United States.[14]

THE FUNDAMENTAL ORDERS OF CONNECTICUT

January 14, 1639

PREAMBLE: We, the inhabitants and residents of Windsor, Hartford, and Wethersfield…knowing where a people are gathered together the word of God requires that to maintain the peace and union of such a people there ought to be an orderly and decent government established according to God…therefore associate…ourselves to be as one public state or commonwealth and do, for ourselves and our successors…enter into combination and confederation together, to maintain and preserve the liberty and purity of the gospel of our Lord Jesus, which we now profess…and also in our civil affairs to be guided and governed according to the laws, rules, orders, and decrees as shall be made, ordered, and decreed, as follows:

1. It is ordered…that there shall be yearly two general assemblies or courts: The one the second Thursday in April, the other the second Thursday in September, following. The first shall be called the Court of Election, wherein shall be yearly chosen…so many magis-

trates and other public officers as shall be found requisite whereof one to be chosen governor for the year ensuing and until another be chosen, and no other magistrate be chosen for more than one year provided always there be six chosen besides the governor; which being chosen and sworn according to an oath recorded for that purpose shall have the power to administer justice according to the laws here established, and for want thereof according to the rule of the word of God; which choice shall be made by all that are admitted freemen and have taken the oath of fidelity…(having been admitted inhabitants by the major part of the town wherein they live) or the major part of such as shall be then present….

4. It is ordered that no person be chosen governor above once in two years, and that the governor be always a member of some approved congregation, and formerly of the magistracy within this jurisdiction; and all the magistrates freemen of this commonwealth….

5. It is ordered…that to the aforesaid Court of Election the several towns shall send their deputies, and when the elections are ended they may proceed in any public service as at other courts. Also the other General Court in September shall be for making laws, and other public occasion, which concerns the good of the commonwealth….

7. It is ordered…that after there are warrants given out for any of the said general courts, the constable…of each town shall forthwith give notice distinctly to the inhabitants of the same… that at a place and time by him or them limited and set, they meet and assemble …to elect and choose certain deputies to be at the General Court then following to agitate the affairs of the commonwealth…. deputies shall be chosen by all that are admitted inhabitants in the several towns and have taken the oath of fidelity; provided that none be chosen a deputy for any general court who is not a freeman of this commonwealth….

8. It is ordered…that Windsor, Hartford, and Wethersfield shall have power, each town…to send four of their freemen as their deputies to every general court; and whatsoever other towns shall be hereafter added to this jurisdiction…shall send so many deputies as the court shall judge meet…which deputies shall have the power of the whole town to give their votes and allowance to all such laws and orders as may be for the public good and unto which the said towns are to be bound.

9. It is ordered…that the deputies thus chosen shall have power and liberty to appoint a time and a place of meeting to gather before any general court to advise and consult of all such things as may concern the good of the public, as also to examine their own elections….

10. It is ordered…that every general court…shall consist of the governor, or someone chosen to moderate the court, and four other magistrates at least, with the major part of the deputies of the

several towns legally chosen; and in case the freemen or major part of them, through neglect or refusal of the governor and major part of the magistrates, shall call a court, it shall consist the supreme power of the commonwealth, and they only shall have power to make laws or repeal them, to grant levies, to admit…freemen, dispose of lands undisposed of to several towns or persons, and…shall have power to call either court or magistrate or any other person whatsoever into question for any misdemeanor, and may for just causes displace or deal otherwise according to the nature of the offense; and…may deal [with]…any other matter that concerns the common good of this commonwealth, except election of magistrates, which shall be done by the whole body of the freemen…. The governor or moderator shall have power to order the court to give liberty of speech, and silence…disorderly speakings, to put all things to vote, and in case the vote be equal to have the casting vote. But none of these courts shall be adjourned or dissolved without the consent of the major part of the court.

11. It is ordered…that when any general court…has agreed upon any… sums of money to be levied upon the several towns within this jurisdiction…a committee [shall be] chosen to set out and appoint what shall be the proportion of every town to pay of the said levy, provided the committees be made up of an equal number out of each town.

3.3 CALVIN'S DILEMMA

Christianity's role in America's early development was not always positive. Protestants quickly forgot Luther's emphasis on liberty of conscience and the creator-redeemer distinction once they themselves wielded the power of government. This confusion began in Geneva under John Calvin.

Although in theory Calvin agreed with Luther that the conscience was free, in practice he had difficulty balancing church and state. The problem arose from a conflict of interest. Calvin had two official responsibilities in Geneva: he was the city's mayor, and he was its chief pastor. As head of both church and state in Geneva, Calvin was unable to keep his two jobs separate. As a pastor he agreed that religious beliefs could not be forced. As a politician he oppressed those who differed with his religious beliefs.

In his *Institutes*, Calvin insists that civil government must ensure "no idolatry, no blasphemy against the name of God, no calumnies against his truth, nor other offences to religion, break out and be disseminated among the people."[15] Calvin did not view this as mixing church and state. In his historical context, a violation like blasphemy was not merely an offense against religion, but also an offense against social decency. Blasphemy—uttering insults at God—was considered an offense against one's neighbor and therefore came under the jurisdiction of the state.

Likewise in America today there are laws against obscenity, public nakedness, unaccepted sexual behavior, opening courts on Sunday, and so on. These laws derive from the religious norms of our culture. In the English Common Law the corresponding crimes were called "Offenses Against God And Religion."[16] Nowadays hardly anyone would argue that a law which forbids someone to run nude in the park mixes politics and religion. Nevertheless, the legal requirement to wear clothes has clear religious roots (compare Genesis 3:7). The practice of clothes-wearing certainly is not universal or transcultural. Wearing clothes is a Judeo-Christian convention that has been seared into our social conscience. We simply take it for granted. It's just decent.[17]

Calvin took the same approach, arguing that laws against blasphemy preserved common decency. Calvin's problem was that he had difficulty separating common decency with his own sense of decency. The arrest and execution of Michael Servetus illustrates this point. Servetus was an eccentric and psychologically unstable genius. A generation before William Harvey, he discovered the cardiopulmonary circulation of blood. He also dabbled in philosophy and religion, and espoused some views that branded him a heretic.

John Calvin

47

Servetus lived in Spain, a staunchly Catholic country, where he openly denied the doctrine of the Trinity. From Spain he exchanged letters with Calvin over that question. Their correspondence was not friendly. Servetus was arrested and put on trial in Spain as a heretic, but escaped from prison before he could be executed. He decided to flee through Switzerland and on his journey stopped in Geneva to hear Calvin preach.

While sitting in church, bothering no one, Servetus was recognized. Although he had committed no criminal acts in Switzerland, he was arrested and put on trial for heresy. The charge against him was that he denied the doctrine of the Trinity. This was his "idolatry and blasphemy." Servetus received the death penalty for his beliefs even though he had done nothing in Switzerland to threaten or harm anyone. The Genevans executed him by burning him at the stake. Calvin supported the arrest and execution of Servetus and acted as one of the prosecutors in the case.

Many of the early Puritans took Calvin's example to mean that government should regulate the content of all religious teaching. For example, when the Puritan movement began to take shape in the late 1500s, some of its early leaders, particularly those in Scotland and in England, simply assumed that a truly "Christian" government would adopt the Puritan form of Christianity and punish non-Puritan forms as heretical. Likewise in New England it was common for Puritans to regard Catholic, Baptist, Quaker, Mennonite, or Methodist beliefs as "public blasphemy." This meant that any form of Christianity other than Puritanism could be outlawed or suppressed.

This was ironic. When Catholics were in control, they punished Protestants for holding incorrect religious beliefs. When Protestants were in control, they punished Catholics for holding incorrect beliefs. Both sides wanted the government to enforce right religion, but neither allowed the other to define right religion. Both Catholics and Protestants agreed that secular government only had authority over outward conduct, but then gave government authority to punish people for holding "incorrect" religious beliefs. Both sides advocated a creator-redeemer distinction only to annul it by saying that an offense against the redeemer was also an offense against the creator.

Both sides were caught in a dilemma. If government had the power to control religion and suppress false beliefs, then government would exercise that power whether controlled by Catholics or Protestants. The Protestant Reformation in Europe and in the American colonies forced people to reexamine the traditional merger between church and state. America in particular was to become the test case for resolving the tension between religious freedom and social conformity.

We struggle with Calvin's dilemma even today. Although we pride ourselves on being committed to freedom of religion, the debate continues whether children should be allowed to pray in public schools. On the other hand, some issues are quite clear. For instance, we rightly do not extend freedom of religion to the father whose religion requires him to sacrifice his firstborn. Whether it be abortion, obscenity, legalization of drugs, homosexuality, or any other "hot" political topic, we always come back to Calvin's dilemma: how far does the freedom to believe and exercise one's beliefs extend? The Puritans said that it ended as soon as the good of the community suffered. But that raises the problem of how we determine what actions are harmful to the community.

3.4 THE PURITAN PREDICAMENT IN AMERICA

The early New England colonies modeled themselves after Calvin's Geneva. This had advantages and disadvantages. On the positive side, it promoted industriousness, literacy, and morality. On the negative side, it encouraged rigidity and oppression. For example, there are numerous recorded instances where Anabaptists, Quakers, and other dissenters were whipped, fined, and imprisoned for having "wrong" beliefs. As the early New England Puritans continued to encounter dissent, they were gradually forced to rediscover the creator-redeemer distinction and the principle of liberty of conscience. At the time of America's founding, these ideals were fully revived. Getting there, however, was a hard road.

3.4.1 ROGER WILLIAMS

In the 1630s, when a religious dissenter named Roger Williams came to Massachusetts, the early Puritans' political theories were put to the test. Williams, who was a Cambridge-educated Puritan, an ordained minister, and the founder of Rhode Island, spent his life championing liberty of conscience. Williams was deeply committed to Luther's understanding of the creator-redeemer distinction, the principle of liberty of conscience, and their implications for the separation of church and state. According to Williams, the civil order in New England was too intertwined with the church.

Roger Williams

Following Luther, Williams wrote, "An enforced uniformity of religion throughout a nation or civil state confounds the civil and religious, [and] denies the principles of Christianity."[18] His criticisms of the Massachusetts government resulted in his expulsion from that colony. He used the occasion to start his own New England colony called Rhode Island. His was the first colony in America where separation of church and state was explicit. He insisted that it was unbiblical for civil magistrates to compel the conscience of citizens, especially in religious matters.[19] According to Williams, such coercion violated the teaching of the New Testament (Luke 9:52–56).[20] As a result, Williams's colony of Rhode Island became an early prototype for the United States.

Williams's tolerant views attracted to Rhode Island many nonconformists and radicals who took unfair advantage of their freedoms. By 1655 Williams had to warn Rhode Island citizens that there was a legitimate role for civil government: government "may judge, resist, compel, and punish such transgressors, according to their deserts and merits."[21] Rhode Island thus forecast the tension throughout America's history between freedom and anarchy. It is a tension with which we continue to wrestle today.

3.4.2 ANNE HUTCHINSON

Meantime, in 1636 a woman from Boston named Anne Hutchinson began to teach doctrines which the Puritan leaders regarded as erroneous.[22] Hutchinson did not believe that good behavior was evidence that a person was right with God. She claimed that the

Anne Hutchinson

Puritan leaders were wrongly preaching that people must obey a set of rules to be accepted by God. They responded by calling her views "antinomian," that is, lawless. The standard Protestant teaching was that people were accepted or saved by God only through God's grace and without following any set of rules. But Protestants were also divided about the necessity of following rules once saved. By charging that the Puritan leaders were preaching that people must obey a set of rules to be saved, Hutchinson was doing the next thing to calling them Roman Catholics, which was the worst insult in colonial New England.

Hutchinson was ordered to trial. The charge against her was not heresy, but "disparaging" (slandering) the ministers, which was considered a disturbance of the peace. In fact, what was at issue between the government and Hutchinson was a matter of Christian doctrine and personal conscience. At her trial one person did speak in her defense, arguing that there "is no law of God that she hath broken nor any law of the country that she hath broke, and therefore deserves no censure."[23] But the majority of the Puritan leaders saw things differently and found her "not fit for our society."[24] She was banished from the colony. These leaders were trying to preserve the Protestant doctrine of separate kingdoms and at the same time trying to regulate religious beliefs through civil laws.

The Trial of Anne Hutchinson

3.4.3 PURITAN DESPERATION

As the seventeenth century progressed, the Puritan predicament in Massachusetts grew worse. The rigid requirements laid on its citizens resulted in increased numbers of persons leaving the church. This crisis led to the Half-Way Covenant (1662), which attempted to preserve the community by allowing unconverted persons to have their children baptized. This measure seemed to indicate a growing toleration among the Puritans. It failed, however, to slow the growing religious diversity among the settlers. More thorough-going measures, culminating in the founding principles of our nation, would be required before genuine liberty of conscience was possible.

With the close of the seventeenth century, the Puritan dilemma came to a head. As more and more settlers opted out of the Puritan system, the Puritan leaders became increasingly anxious about their society. This anxiety led to the preaching of sermons known as *jeremiads*. A jeremiad was a fiery sermon warning of destruction to the community if people did not repent and return to God. These sermons fell largely on deaf ears. The religion-weary Massachusetts Puritans were less intent on reforming their lives than on subduing the Native Americans.

In 1675 the violent King Philip's War broke out between the Puritans and the Native Americans. This war was named after Philip Metacomet, the sachem (chief) of the Wampanoag tribe. Philip resented the colonists' intrusion and control in the affairs of his people. Fighting between Native Americans and New Englanders first broke out in a frontier settlement, but quickly spread throughout southern New England. Philip's raiding parties destroyed many New England towns, killing or capturing their inhabitants. In the end, however, the colonists proved victorious. In August 1676 they trapped and killed Philip. Despite the colonists' victory, many Puritan leaders viewed this war as God's judgment on the declining Puritan community.

3.4.4 THE SALEM WITCH TRIALS

Anxiety among Puritan leaders about the declining state of religion in Massachusetts created a climate of tension and distrust. This climate made the colony ripe for a witch-

Salem Witch Trial

Witchcraft Trial of George Jacobs

hunt. Their community was slowly collapsing and in their minds only one perpetrator could be responsible: the devil. When a West Indian servant lady in Salem named Tituba was observed engaging in her native religious practices, a terrible crisis ensued. A group of teenage girls who witnessed Tituba's practices accused her of witchcraft to avoid being suspected themselves. The attention the teenage girls received gave them a sense of power. They got carried away and started accusing others of witchcraft, apparently for revenge, or perhaps for amusement.

The judges of the court at Salem were Puritans lamenting the decline of society. They were looking for a scapegoat. Coupled with the adolescent accusers' sense of power and the Puritan leaders' anxiety about society, the misunderstanding of Tituba's religious practices provided all the ingredients for a legal fiasco.[25] The notorious witch trials of Salem and the subsequent executions became a permanent blot against the Massachusetts Puritans.

The Puritan predicament culminated in the Salem witch trials. Within a few years after the trials, Puritan leaders acknowledged the terrible tragedy that occurred in Salem in 1692. The bitter experience of these trials taught the colonies a valuable lesson. The next hundred years of political thought in the colonies would focus on recovering the Protestant commitment to liberty of conscience, reviving the creator-redeemer distinction, and providing a clearer division between church and state.

The witch trials had a profound influence on the Founders of our nation. The way the trials were mishandled pressed hard on the Founders' minds. The trials showed the Founders what they needed to guard against if they were to preserve liberty and justice. No other single event had as great an impact on the American Bill of Rights, which was drafted in 1791. The first, fourth, fifth, sixth, and eighth amendments to the United States Constitution provided safeguards against the way justice was misadministered in Salem.

3.5 THE FIRST GREAT AWAKENING

During the early eighteenth century, the English monarchs treated the American colonies with what historians call "salutary neglect." Essentially, this meant that the crown did not interfere with the colonists' activities so long as they were operating peacefully and contributing toward the prosperity of Great Britain.[26] England's more pressing concern was with the Jacobites (those who remained loyal to the Stuart family).[27] After James II Stuart was deposed from his throne in 1688, he and his family continued trying to regain it by force. His heirs became known as the Pretenders, and they persistently plotted to reassert their place on the throne. Besides pressure from the Jacobites, England was also at war with France.

The problems in England left the American colonists free to pursue the desire of their hearts. What was their desire? For the Puritans who left England in search of freedom, it was summed up in the words of Calvin: "The principal care and solicitude of our life should be to seek God and to aspire to Him with all affection of heart."[28] This goal was inscribed upon the hearts of most Americans from the time they could talk. After the Salem witch trials, however, many hearts turned away, and newcomers and newborns were increasingly indifferent to the Puritan vision.

Americans were steeped in Christianity, the Bible, and church politics. The outward trappings of Christianity were evident everywhere. At the same time, however, religion was becoming mechanical and not from the heart. The colonists seemed to have lost their grandparents' zeal for the faith. A 1727 New England earthquake was interpreted by some as God's displeasure at the colonists' lukewarm faith. In the 1730s a diphtheria outbreak heightened these suspicions. What is more, doubts were being raised about whether the majority of the clergy were themselves sincere Christians.[29]

Amidst this turmoil America experienced a religious revival. This event is usually called the Great Awakening. The Great Awakening can be traced back to Halle, Germany, where Theodore Freylinghuysen attended seminary. There in the late seventeenth century a group of Lutherans called *pietists* emphasized joyful devotion to God as the essence of Christianity. Freylinghuysen caught the spirit and carried it to New Jersey where he preached among Dutch settlers during the 1720s. He inspired a family of preachers from Scotland named the Tennents, who spread the movement among the Scottish-Irish immigrants.[30] As part of their efforts they established the Log Seminary. A student of the Log Seminary named Samuel Blair went on to found his own Log College and enrolled Samuel Finley and Samuel Davies, both of whom later became presidents of the College of New Jersey (the future Princeton University).[31]

Ministers at Oxford University in England also experienced a burst of energy at this time. Led by John Wesley, they were first called the Holy Club, but eventually their disciplined approach to religion earned them the label Methodists. Among them was a charismatic orator named George Whitefield (pronounced *WIT-feeld*). Wesley and Whitefield both traveled to America as evangelists. Whitefield stayed in America much longer than Wesley. He traveled from New England to

John Wesley

George Whitefield

the Deep South preaching wherever he could, usually in public squares. Whitefield's voice was so strong that Benjamin Franklin calculated it was possible for 30,000 people to hear him at a given time.[32] Whitefield's ability to move people's emotions was extraordinary. Franklin describes an occasion when he was determined not to put any money into Whitefield's collection plate:

> *I perceived he intended to finish with a collection, and I silently resolved he should get nothing from me. I had in my pocket a handful of copper money, three or four silver dollars, and five pistoles of gold. As he proceeded, I began to soften and concluded to give him the coppers. Another stroke of his oratory made me ashamed of that and determined me to give the silver; and he finished so admirably that I emptied my pocket wholly into the collector's dish, gold and all. At this sermon there was also one...who had by precaution emptied his pockets before he came from his home; toward the conclusion of the discourse, however, he felt a strong desire to give and applied to a neighbor who stood near him to borrow some money for the purpose.... His answer was, "At any other time, Friend Hopkinson, I would lend to thee freely, but not now; for thee seems to be out of thy right senses."[33]*

If Whitefield could touch a heart as critical as Franklin's, his impact on people eager to be converted was even greater.

During Whitefield's stay in America, he became the friend of Jonathan Edwards. Edwards had been a child prodigy. Entering Yale at age twelve, he immediately began unraveling complex philosophical treatises. Upon his conversion he became committed to two central ideas: (1) true Christianity always penetrates and affects the heart, and (2) God exercises full control over all of the universe.

Jonathan Edwards

54

Edwards pastored a Massachusetts church where he became a central figure in the Great Awakening. There he preached his most famous sermon, "Sinners in the Hands of an Angry God." In it he emphasized the urgency of God's redemption and humanity's utter dependence on God's grace. That sermon marked the high point of a tremendous religious awakening that swept the colonies between 1735 and 1750. People would literally fall down, overcome by emotion at the gravity of their sin and the forgiveness offered by God.

How was this awakening to be explained? Edwards attributed the awakening to God. This is the explanation that the colonists themselves provided. Edwards, in "Some Thoughts Concerning the Recent Revival" and "Narrative of Surprising Conversions," concluded that the religious intensification that occurred in the early eighteenth century was just that—surprising. The awakening was considered a providential work of God's spirit.

As a result of his brilliance, fame and piety, Edwards was in the 1750s invited to assume the presidency of the College of New Jersey. He accepted the offer. Soon after he arrived he was informed about a scientific experiment to develop a vaccine for smallpox. Those conducting the experiment needed volunteers as subjects. Edwards, a firm believer in the progress of science, felt it would set a good example if he volunteered to receive the inoculation. He did, but became ill with smallpox. After a brief period of recovery, he eventually succumbed to the disease. Edwards died in 1758, a martyr for science.

This early end to Edwards's life meant a drastic change for the fate of the colonies. Edwards was one of the two most famous American celebrities of his era. Once Edwards was gone, Benjamin Franklin stood alone as the most influential personality in the colonies. Franklin's ideals differed significantly from those of Edwards. Edwards was an ardent defender of orthodox Christianity. Franklin, though raised as a Presbyterian, became increasingly attracted to the anti-Christian views of the French Enlightenment (see section 2.5). Edwards did not live long enough to take on Franklin's writings. Franklin's ideals, as proclaimed in his *Poor Richard's Almanac*, became ingrained in the minds of Americans. Had Edwards lived, he would likely have been a member of the Continental Congress and the Constitutional Convention, alongside Franklin.

The Great Awakening also made an impact on Virginia. At the urging of his Log College mentors,

Poor Richard, 1733.

AN

Almanack

For the Year of Christ

1733,

Being the First after LEAP YEAR:

And makes since the Creation	Years
By the Account of the Eastern *Greeks*	7241
By the Latin Church, when ☉ ent. ♈	6932
By the Computation of *W.W*	5742
By the *Roman* Chronology	5682
By the *Jewish* Rabbies	5494

Wherein is contained

The Lunations, Eclipses, Judgment of the Weather, Spring Tides, Planets Motions & mutual Aspects, Sun and Moon's Rising and Setting, Length of Days, Time of High Water, Fairs, Courts, and observable Days

Fitted to the Latitude of Forty Degrees, and a Meridian of Five Hours West from *London*, but may without sensible Error, serve all the adjacent Places, even from *Newfoundland* to *South-Carolina.*

By *RICHARD SAUNDERS*, Philom.

PHILADELPHIA:

Printed and sold by *B. FRANKLIN*, at the New Printing Office near the Market.

The Third Impression.

Title page of Poor Richard's Almanac

Samuel Davies took the revival to Virginia. He started preaching there in 1748, and soon a revival was in full swing. During that time the government of Virginia officially endorsed the Anglican church, giving it preferential treatment and collecting tax revenues for it. Davies disapproved and became a champion of those in Virginia who were not Anglican, namely the Baptists and Presbyterians.[34] Davies's most famous disciple was a young man named Patrick Henry. Henry went on to become the orator who with his fiery speeches launched Virginia into the American Revolution.

After his time in Virginia, Davies traveled to Britain to rally support for the Presbyterian colleges in the colonies.[35] While there, Davies had the opportunity to preach to King George II. He reportedly chastised the king for not paying close attention to his sermon.[36] Upon his return to America, the trustees of the College of New Jersey called on Davies to assume the office of president (the post that Jonathan Edwards had just vacated by his untimely death). When King George II died, Davies preached a sermon praising George for his policy of "salutary neglect" and warning that any other royal policy would not be tolerated. A few years later George III changed that policy of neglect to one of interference. The consequence was the birth of a new nation.

3.6 THE IMPACT OF THE AWAKENING

Benjamin Franklin

The majority of people who founded the United States of America either experienced, or were children of those who experienced, the religious awakening of the 1740s. For example, Benjamin Rush, a central figure at the Continental Congress and a signer of the Declaration of Independence, attributed the development of his ideals to the Great Awakening preachers (the Tennents and Whitefield).[37] Patrick Henry related that he was "first taught what an orator should be" by listening to Samuel Davies's sermons.[38] The effect of the awakening upon Samuel Adams's political activism has been well documented.[39] Benjamin Franklin's early attempts at colonial union paralleled the intercolonial endeavors of the revivalists.[40]

The Great Awakening advanced higher education throughout the colonies. Not only did it stimulate the colonists' love of learning (especially for the Bible), but by increasing the number of new Christians, the awakening increased the need for educated clergy. Princeton, Brown, Rutgers, Columbia, and Dartmouth were all established because the awakening created a demand for more clergy (see chapter 4).

There is a close connection between the Great Awakening and America's founding. Alan Heimert has argued persuasively that the awakening produced and cultivated the social climate necessary for the revolution.[41] Keith Griffin has argued that the theology of the awakening supplied the political theory that was responsible for the revolution.[42] The Christian message of sin and redemption provided a common reference point for all Americans and bred America's first traveling celebrities.[43] The awakening was the first successful intercolonial event. It united the colonies in a common bond. This bond would eventually become the union declared in Philadelphia in 1776.

At the forefront of the Founders' political consciousness was their religious heritage: (1) They embraced Luther's and Calvin's theories concerning the creator-redeemer distinction and resistance to leaders who encroach upon it. (2) They looked to the English Puritan revolutions of the seventeenth century as their glorious legacy in the same way we look to the American Revolution today. (3) They were steeped in Calvinist resistance theories as expressed by seventeenth-century writers like Milton, Rutherford, Sidney, and Locke. (4) They employed the covenantal model of government as derived from the Christian Scriptures to organize their New England communities. (5) They were raised on the preachers of the Great Awakening the way we are raised today on television. Christian ideals shaped and permeated the Founders' political worldview.

THE SOCIO-CULTURAL BACKDROP FOR THE FOUNDING OF THE UNITED STATES

As the great majority of early settlers of the country were from Great Britain, they declared that the common law of England should be the law here. But Christianity is the basis of the common law of England, and is therefore of the law of this country.... [The early settlers] introduced their religion into their families, their schools, and their colleges.... They formed themselves as Christians into municipal and state organizations. They acknowledged God in their legislative assemblies. They prescribed oaths to be taken in his name. They closed their courts, their places of business, their legislatures, and all places under the public control, on the Lord's Day. They declared Christianity to be part of the common law of the land. In the process of time thousands have come among us, who are neither Protestants nor Christians. Some are papists, some Jews, some infidels, and some atheists. All are welcomed; all are admitted to equal rights and privileges. All are allowed to acquire property, and to vote in every election, made eligible to all offices, and invested with equal influence in all public affairs. All are allowed to worship as they please, or not to worship at all, if they see fit. No man is required to profess any form of faith, or to join any religious association.... Christianity does not teach that men can be made religious by law. ★

- Charles Hodge

PROLOGUE: THE ROLE OF NEW ENGLAND AND VIRGINIA IN THE DEVELOPMENT OF AMERICAN IDEALS

THE ENGLISH COMMON LAW

At the founding of our nation, two principal centers shaped American culture: New England and Virginia. New England was the cradle and Virginia was the nursery of our American identity. Although Virginia was chronologically the first region in America settled by the English, New England quickly became the most populated and culturally distinctive region in the seventeenth century.

It was in New England that all children were first required by law to attend school. For more than half a century it was only in New England that a person could attend college. It was in New England that constitutional and republican forms of local government first flourished. It was in New England that the political response to religious dissent first became an issue. New England was the soil that sprouted America's first celebrities: intellectuals like Jonathan Edwards and Benjamin Franklin, and patriots like Samuel Adams and Paul Revere. It was in New England that the call to separate from England first went out. It was in New England that the first shots in the war for independence were fired.

The New England Puritans largely defined the values and norms of America's culture leading up to the Revolution. But as the Revolution approached, Virginians took center stage. The Revolutionary War began in New England but *ended* in Virginia at the hands of George Washington, who himself was a Virginian. When the United States was founded, Virginia was the largest colony in America. It included present-day West Virginia, Kentucky, Ohio, Indiana, and Illinois. Four of the first five presidents of the United States were from Virginia. The site for the United States capital was chosen to be on the border of Virginia by the Potomac River, and named for the Virginian who chose it.

At the founding of the United States it was Virginians who wrote (1) the birthing document of the nation (the Declaration of Independence); (2) the rules for the establishment of townships and for new territories to become states (the Northwest Ordinance); (3) the lion's share of the Federal Constitution; (4) the Bill of Rights; (5) the first executive orders; (6) the rules for Parliamentary Practice in the United States Congress; and (7) the *Marbury v. Madison* decision which established the Supreme Court's role regarding judicial review. Shortly thereafter it was a Virginian (Thomas Jefferson) who doubled the size of the United States by purchasing the Louisiana territory. Another Virginian established the end of colonialism in the Western Hemisphere (the Monroe Doctrine).

New England and Virginia were the soil in which the United States blossomed. From New England and Virginia the United States received its most permanent educational, social, cultural, and political imprints. In understanding the genesis of our American ideals, it is therefore crucial to understand the socio-cultural backdrop of these colonies. In this unit we will examine four aspects of America's socio-cultural history: (1) the common laws enforced in colonial American municipalities; (2) the educational institutions that shaped the minds of the young; (3) the family structures and customs of the middle class; and (4) the nomenclature (naming patterns) of one of the earliest American communities.

4.1 THE COMMON LAW AND CHRISTIAN MORALITY

When the English colonized America, they did not start from scratch in writing laws for themselves. They embraced the English laws as their own. The English legal tradition,

King Alfred

called the Common Law, has ancient origins and is grounded in Judeo-Christian morality. About A.D. 890 King Alfred the Great had the laws of England codified. He simply took the Mosaic Law (as found in the Old Testament) and expanded and modified it, applying it to the circumstances of the people of England at that time.

As time went on and new legal issues arose, the Common Law was expanded. It began to include more detailed guidance about civil rights, as well as more specific moral laws regulating proper behavior. In the thirteenth century, Henri Bracton wrote *De Legibus et Consuetudinibus Angliae* (On the Laws and Customs of England).[1] Bracton put in writing the judicial practices and decisions that had been in usage from time immemorial. In the centuries that followed a number of legal scholars continued to clarify and expand the Common Law. Most notable were Sir Edward Coke and Sir William Blackstone. Coke's and Blackstone's writings gave early Americans their law.

The Common Law was thus a body of legal principles that developed over time as a result of traditional and time-tested judicial decisions. The Common Law followed Judeo-Christian morality closely. Behaviors that were considered unlawful included:

Sabbath-Breaking

Witchcraft

Cursing

Public Exposure

Fornication and Adultery

Incest

Homosexuality

Polygamy

Arbitrary Divorce

Prostitution

Gambling

Drunk and Disorderly Conduct

The Common Law prohibited these behaviors not because they were harmful to other persons, but because they were thought offensive to God and religion. Blackstone clearly delineated between offenses to persons and offenses to God and religion. Blackstone argued that these behaviors were regulated by the "Revealed Law" (i.e., the Bible).

The Common Law was more than just a list of prohibitions. For instance, it endorsed public care for the poor and infirmed, or what we now call welfare programs. The Common Law based public welfare directly on biblical commands in the Old and New Testaments.[2]

When the United States was founded in 1776, the Founders did not dispense with the English Common Law. On the contrary, to this day most states continue to defer to the Common Law.[3] When the state legislatures began to write their own legal codes, they used Blackstone's system as a guide. As a result, state laws generally included a heading titled "Offences Against God and Religion."[4] Eventually, some of these laws were given a nickname: Blue Laws.

In our day many of these laws are slowly being repealed on the grounds that they are explicitly religious. The consequences for our culture have been profound. Harold Berman, a foremost scholar on the Common Law, observes the current trend:

The law is becoming more fragmented, more subjective, geared more to expediency and less to morality, concerned more with immediate consequences and less with consistency or continuity. Thus the historical soil of the Western legal tradition is being washed away in the twentieth century, and the tradition itself is threatened with collapse.... This did not occur at once, since the predominant system of beliefs throughout the West remained Christian. It is only in the twentieth century that the Christian foundations of Western law have been almost totally rejected.... Thus not only legal thought but also the very structure of Western legal institutions have been removed from their spiritual foundations, and those foundations, in turn, are left devoid of the structure that once stood upon them.[5]

SIR WILLIAM BLACKSTONE, KNT.
COMMENTARIES ON THE LAW

BOOK IV, CHAPTER IV
OFFENCES AGAINST GOD AND RELIGION

Defined. These are crimes which more immediately offend God, by openly transgressing the precepts of religion, either natural or revealed, and mediately, by their bad example and consequence, the law of society also, which renders them amenable to censure.

Basis of Judicial Oaths. The belief in a future state of rewards and punishments, the entertaining just ideas of the attributes of the Supreme Being, and a firm persuasion that He superintends and will finally compensate every action in human life, are the grand foundation of judicial oaths, which call God to witness the truth of those facts, which perhaps may only be known to him and the party attesting. All moral evidence, all confidence in human veracity [are] weakened by apostasy, and overthrown by total infidelity.

Gross Impieties. We proceed now to consider some gross impieties and immoralities, which are punished by our municipal law, frequently in concurrence with the ecclesiastical; the spiritual court punishing *pro salute animae*, for the safety of the soul, while the temporal courts correct more for the sake of example, than for private amendment.

Blasphemy. An offence against God and religion is that of blasphemy against the Almighty, by denying His being or providence, or by contumelious reproaches of Christ. Also all profane scoffing at the holy scriptures, or exposing them to contempt and ridicule. This is punished by fine and imprisonment, or infamous corporal punishment.

Cursing. This is somewhat allied to blasphemy. By statute of George II, which repeals all former acts, every laborer, sailor, or soldier profanely swearing, shall forfeit one shilling for every offence, and every other person under the degree of a gentleman, two shillings; and every gentleman or person of rank, five shillings, for the poor of the parish, and on the second offence, double, and the third offence, treble. In default of payment, the offender shall be sent to the house of correction for ten days. Profanity was expressly forbidden in stage plays.

Profanation of the Lord's Day. This offence is vulgarly called Sabbath-Breaking, and is punished by municipal law. Beside the indecency and scandal of permitting any regular business to be publicly transacted on that day in a country professing Christianity, and the corruption of morals which usually follows its profanation, the keeping this day holy, as a time of relaxation, as well as for public worship, is of admirable service to a state, considered merely as a civil institution. It humanizes, by the help of conversation and society, the manners of the lower classes, which would otherwise degenerate into a wild ferocity and savage selfishness of spirit; it enables the industrious workman to pursue his occupation during the ensuing week with health and cheerfulness; it imprints upon the minds of the people that sense of their duty to their God, so necessary to make them good citizens, but which would be defaced by an unremitted continuance of labor, without any stated time to recall them to the worship of their Maker.

Drunkenness. By statute of James I, this vice was punished by a fine of five shillings, or by sitting six hours in the stocks, by which time it was presumed that the culprit would become sobered, and not liable to do the mischief.

Open Lewdness. This is either by frequenting houses of ill-fame, which is an indictable offence, or by some grossly scandalous and public indecency, for which the punishment is fine and imprisonment. In the year 1650, not only were incest and adultery capital crimes, but also the repeated acts of keeping a brothel or committing fornication, were upon a second conviction, made felony, without benefit of clergy.

4.2 THE COMMON LAW AND THE FOUNDING

The great achievement of the Founders was to form an independent representative republic that incorporated all thirteen colonies. Nevertheless, the legal basis for that achievement was long-standing. The ideas upon which the Founders acted had been consciously and intentionally nurtured through the centuries by the leading representatives of the English Common Law. The core concepts of law and rights, which were a by-product of the Common Law, were the shared heritage of both Catholics and Protestants. *The Common Law was generally founded upon biblical law.* It was proclaimed and maintained by major spokespersons of both traditions at practically all points in the history of Europe and England after the twelfth century. The Common Law provided the basic theory of law and rights at the time of American independence. It provided a ground of consensus for the Founders as well as for the rest of America.

Magna Carta

4.2.1 THE MAGNA CARTA

The Magna Carta, signed in 1215, was England's most important legal document—perhaps the most significant in Western History.[6] This document defined the legal rights of freemen in England. It was written by Cardinal Stephen Langton (d. 1228). Langton had taught theology at Paris before being sent to England to become the Archbishop of Canterbury.[7] Langton was an expert in theology and political theory. M. Stanton Evans describes the Magna Carta's political and religious context.[8]

As might be expected from biblical ideas of kingship, the foremost political concept of the Middle Ages was constitutionalism—establishing limits on the power of kings…. Of the several sources that embodied this idea of limits, the foremost, by a tremendous length, was the church…. On net balance, it is fair to say, the Catholic Church of the Middle Ages was the institution in Western history that did the most to advance the cause of constitutional statecraft. This resulted from its constant readiness, in the spirit of Hebrew prophets, to challenge the might of kings and emperors if they transgressed the teachings of religion.[9]

Siding with the nobility of England in a dispute with Prince John, Langton drafted the Magna Carta, which John was then forced to sign. By signing it, John promised to protect the rights of the church, the rights of Christians, and the rights of English citizens generally.[10] The first article (of the sixty-three that are listed in the Magna Carta) guarantees religious liberty. The rest flow from that basic foundation.[11]

As a Catholic theologian, Langton appealed to the Catholic church's own legal tradition, known as

King John signing the Magna Carta

canon law, in drafting the Magna Carta. Before the twelfth century ended, a group of Catholic lawyers called *canon lawyers* had formulated the concept of inalienable rights. They understood that there were rights attached to each individual. Moreover, those rights were unchangeable and permanent. They were "personal rights" or "rights of the person." They could be defended against all the world. Here we see for the first time the concept of inalienable rights. As Richard Tuck notes, "It was the canon lawyers who developed and applied such important maxims as the principle that 'personal [rights] cannot be transferred to others nor be the subject of contracts.' "[12]

The Magna Carta made individual rights part of England's social order. It established principles that Jefferson and the Founders relied upon nearly 600 years later. Legal historian Richard Perry remarks:

> *The American colonists…viewed the Magna Carta as a written constitution limiting the power of government and securing to the individual the rights of trial by jury…and the guarantee that no person could be deprived of life, liberty, or property without due process of law.*[13]

During the period leading up to the American Revolution, the Magna Carta was the most routinely invoked source to support the colonists' grievances against King George III.

Within a decade of the signing of the Magna Carta, Henry Bracton was born. Bracton was the Catholic legal scholar who later became known as the father of the English Common Law. During Bracton's time the Common Law of England was expressly Catholic. After Henry VIII made himself head of the Church of England in 1534, both England and the Common Law became formally Protestant. But England's shift from Catholicism to Protestantism made no material change in the Common Law. Its basic principles of law and rights remained the same. None was denied or changed. The Common Law was simply viewed as British rather than as Catholic or Protestant. Throughout its history the Common Law remained squarely and explicitly rooted within a Christian worldview.

4.2.2 EDWARD COKE

The principal authority on the Common Law during the seventeenth century was Sir Edward Coke (1552–1634; his name is pronounced "Cook"). Coke was the chief justice of the Court of Common Pleas. He helped frame the 1628 Petition of Right, which presented the most thorough-going statement of English civil liberties up to that time. His most significant work is his *Institutes of the Laws of England* (1628). Coke's *Institutes* was the standard textbook in the colonies for learning the principles of law and rights.[14]

Sir Edward Coke

Coke came into conflict with King James I by presenting him with Bracton's argument that the king is under God and under the law. James and his son Charles held to the Græco-Roman theory of "Divine Right of Kings." On this theory, the king's authority was absolute. This collision of views led to a conflict with Parliament in 1628. Coke was then a member of Parliament. Because of this conflict, Charles I shut down that Parliament for twelve years. Charles's absolutist policies caused 20,000 Puritans to leave England and come to America. Here was an important motive for the settlement of America: the people's belief in a higher law than that of the king. This belief was inherited from the Common Law.

4.2.3 WILLIAM BLACKSTONE

Sir William Blackstone (1723–80) taught law at Oxford and quickly gained the reputation of being the greatest living expert on the British Common Law. In 1765 he published the four-volume *Commentaries on the Laws of England*. Blackstone's *Commentaries* won instant acclaim throughout England. In the colonies they were not only a sensation—they became a weapon.[15]

The Founders of the United States cited Blackstone twice as often as they cited Locke.[16] Throughout the colonies people began citing Blackstone as an authority on law, rights, and liberties. In the ten years before the Revolution, more copies of Blackstone's *Commentaries* were sold in the colonies than in England itself. Seeing government's purpose as the protection of the people, Blackstone echoed Locke's view on the foundation of government:

For the principal aim of society is to protect individuals in the enjoyment of those absolute rights, which were vested in them by the immutable laws of nature…. Hence it follows, that the first and primary end of human laws is to maintain and regulate these absolute rights of individuals.[17]

Every element of the Founders' understanding of legal rights had already been stated in Blackstone's *Commentaries*. Blackstone showed how the English Common Law affirmed the principle of inalienable rights. Blackstone called them natural rights and absolute rights. But they were identical to what Jefferson would call *inalienable* rights. According to Blackstone:

Those rights, then, which God and nature have established, and are therefore called natural rights, such as are life and liberty, need not the aid of human laws to be more effectually invested in every man than they are; neither do they receive any additional strength when declared by the municipal laws to be inviolable. On the contrary, no human legislature has power to abridge or destroy them, unless the owner shall himself commit some act that amounts to a forfeiture.[18]

Rights are…first, those which concern and are annexed to the persons of men, and are then called jus personarum or the rights of persons…. Natural persons are such as the God of nature formed us.[19]

By the absolute rights of individuals we mean those which are so in their primary and strictest sense, such as would belong to their persons merely in a state of nature, and which every man is entitled to enjoy whether out of society or in it.[20]

Natural liberty...[is] a right inherent in us by birth, and one of the gifts of God to man at his creation.[21]

Several key points stand out in Blackstone's comments about rights. First, the most important rights are God-given. They are not government created. Government's laws cannot make those rights stronger or weaker. Second, they can only be lost if a person forfeits them. The rights are permanent as long as a person lives honestly and justly. But they can be taken away as punishment for crime or for some other violation of the laws of nature. Third, they are part of human nature itself because God attaches them to humanity—they are "annexed" to personhood. Fourth, these rights are absolute, not in the sense of being unlimited or boundless—their limits are set by the laws of nature. Rather, they are absolute in the sense that they are not created by society or government. They are what they are and will never change.

The key difference between Britain and America was not how the rights were defined but how they would be protected. The British system of government was not well-suited for protecting them. It gave the king and Parliament broad powers based on customs and traditions. These powers were called prerogatives, meaning that they were outside the restrictions of ordinary laws. The king's power was called the royal prerogative. It was similar to emergency power. The king, because he was king, could exercise extraordinary powers even if it meant denying people's absolute rights.

The Parliament's power was called parliamentary supremacy. It meant that for some purposes there were no effective limits on the legislature's power. Since England did not have a written constitution to limit its power, Parliament could pass any law it wished. There was no separate supreme court in England. The highest court was controlled by the Parliament and lacked the power to declare laws unconstitutional. Therefore, where lawmaking was concerned, Parliament was supreme. If Parliament's laws denied people's absolute rights, there was no way to stop it.

In the British system, the king and Parliament were free to treat all rights as alienable. Even though the British Common Law said that people possessed inalienable rights, the British government functioned as if such rights did not exist.

The American Founders decided to take Blackstone seriously. If certain rights are truly inalienable, they reasoned, then these rights could be defended—even against the king and Parliament. Furthermore, if inalienable rights were the basis of government, it was wrong for the king and Parliament to nullify these rights with arbitrary power. The form of government would have to be changed. It could no longer be based on royal prerogative and parliamentary supremacy. The new government would be based on inalienable rights. Any powers contrary to those rights would have to be abolished.

Thomas Jefferson

4.2.4 THOMAS JEFFERSON

When America declared its independence from England, Thomas Jefferson (1743–1826) was given the task of explaining why. The Continental Congress picked Jefferson to be a member of the five-man committee assigned to write the Declaration of Independence.[22] The committee insisted that Jefferson write the original draft. Why did they pick Jefferson? He was barely thirty-three. Adams was Harvard-trained and older; why not choose him? Franklin had the greater celebrity; why not have him write it?

The main reason is that Jefferson had mastered the principles of British liberty and the Common Law. As a student at the College of William and Mary, Jefferson had been a first-rate disciple of Coke through the tutelage of George Wythe and other legal experts.[23] After finishing college and his legal studies Jefferson went into politics. He became a legislator, representing his county in the House of Burgesses, the Virginia colonial legislature. From 1765 until 1774, the tension between America and England grew steadily. During that time, Jefferson paid close attention to the ongoing controversy about rights and liberty, developing his own deeply held convictions. During the Stamp Act crisis (see section 8.2), Jefferson would occasionally slip away to the capitol building to listen to Patrick Henry's fiery speeches. Henry had demanded, "Give me liberty, or give me death."

Later, as a delegate to the Continental Congress in Philadelphia, Jefferson learned first-hand what the leaders of the other colonies were saying about rights. From 1774 to 1776, the Continental Congress wrote numerous letters and appeals to the king, explaining their position. Jefferson was able to integrate, synthesize, and harmonize those various arguments and made them his own. Jefferson was at that time reading Blackstone. His reading of Blackstone merely confirmed what he had already learned from Coke's *Institutes* and from other sources, like Sidney and Locke, about individual rights.[24]

Jefferson wrote his *Summary View of the Rights of British America* in 1774.[25] He had a talent for explaining matters clearly and completely, yet with persuasive simplicity and disarming courtesy. Jefferson's cogently reasoned *Summary* left no doubt in anyone's mind who their spokesman should be.

Jefferson's *Summary View of the Rights of British America* explains in impressive detail what the Declaration of Independence states more concisely. Society is built on two pillars, law and rights. The two are inseparable. Both rest on a simple and powerful idea: the God who created nature, and who established a universal law called the law of nature, also created human beings, endowing each with inalienable rights.

Jefferson's *Summary* echoed all the same language of law and rights found in Coke and Blackstone. Man's life in society is governed and regulated by universal law, a moral code laid down by the Creator. This fundamental law is called the law of nature. The law of nature tells a person how to live justly with other persons, and it establishes certain rights that belong to everyone.

These rights are a part of what it means to be a person. They are attached to personhood itself: every human has those rights simply by being created. They are a part of our natural existence. To deny these rights to anyone is to deny that person's humanity. Since these rights are given by the Creator and defined by the Creator's law, no earthly ruler can ignore them, avoid them, or diminish them.

Jefferson repeated these ideas in the opening sentences of the Declaration of Independence. Using the "laws of nature and of nature's God" as the starting point, he proclaimed that "all men are created equal" and "endowed by their Creator with certain unalienable rights" including "life, liberty, and the pursuit of happiness."[26]

If the British view of legal rights was so similar to that of the American Founders, how was the American view unique? Why did Jefferson and the Founders believe that a complete separation from England was necessary for their rights to be protected?

The short answer is that the king and Parliament often disregarded those rights. For centuries, common law judges and legal scholars had said that the rights existed. But England's political system failed to honor those rights and sometimes denied them entirely. Under the British form of government, the king and Parliament were too powerful. Nothing could stop them from violating people's rights.

In sum, the ideas of the Founders regarding inalienable rights as the basis of government were not unique. It was already part of the English Common Law tradition, a tradition explicitly rooted in medieval Christian legal and political theory.

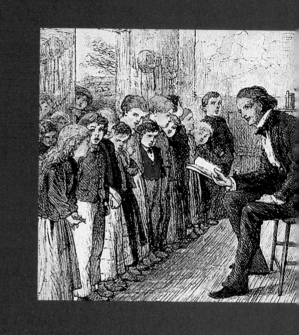

COLONIAL EDUCATION

5.1 THE NEW ENGLAND PRIMER

In early American culture, the institutions that were most responsible for shaping the minds of young people were the colonial schools. The colonial schools played a crucial role in the intellectual development of the Founders of our nation. What was the motivation for establishing schools in America? The Puritans had one answer: to promote knowledge of the Bible.

Illiteracy was a great evil for the Puritans because it barred people access to the Bible. Because the Bible was seen as essential to salvation,[1] literacy was highly valued in New England. Accordingly, as early as 1647 the New England Puritans required that "every township within this jurisdiction, after the Lord hath increased them to the number of fifty householders, shall then forthwith appoint one within their towns to teach all such children as shall resort to him to write and read."[2] As a result, the American colonies had an extremely high literacy rate. Since then the United States has continued to enjoy that distinction, although illiteracy is currently increasing.

For their textbook of choice, Puritans opted for the *New England Primer*. It was a small book filled with alphabets, lessons, verses, prayers, and the Westminster Catechism. Five million copies of the text are reported to have existed in the colonies.[3] This made the *Primer* the second best-selling book in the American colonies (the Bible was number one). Since there were only about 4 million people in America at the time of the Revolution (and only about 2 million of European descent), the *Primers* must have been everywhere.

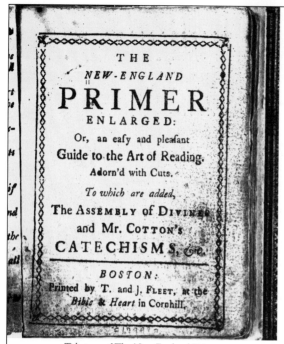

Title page of <u>The New England Primer</u>

The New England Primer established a national tradition of schools and schoolbooks that celebrated both literacy and Christian character by teaching "millions to read, and not one to sin."[4] Through the Westminster Catechism, the *Primer* gave many of the Founders their first encounter with the ideals of the Protestant Reformation. The teaching of this Catechism was enforced by law in New England.[5]

An examination of the alphabet lesson of the *Primer* reveals its explicitly Puritan tone. The accompanying rhyme for more than half of the letters makes reference to a biblical story. The doctrine of "original sin" is the very first of the lessons: **A**—In Adam's fall, we sinned all. The brevity of life is also an emphasis throughout the *Primer*: **G**—As runs the **G**lass, man's life doth pass; **T**—**T**ime cuts down all, both great and small [accompanied by an illustration of the grim reaper].

Later the *Primer* offers the following advice: "At night lie down prepared to have, thy sleep, thy death, thy bed, thy grave." Many twentieth-century parents continue this advice, teaching their children the *Primer's* prayer, which goes like this:

> *Now I lay me down to sleep*
> *I pray the Lord my soul to keep*
> *If I should die before I wake*
> *I pray the Lord my soul to take*[6]

Although this emphasis on death may strike us as morbid, the Puritans had good reasons for it. First, child mortality was very high in the colonial period. Smallpox and a host of other fatal conditions came quickly. The Puritans felt that they needed to prepare their families for that reality. Second, the prospect of death reminded the Puritans that they needed to be more concerned with the state of their souls than with temporal distractions. By making children aware of death, the *Primer* attempted to instill in children an interest in spiritual and eternal matters, and especially a hunger to study the Bible.

The *Primer* also conveyed the Puritan view of discipline. **I**—The **I**dle fool, is whipped at school; **J**—**J**ob feels the rod, yet blesses God. These two, taken in conjunction, reflect a practice that goes back to the medieval period where the schoolmaster administers corporal punishment and then makes the student kiss the paddle.[7] This emphasis on discipline was also related to the Puritan preoccupation with the afterlife. The Puritans believed that a spanking might save one's soul, or, as Cotton Mather put it: "better whipped than damned."[8]

THE NEW ENGLAND PRIMER: THE ALPHABET

In Adam's fall
We sinned all.

Thy life to mend,
God's Book attend.

The Cat doth play,
And after slay.

A Dog will bite
A thief at night.

The Eagle's flight
Is out of sight.

The idle Fool
Is whipped at school.

As runs the Glass,
Man's life doth pass.

My book and Heart
Shall never part.

Job feels the rod,
Yet blesses God.

Proud Korah's troop
Was swallowed up.

The Lion bold
The Lamb doth hold.

The Moon gives light
In time of night.

Nightingales sing
In time of spring.

The royal Oak, it was the tree
That saved his royal majesty.

Peter denies
His Lord, and cries.

Queen Esther comes in royal state,
To save the Jews from dismal fate.

Rachel doth mourn
For her first-born.

Samuel anoints
Whom God appoints.

Time cuts down all,
Both great and small.

Uriah's beauteous wife
Made David seek his life.

Whales in the sea
God's voice obey.

Xerxes the Great did die,
And so must you and I.

Youth forward slips—
Death soonest nips.

Zaccheus, he
Did climb the tree,
His Lord to see.

Lesson from <u>The New England Primer</u>

5.2 LATIN AND APPRENTICESHIPS

In the Southern colonies schooling typically took place at home or with a personal tutor. Often these tutors were clergymen who took students into their homes as boarders and mentored them until they were old enough to go to college or to become an apprentice to a craftsman.[9] Apprenticeships were an important part of the educational process in the South as well as in the North. At fourteen, a boy might be apprenticed to a craftsman or merchant to learn a trade from the ground up. It normally took seven years of intense labor to master the necessary skills, with the apprentice living in the master's home.[10]

Grade school students, male and female, were taught Latin and English side by side as early as they were able to begin their schooling. In the early eighteenth century, a child's study of Latin was considered a sign of orthodox religious observance.[11] The ability to read Latin was the most important skill for anyone intending to enter professional public service. Fluency in not just reading but also writing Latin was the minimum requirement for acceptance into any college.

In disciplines like law and theology, many important textbooks were only printed in classical languages. Therefore, a very early start in Latin, Greek, and maybe even Hebrew was the norm rather than the exception in New England and Virginia. The classical education in the early lives of the Founders contributed significantly to the success of America's birth. As Samuel Eliot Morison, the dean of colonial American history, notes:

A Colonial classroom

American revolutionary leaders, both North and South, Madison, Wythe, and Jefferson, the Rutledges and Pinckneys, as well as Hamilton, Jay, and the Adamses and Trumbulls, could never have rendered their distinguished services to the young republic without that classical learning which is denied to most Americans today.[12]

5.3 AMERICA'S FIRST FOUR COLLEGES

America's first colleges played a crucial role in the birth of the United States.[13] They were essentially Christian seminaries—places for training Christian ministers. They were also places for "the conditioning of minds for rebellion."[14] According to Leonard Tucker,

The colleges deserve considerable credit for effecting the political dissolution with Great Britain and establishing the new nation. For the most part, they served to instill the principles of Whiggism into the minds of men who were soon to shape America's destiny.... It is certainly not coincidental that the excellent leadership which was largely responsible for the success of the Revolution was made up primarily of college-trained men.[15]

In this section we examine America's first four colleges: Harvard, the College of William and Mary, Yale, and Princeton.

5.3.1 HARVARD

Among the few thousand Europeans who immigrated to Boston in the early part of the seventeenth century, at least 130 were theologically educated. Over 100 were trained at Cambridge and almost thirty at Oxford.[16] It was no surprise, therefore, that these Oxbridge graduates should desire to establish a college on this side of the Atlantic. They were especially "dreading to leave an illiterate ministry to the churches."[17] This concern was responsible for the establishment of all our first educational institutions of higher learning. The first four colleges in America were established for the express purpose of theological training.

The first of these institutions was founded in 1636. In his will, a Puritan named John Harvard left his library of 400 books for establishing a "seminary" in the Boston area.[18] In return, the school took the name of its first donor. Students were to understand their education in the following terms:

The maine end of [a student's] life and studies is to know God and Jesus Christ, which is eternal life, John 17.3, and therefore to lay Christ in the bottome, as the only foundation of all found knowledge and learning.[19]

From 1636 till 1693, Harvard was the only institution this side of the Atlantic where a young person could receive a college education. Committed to Puritanism, Harvard eventually adopted the Westminster Confession as its statement of faith and required professors to uphold it.[20] Harvard, as well as all of the other colonial colleges, was an explicitly Christian institution.

Harvard College

The majority of the books read at Harvard were theological. For example, in 1730, 58 percent of the books available there were theological texts whereas only 8 percent pertained to the physical sciences.[21] As late as 1773, in the midst of the political problems with Britain, Harvard's library contained 246 theological books but only 20 on politics.[22] Why? The colonists considered theology the queen of all disciplines and the foundation of politics. If one was interested in government, one had to read theology. If one was interested in any discipline whatsoever, one first had to look at it theologically. These theology textbooks at Harvard shaped the political minds of some of our country's most notable Founders: John Adams, John Hancock, Elbridge Gerry, Jonathan Mayhew, Samuel Adams, and James Otis.

By teaching their students the political resistance theories of Calvin and the English Puritans, the professors at Harvard played an important role in precipitating the American Revolution. Samuel Eliot Morison claims a direct link between the classical Protestant curriculum at Harvard and the patriotic fervor that ignited the Revolution.[23] The only book at Harvard used as a political science text was Burlamaqui's *Principles of Natural Law.* Burlamaqui outlined the logic for colonial independence.[24]

The political ideals embraced by Puritans at Harvard unquestionably anticipated the coming conflict with England. As early as 1729 a student at Harvard was arguing that the Bible does not require unconditional obedience to the government.[25] In 1733 a student argued *vox populi est vox Dei* (the voice of the people is the voice of God).[26] Ten years later a student named Samuel Adams proposed the following commencement thesis: "It is lawful to resist the Supreme Magistrate, if the Commonwealth cannot otherwise be preserved."[27]

During the reign of George III, disputations against tyranny became commonplace at Harvard. To register their protest against English interference, students at Harvard resolved to abstain from drinking tea and determined to use only paper manufactured in America for their degrees.[28]

Harvard played a significant role in the founding of America. The Founders understood and acknowledged this fact. After the American Revolution, for example, John Hancock declared that Harvard was "the parent and nurse of the late happy Revolution in this Commonwealth."[29]

LAWS AND STATUTES
FOR STUDENTS OF HARVARD COLLEGE
(CA. 1700)

STATUTES, LAWS AND PRIVILEGES, APPROVED AND SANCTIONED BY THE PRESIDENT AND FELLOWS OF HARVARD COLLEGE AT CAMBRIDGE IN NEW ENGLAND: TO WHICH BOTH SCHOLARS AND STUDENTS, CANDIDATES FOR ADMISSION AS WELL AS THOSE ADMITTED, ARE REQUIRED TO CONFORM, FOR THE PROMOTION OF LEARNING AND GOOD MORALS.

[ADMISSION REQUIREMENTS:]

1. Everyone competent to read Cicero or any other classic author of that kind extemporaneously, and also to speak and write Latin prose and verse with tolerable skill and without assistance, and of declining the Greek nouns and verbs, may expect to be admitted to the College: if deficient in any of these qualifications, he cannot under any circumstances be admitted.

2. All persons admitted to the College must board at the Commons, and must each pay three pounds to the steward on their entrance, and must discharge all arrears at the end of every three months;

nor shall any undergraduate of the institution be allowed to board out of the College, unless by special permission of the President, or his tutor. If leave to do so shall be granted by either of these officers, the student shall faithfully observe the usual rules of the Common; but if any ever shall leave College for private quarters, without permission of the President or Tutor, he shall not enjoy any privilege of the institution.

[SCHOOL POLICIES:]

3. While the youth is here, he will be required to be diligent, and to observe study-hours with the same strictness as he does those of public recitation.

4. Every student must regard it as his duty to attend all College exercises, secular and religious, public and private. While in the Freshman class, he must speak in public on the stage eight times a year. Sophisters [sophomores] must be present at a public debate twice a week. Both bachelors and sophisters must write out an analysis in some branch of sacred literature: bachelors will discuss in public philosophical questions once a

fortnight, under the superintendence of the President: in the President's absence, the two senior tutors will act as a moderator by turns.

5. No one must, under any pretext, be found in the society of any depraved or dissolute person.

6. No one in the lower class shall leave town without express permission from the President or tutors: nor shall any student, to whatever class he may belong, visit any shop or tavern, to eat and drink, unless invited by a parent, guardian, step-parent, or some such relative.

7. No student shall buy, sell or exchange any thing without the approval of his parents, guardians or tutors. Whoever shall violate this rule, shall be fined by the President or tutor, according to the magnitude of the offense.

8. All students must refrain from wearing rich and showy clothing, nor must anyone go out of the college yard, unless in his gown, coat, or cloak.

9. Every undergraduate shall be called by his surname only, unless he is a commoner, or the oldest son of a gentleman, or the child of a noble house.

10. Every commoner shall pay five pounds for the perpetual use of the college, before admission.

11. Every scholar in the lower class shall pay his tutor two pounds a year; unless he be a commoner, when he shall pay three pounds a year.

12. No person in a higher class, Tutors and Fellows of the college excepted, shall be allowed to force a freshman or junior to go on errands or do other services, by blows, threats or language of any kind. And any undergraduate who violates this rule, shall be punished by bodily chastisement, expulsion, or such other mode as shall seem adviseable to the President and Fellows.

13. Students of all grades are to abstain from dice, cards and every species of gaming for money, under penalty, in the case of a graduate, of twenty shillings for each offense; and, if the offender is an undergraduate, he shall be liable to punishment, as the discretion of the President or tutor shall assign.

14. If any student is absent from prayers, or recitation, unless necessarily detained, or by permission of the President or tutor, he shall be liable to an admonition; and if he commit the offence more than once in a week, to such other punishment as the President or tutor shall assign.

15. No student shall be absent from his studies or stated exercises for any reason, (unless it is first made known to the President or tutor, and by them approved) with the exception of the half-hour allowed for lunch, and half-hour for dinner and also for supper, until nine o'clock.

16. If any student shall, either through wilfulness or negligence, violate any law of God or of this college, after being twice admonished, he shall suffer severe punishment, at the discretion of the President or his tutor. But in high-

handed offences, no such modified forms of punishment need be expected.

[GRADUATION REQUIREMENTS:]

17. Every student who, on trial, shall be able to translate from the original Latin text, and logically to explain the Holy Scriptures, both of the Old and New Testament, and shall also be thoroughly acquainted with the principles of natural and moral philosophy, and shall be blameless in life and character, and approved at public examination by the President and the Fellows of the College, may receive the first degree. Otherwise, no one shall be admitted to the first degree in Arts, unless at the end of three years and ten months from the time of his admission.

18. Every scholar who has maintained a good standing, and exhibited a written synopsis of logic, natural and moral philosophy, arithmetic and astronomy, and shall be prepared to defend a proposition or thesis; shall also be versed in the original languages, as aforesaid: and who carries with him a reputation for upright character and diligence in study, and shall pass successfully a public examination, shall be admitted to the second, or Master's, degree.[30]

5.3.2 THE COLLEGE OF WILLIAM AND MARY

The College of William and Mary began for the same reason as Harvard. Fearing that their colony would lack educated clergy, the Virginians decided to establish a seminary on their own soil:

Whereas the want of able & faithful ministers in this country deprives us of these great blessings and mercies that always attends upon the service of God which want by reason of our great distance from our native country cannot in probability be always supplied from thence. BE IT ENACTED that for the advance of learning, education of youth, supply of the ministry and promotion of piety there be land taken upon purchases for a college and freeschool and there be with as much speed as may be convenient housing erected thereon for entertainment of students and scholars.[31]

William and Mary was founded in 1693 to propagate the Christian gospel.[32]

During the revolutionary conflict a fraternity was established at William and Mary that has since become the hallmark of academic excellence. In 1776 a group of students founded a society designated by three Greek letters: *phi beta kappa* (ΦΒΚ). Those admitted to the society swore the following oath:

I, A.B., do swear on the holy Evangelists of Almighty God, or otherwise, as calling the Supreme Being to attest this my oath, declaring that I will, with all my possible efforts,

William and Mary College

endeavour to prove true, just, and deeply attached to this our growing fraternity.[33]

The College of William and Mary excelled her colonial sister colleges in teaching students the Common Law of England. This emphasis on legal education did more than just provide Virginians with tools for litigation. Students at William and Mary extracted the political philosophy that was written between the lines of their legal case books. This political philosophy proved explosive once articulated by such students as Thomas Jefferson. According to J. E. Morpurgo,

> *A taste for reading of law-books was by no means uncommon among the students of William and Mary. Even those who had no intention of progressing to the practice of law were infected by the enthusiasm…by the growing realization that the aspirations of America were closely related to the principles of English law.*[34]

Thomas Jefferson credited his law tutor at the College of William and Mary, George Wythe, as having the greatest impact upon his intellectual development.[35] Professor Wythe was a devout Christian. His name is the first of the Virginia signers on the Declaration of Independence. Imogene Brown describes Wythe's significance as follows:

> *[Wythe] is seldom in the reiterated and resounding chorus which includes Washington, Jefferson, Adams and Madison. Yet as much as any of these he was responsible for certain characteristics of the American nation…. He played a considerable part in almost every event and in every advance that turned Colony into Commonwealth; in all the debates that brought together as one nation thirteen disparate colonies he was either present and vocal or else his opinion was tacitly represented by one of his former pupils.*[36]

5.3.3 YALE

Yale was founded in New Haven, Connecticut, in 1701 as an alternative to Harvard. Discontented with Harvard's rigid Puritanism, ten ministers founded Yale out of "their sincere Regard to & Zeal for upholding & Propagating of the Christian Protestant Religion by a succession of Learned & Orthodox men."[37]

> *At the first meeting of Yale's trustees in November, 1701, the seven clergymen in attendance began their deliberations by writing a statement of purpose. They recalled the "Grand errand" of their "blessed fathers" who had left Europe and come to America "to plant, and under the Divine blessing to propagate in this Wilderness, the blessed Reformed, Protestant Religion, in the purity of its Order, and Worship."…With that goal in mind, the trustees established the collegiate school…. Yale's principal purpose was to train orthodox men in general and orthodox ministers in particular; instruction in Reformed theology was the only aspect of the curriculum legislated by the trustees.*[38]

Yale's early supporters dubbed it the "school of the prophets," alluding to the schools by that name in the Old Testament.[39] All students were required "to recite the Assemblies Catechism in Latin."[40] Yale's most famous graduate was Jonathan Edwards. Edwards was a central figure in the revivals that swept New England in the mid-eighteenth century. He became the third president of Princeton and there died after being inoculated with smallpox

Yale College

vaccine (see chapter 3).

Yale had an enormous influence on the developing Ivy League. The first three presidents of Princeton were Yale graduates: Jonathan Edwards, Aaron Burr Sr., and Jonathan Dickinson. Dartmouth's first president and founder, Eleazar Wheelock, was a Yale alumnus. The first president of Columbia University, Samuel Johnson, was also a graduate of Yale.[41]

Yale's influence on the founding of the United States was significant. Although historians have long recognized that Yale produced a large number of the Revolution's military officers,[42] more recently historians have begun to note Yale's role

> as a "seminary of sedition," as an institution that had much to do with implanting the seeds of liberty in the fertile revolutionary soil of Puritan Connecticut. This aspect of Yale's history is really the unknown chapter.... It bears greater significance than the contributions made by the men of Yale on the field of battle.[43]

Yale's professors and students were Whigs, who steadfastly resisted intrusions by the British Crown.[44] During the Revolution, Tories loyal to King George III identified Yale as "a nursery of sedition"[45] and its library as "a mine of heresy."[46] The commencement theses given in the pre-Revolutionary era at Yale mirrored those at Harvard.

A 1763 thesis argued the negative to the question: "Whether rebellion in any republic is more often to be attributed to the rebellious attitude of the subjects rather than to the laws of the legislators?" In 1766, a year after the king's decision to tax the colonies in the notorious Stamp Act (see section 8.2), a student argued the affirmative to the question: "Whether the Supreme power of the Republic can be limited by the original Constitution?" Because Parliament legislated taxes, another student in 1768 argued the negative to the question: "Whether the legislature, after a pact has been drawn up, has any authority to violate the Constitution?"[47]

By the early 1770s Yale was seeking a break with Britain and the establishment of an

American Constitution. In 1774 the president of Yale, Ezra Stiles, warned, "If oppression proceeds…a public spirit of enterprise may originate an American Magna Charta…. *There will be a Runnymede in America.*"[48] (Runnymede is where the Magna Carta was signed.) According to one student of Stiles, his fire for liberty "was kindled at the altar of the English and New England Puritans."[49]

The patriotism of Yale's Puritan graduates was second to none. When the war broke out at Lexington, Massachusetts, 100 Yale students rushed to fight.[50] Timothy Dwight, who would later become the president of Yale, was largely responsible for this enthusiasm. When a 1773 Yale graduate named Nathan Hale (who had been a disciple of Dwight) was captured by the British at Manhattan, his execu-

Ezra Stiles

tion was ordered the next day. Even though Hale's last request was for a Bible, the British rejected his plea. Just before he was hanged, he uttered the famous words: "I only regret that I have but one life to lose for my country."[51]

Nathan Hale was only one of the participants in the founding who was trained at Yale. Four Yale graduates signed the Declaration of Independence: Philip Livingston, Lyman Hall, Lewis Morris, and Oliver Wolcott.[52] The artist who painted *The Signing of the Declaration* was John Trumbull. He received his master's degree from Yale in 1770. Noah Webster, the grand scholar of the American language, also received his training from the Puritans at Yale.

The Execution of Nathan Hale

83

5.3.4 Princeton (The College of New Jersey)

When the religious revival known as the Great Awakening broke out in the mid-seventeenth century, a fresh interest in religion blossomed in the Middle Colonies. As a result, more ministers were needed, and this in turn necessitated a local training ground for ministers. When the Presbyterian Synod of New York founded the College of New Jersey (Princeton), it presented the following rationale:

The difficulty, (and in some cases impossibility,) of sending youth two, three, four, or five

Princeton College

hundred miles or more, to the colleges in New England, is also evident at first sight. Now it is from the college of New Jersey only, that we can expect a remedy of these inconveniences;…it is on that the Presbyterian churches, through the six colonies above mentioned [New York, New Jersey, Pennsylvania, Maryland, Virginia, and Carolina], principally depend for a supply of accomplished ministers.[53]

Just as with Harvard, William and Mary, and Yale, so too the College of New Jersey was founded as a theological seminary.[54] Yale-trained theologians like Aaron Burr Sr. were appointed as presidents in its earliest years. Jonathan Edwards and John Witherspoon, both presidents at Princeton, were first-rate Christian philosophers and, with Benjamin Franklin, among the most influential men in the colonies prior to the Revolution. Samuel Davies, the Virginia revivalist who sparked Patrick Henry during the Great Awakening, finished his career as president of Princeton.

Of all the early schools that were dedicated to advancing Christianity into all parts of the world, Princeton was second to none. Princetonians were not content simply to advance Christianity within America. They were at the forefront of the growing overseas missionary movement. Graduates from the college, and later from Princeton Theological Seminary, began an alliance with Christians in Paris. That alliance eventually evolved into the World Evangelical Alliance and later into the World Council of Churches.[55]

During the 1760s, Anglicans in London felt that one way to tranquilize the Americans was to take control of the college at Princeton.[56] John Witherspoon, a devoted Christian, was president of the college during the founding era. He had as wide an influence on American patriots as any other teacher in the colonies.[57] The political implications of Witherspoon's theology are evident in the United States Constitution.[58]

By 1770, Witherspoon had made the conflict with England a focus of the curriculum at Princeton.[59] One student's thesis defended the colonists' boycott of British goods.[60] His own son, James Witherspoon, argued a thesis urging the classical resistance theories of the earlier Puritans. He subsequently joined the patriot army and was killed in battle.[61]

John Witherspoon

The British labeled John Witherspoon "a political firebrand." One British officer said that Witherspoon "had no less share in the Revolution than Washington himself. He poisons the minds of his young students and through them the Continent."[62] Several Princetonians were members of the Continental Congress, and

84

signed the Declaration of Independence. Those who learned their political theories at Princeton included James Madison, Henry Lee, Richard Stockton, and Benjamin Rush.

More alumni from Princeton attended the Constitutional Convention of 1787 than from any other American or British institution. Representing the states were nine Princeton alumni:

Alexander Martin 1756 (North Carolina)   *Gunning Bedford Jr. 1771 (Delaware)*
William Paterson 1763 (New Jersey)   *James Madison 1771 (Virginia)*
Oliver Ellsworth 1766 (Connecticut)   *William R. Davie 1776 (North Carolina)*
Luther Martin 1766 (Maryland)   *Jonathan Dayton 1776 (New Jersey)*
William C. Houston 1768 (New Jersey)[63]

The main college building at Princeton is Nassau Hall. It played an important role in America's founding. When the British occupied Philadelphia shortly after the war began, the Second Continental Congress relocated to Princeton. There they monitored the progress of the war. Just after Washington crossed the Delaware River and captured Trenton on Christmas Day of 1776, he turned his army toward Princeton (which is about fifteen miles from Trenton) and there won a crucial victory against Cornwallis.

The British had been holed up in Nassau Hall when Alexander Hamilton assaulted it and induced their evacuation. To this day the building displays battle scars from the cannonballs that struck it in January of 1777. Later Washington returned to Princeton to pose for a portrait by Charles Wilson Peale. That portrait was hung in Nassau Hall in the place where King George III's portrait had been displayed before it was destroyed in the battle. Peale's portrait of Washington remains hanging in Nassau Hall to this day.

Washington crossing the Delaware

FAMILY LIFE IN NEW ENGLAND

The Bible and the nuclear family were the cornerstones of New England society.[1] The intense cohesion of New England families was in part logistical. Not only was travel extremely limited, but people had few places to go even if they could. Houses were small and families were big. Families with more than a dozen children were common.[2] As a result, "they even slept together, entire households in a single room—servants, masters, children—two, three, even four to a bed."[3] There was a minimal sense of individuality.

The family was an organic unity that survived through an interdependency of its members. Husband and wife worked as one. As a result, laws prevented husband and wife from being apart for extended periods.[4] This closeness tremendously affected the way Puritans interacted with family members and neighbors. There were very few secrets. When there was a quarrel or domestic abuse, everyone knew it, and the community intervened. This chapter provides a window into Puritan family life.

Puritan wedding

In finding a spouse, the Puritans had very different values from most twentieth-century Americans. Our culture generally endorses a consumer approach to courting—"playing the field" until you find someone that you are attracted to and that you love. The New England Puritans, by contrast, understood love as the *result* of marriage, not as the *reason* for it.

Because Puritans regarded everything as under the control of God, to be married to someone meant that God had chosen that person specifically for you. The foundation for love was therefore that God had chosen your spouse. Although marriages were not arranged,[5] whatever circumstances brought about the marriage were deemed God's will, and therefore the spouse was God's choice for one's mate.[6]

This approach to marriage, which is so foreign to our current sensibilities, had advantages.[7] Divorce was extremely rare. This was in part because adultery was a capital offense.[8] But more so, it was because, unlike marriages today (half of which fail), marriage was not based on attraction. This meant that if one's spouse grew unattractive, the grounds for the marriage bond were unaffected.

Whereas our present consumer approach to marriage leads to the practice of "trading it in when it gets old," the Puritans had the process reversed. Today we start by "falling in love," and after several years often "fall out of love." In Puritan New England love was not supposed to be there at the beginning; it was supposed to develop over time. As a result of their sacred bond, a Puritan husband and wife were expected to cultivate an attraction for each other. There was no such thing as "falling out of love." Love was not an emotion so much as a frame of mind that one nurtured.

The process of growing to love one another worked like this. If a man and a woman determined that they might be suitable for one another, an espousal period was established. The theologian William Ames wrote: "By this means the minds of the betrothed are prepared and disposed to those affections, which in matrimony are requisite."[9] This was a time, not to find out if one liked the other person, but to find out if one had the ability to overcome one's dislikes. There is an abundance of evidence to prove that once they were married, Puritan couples did indeed develop a deep affection for one another.[10] Anne Bradstreet's poems to her husband exemplify the letters and writings of Puritan women.

88

TO MY DEAR AND LOVING HUSBAND
WRITTEN 1678
BY ANNE BRADSTREET

If ever two were one, then surely we

If ever man were loved by wife, then thee;

If ever wife was happy in a man

Compare with me, ye women, if you can.

I prize thy love more than whole mines of gold

Or all the riches that the east doth hold.

My love is such that rivers cannot quench,

Nor ought but love from thee, give recompense.

Thy love is such I can no way repay,

The heavens reward thee manifold I pray.

Then while we live, in love let so persever

That when we live no more we shall live ever.[11]

The letters of John and Margaret Winthrop exhibit this kind of relationship also, and a thorough study of other available letters "demonstrate[s] that the Winthrops were not an exceptional case."[12] Thomas Hooker gave an example of the ideal love that a Puritan man has for his wife:

The man whose heart is endeared to the woman he loves, he dreams of her in the night, hath her in his eye and apprehension when he awakes, museth on her as he sits at table, walks with her when he travels, and parlies with her in each place were he comes.[13]

After conducting his extensive study of Puritan marriage, Edmund Morgan concluded: "the Puritans were a much earthier lot than their modern critics have imagined.... The Puritans were neither prudes nor ascetics. They knew how to laugh and they knew how to love."[14]

6.2 THE ROLE OF WOMEN: DOMESTIC AFFAIRS

The Puritans viewed the place of women always through the lens of Genesis 2:18: "And the Lord God said, 'It is not good that the man should be alone; I will make him a

Puritan family life

help meet for him.'" Women, then, according to the Puritans were "Creatures without which there is no comfortable living for man."[15]

Today, in an age that stresses women's independence, this conception of the role of women seems narrow and oppressive. But in a community that viewed the nuclear family as the basis for society, it was absolutely crucial to see women as inseparable from men and vice versa. This view had been encoded in the Common Law of England and embraced by all Americans well into the nineteenth century. The Common Law stated:

> By marriage, the husband and wife are one person in law; that is, the very being or legal existence of the woman is suspended during the marriage, or at least is incorporated and consolidated into that of the husband, under whose wing, protection, and cover she performs every thing; and is...under the protection and influence of her husband, her baron, or lord. The husband is bound to provide his wife with necessaries, by law, as much as himself; and if she contracts debts for them, he is obliged to pay them.[16]

Granted, the Common Law endorsed a *patriarchy* (i.e., leadership by men). But for the Puritans, a man's example of leadership was Jesus Christ, who sacrificed himself for the very people he led. Thomas Hooker, the founder of Connecticut, put it this way:

> All [the husband] hath, is at [the wife's] command. All he can do, is wholly improved for her content and comfort. She lies in his Bosom, and his heart trusts in her, which forceth all to confess, that the stream of his affection, like a mighty current, runs with full tide and strength.[17]

Since the responsibility for a woman's comfort and security rested with her husband, according to John Winthrop,

> [A Puritan wife] is to be subject to [her husband], yet in a way of liberty, not of bondage; and a true wife accounts her subjection her honor and freedom, and would not think her condition safe and free, but in her subjection to her husband's authority.[18]

Did colonial patriarchy lead to domestic abuses? In some cases, yes.[19] It is, however, ironic that currently in America, in a culture that denounces patriarchy, there are far more problems with domestic abuse than the Puritans ever came close to encountering.[20] The laws in colonial New England against domestic abuse were tough:

> Husband and wives were forbidden by law to strike each other, and the courts enforced the provision on numerous occasions. But they did not stop there. Henry Flood was required to give bond for good behavior because he had abused his wife by "ill words calling her whore and cursing of her."...James Harris was fined ten shillings and required to give

Puritan family

bond for good behavior by the Suffolk County Court because of "disorderly carriage in his family neglecting and refusing to provide for them and for quarrelling with his wife."[21]

The courts had a vested interest in preserving marital harmony. Since they linked the peace of the community to the peace of the family, they refused to tolerate domestic abuse. Domestic abuse occurred rarely in colonial New England.

Besides the strict laws against it, another reason for the low incidence of domestic abuse may have been the Puritan practice of spiritual disciplines. The law required fathers, for instance, to set aside a time of worship at the beginning and end of each day. Singing, praying, and Bible reading were all a part of Puritan family worship. Such spiritual disciplines may have helped to deter serious long-term domestic conflicts.

It is a mistake to think that Puritan women had minimal decision-making powers. Puritans took the thirty-first chapter of Proverbs as their guide for the role of women. That portion of the Bible accords women a central role in family management, including economic and business affairs. Samuel Sewall, one of the early leaders of Massachusetts, preferred that his wife manage the family finances: "If I want I will borrow of her. She has a better faculty than I at managing Affairs."[22] This arrangement was not unique to Sewall. Other men, including ministers, conceded that their wives were as capable, if not more so, as administrators of the family.[23]

Puritans felt that women were spiritually superior to men.[24] Historians have recognized the overwhelming evidence that colonial women excelled men in church participation.[25] Since the churches were the centers of the community, women therefore had a powerful voice, whether explicit or implicit, in the direction of the community.

In distinguishing gender roles, the

Samuel Sewall

Puritans claimed to be following the law of nature. Women, by virtue of their natural ability to bear and nurse children, were called to domestic life. Men, by virtue of their physical strength and their freedom from pregnancy, were better suited to go out of the home

Puritan wife

for extended periods. They were therefore called to public pursuits. The Puritans did not regard one calling as superior to the other. The callings of men and women were different and complementary.

Besides stressing the education of their children (see chapter 5), the Puritans also stressed the *vocatio*, or calling, of their children's lives. The Puritans believed no child could expect God's blessing in life unless that child understood the calling God had for him or her.[26] Usually between the age of ten and fourteen a young person was expected to discern his or her calling.[27]

How was a young person to discern this calling? The Puritans pointed their children to two types of evidence: *internal* and *external* evidence. Internal confirmation of a call consisted essentially of the inclinations, desires, and passions of the individual. A person was considered best suited for a vocation if he or she thoroughly enjoyed the work it presented. External confirmation consisted primarily of the assessment of others. Their perceptions would either affirm or negate that the person had the talents to do well in the vocation.

Parents provided the most important external confirmation. Next came other family members and the community. When Josiah Cotton sought external confirmation of his call from his brother John, he was told to evaluate "your own inclinations, and qualifications. I perceive two stand candidates with you, the practice of Physick and Theology."[28]

Young women did not have as difficult a time discerning their calling

Puritan girl

92

as young men, "because there was little likelihood of their ever following any career but that of a housewife, whether as a daughter, wife, or mother."[29] As soon as she was able, a young woman spent her growing years helping to care for the younger children in her family and learning all the skills she would eventually need to manage her own household as a wife and mother.

The most common method of helping a young man discern his calling was apprenticeships. Often the oldest son followed the father's calling. For the more affluent, college was an option. Parents worked hard to help their children develop the skills necessary to fulfill their calling. The most esteemed calling among colonial New Englanders, and the one which many parents wished for their sons, was to be a minister of the gospel.[30] To fulfill this calling, however, generally required a college education.

Because pursuing one's calling was hard work, teenage boredom, rebelliousness, and delinquency were virtually unknown in New England. Young people had no time for it. Once they did enter the adult world, they never considered their work just a job. It was their vocation, their way of serving God, and they took pride and joy in it as such.

A CHRISTIAN AT HIS CALLING
COTTON MATHER
1701

Cotton Mather

Every Christian ordinarily should have a *calling*. That is to say, there should be some special business, and some settled business, wherein a Christian should for the most part spend the most of his time; and this, that so he may glorify God....

There is a variety of callings in the world; even as there are various objects, about which the *callings* of men are conversant, and various designs unto which the *callings* of men are intended. Some *callings*, are more immediately, to serve the souls of our neighbors; and some their *safety* and some their *defense*; and some their bodies; and some their *estates*; and some their *delights*. But it is not lawful for a Christian ordinarily to live without some *calling* or another, until infirmities have unhappily disabled him. Indeed a man cannot live without the help of other men. But how can a man reasonably look for the help of other men, if he be not in some calling helpful to other men?...

A Christian should have it contrived, that his calling be *agreeable*, as well as *allowable*. It is a wonderful inconvenience for a man to have a calling that won't agree with him. See to it, O parents, that when you choose callings for your children, you wisely consult their *capacities*, and their *inclinations*; lest you ruin them....

It is the singular favor of God, unto a man, that he can attend his occupation with *contentment* and *satisfaction*. That one man has a spirit formed and fitted for one occupation, and another man for another, this is from the operation that God, who forms the spirit of man within him.... Count not your business to be your *burden* or your *blemish*. Let not a proud heart make you ashamed of that business wherein you may be a *blessing*. For my part, I can't see an honest man hard at work in the way of his occupation, be it never so [insignificant] (and tho' perhaps driving of a wheel barrow) [without finding] my heart sensibly touched with respect for such a man. It is possible, you may think, that you may see others in some greater and richer business; and you may think that you might be yourselves greater and richer, if you were in some other business. Yea, but has not the God of heaven cast you into that business, which now takes you up?

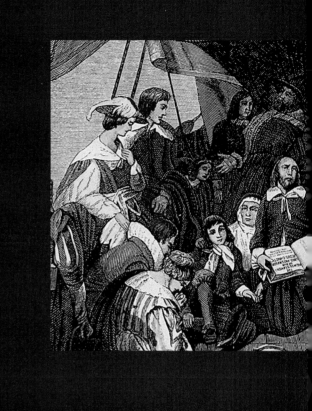

NOMENCLATURE

Naming practices express the values and ideals of a culture. A comprehensive study of first names, therefore, provides a unique window into the common ideals of a society. In this chapter we examine the nomenclature (i.e., naming practices) of the first New England settlers. This examination reveals a culture permeated with biblical ideals and values.

Men	Women
John	Agnes
William	Alice
Thomas	Cicely
Richard	Joan
Robert	Matilda
Henry	Margaret
Roger	Elizabeth
Walter	Isabel
Hugh	Helen
Rolf	Elaine
Edmund	Emma
Nicholas	Katherine
Philip	Mabel
	Sybil
	Beatrice

To understand the significance of the New Englanders' nomenclature, one must first understand how previous generations named their children. Before the Protestant Reformation, the English used only about twenty different names for males and another twenty for females.[1] Elsdon Smith, in his *Story of Our Names*, lists thirteen of the period's most common men's names and fifteen of the most common women's names. These represented 90 percent of all names used.[2]

Only three out of the thirteen medieval men's names come from the Bible: John, Thomas, and Philip. All three are from the New Testament. Of the women's names only one, Elizabeth, is from the Bible. This name too is from the New Testament. Old Testament names seem not to have been used. Outside these four New Testament names, the bulk of the names on this list have Norman origins.

Most of these names had been used for over a millennium, dating back to when the Normans used an early Indo-European language. When the Norman names were first used, they had specific meanings. But by the time the Normans came to England with William the Conqueror, their language had changed and the meanings of the names had been forgotten.[3]

Between the Norman conquest and the Protestant Reformation, children were named to honor a relative, a political leader, or an admired friend.[4] For example, compare the men's names on the above list with the following list of Norman leaders:

ROBERT I, *Duke of Normandy, Father of the Conqueror*
WILLIAM, *the Conqueror*
HENRY, *the Conqueror's son, King of England*
HUGH *Capet, the most prominent King of France*
EDMUND *the Magnificent, King of England*
EDMUND *Ironside, King of England*
RICHARD *De Clare, "Strongbow," conqueror of Ireland*[5]

The Reformation marked a significant shift in English naming patterns.[6] Increasingly biblical and religious names came into use in England. That shift became particularly evident with the passengers of the *Mayflower*.

William the Conqueror

98

THE NOMENCLATURE OF THE FIRST TWO GENERATIONS OF PILGRIMS AT PLYMOUTH

First Generation	Children
John Alden (married William Mullins's daughter, of the second generation)	John Joseph David Jonathan Elizabeth Ruth Sarah Mary
Isaac Allerton Mary Allerton	Bartholomew Remember Mary Isaac John Hooke
John Allerton	
John Billington Ellen Billington	John Francis
William Bradford Dorothy Bradford	John Joseph William Mercy
William Brewster Mary Brewster	Love Wrestling Patience Fear Jonathan
Richard Britteridge	
Peter Brown	(4 Children)
William Button	
John Carver Katherine Carver	
James Chilton (and Wife)	Mary

First Generation (continued)	Children (continued)
Richard Clark	
Francis Cooke Esther Cooke	John Jacob Jane Esther Mary
Humility Cooper	
John Crackston	John
Edward Doty Faith Doty	William Edward Isaac Thomas Joseph John Faith Desire
Francis Eaton Sarah Eaton	Samuel Benjamin Rachel
Thomas English	
Moses Fletcher	
Edward Fuller Ann Fuller	Samuel Matthew
Samuel Fuller Bridget Fuller	Samuel Mercy
Richard Gardiner	
John Goodman	
William Holbeck	
Stephen Hopkins Elizabeth Hopkins	Giles Oceanus (born during passage) Caleb Constanta Damaris Deborah Ruth

First Generation (continued)	Children (continued)
John Howland Elizabeth Howland	John Jabez Joseph Isaac Desire Hope Lydia Hannah Ruth Elizabeth
John Langmore	
William Latham	
Edward Lester	
Edmund Margeson	
Christopher Martin (and Wife)	
Desire Minter	
Ellen Moore	
Jasper Moore	
William Mullins Alice Mullins	William Joseph Priscilla
Digory Priest	
Solomon Prower	
John Rigsdale Alice Rigsdale	
Thomas Rogers	Joseph
Henry Sampson Anne Sampson	Stephen James John Caleb Elizabeth Hannah Mary Dorcas

First Generation (continued)	Children (continued)
George Soule Mary Soule	George Zachariah John Nathaniel Benjamin Patience Elizabeth Mary
Myles Standish Rose Standish	Alexander Myles Charles Josiah Lora
Elias Story	
Edward Thompson	
Edward Tilley Anne Tilley	
John Tilley (& Wife)	Elizabeth
Thomas Tinker (& Wife)	(Son)
Ely Trevor	
William Trevor	
John Turner	(two Sons)
Richard Warren Elizabeth Warren	Nathaniel Joseph Mary Ann Sarah Elizabeth Abigail
William White Susanna White	Resolved Peregrine
Roger Wilder	
Thomas Williams	

First Generation (continued)	Children (continued)
Edward Winslow Elizabeth Winslow	Edward (died young) John Elizabeth Edward
Gilbert Winslow	

7.2 EARLY AMERICAN NAMES

The most famous group of English settlers to America were the Pilgrims who settled Plymouth, Massachusetts, in 1620. William Bradford (who was both a passenger on the *Mayflower* and the governor of the colony at Plymouth) listed the names of all the *Mayflower* passengers in his 1650 history of the colony.[7] Although his list is thorough, he identified some individuals without mentioning their first names.

James Savage filled in most of those blanks in his *Genealogical Dictionary of the First Settlers of New England*.[8] Combining these two sources, one may construct a virtually complete list of the names of all the *Mayflower* passengers and their children—a total of 170 names. The following analysis of that list reveals how these first settlers' ideals are silently embedded in their names.

THE

HISTORY

OF THE

COLONY

OF

MASSACHUSETS-BAY,

Title page, The History of the Colony

103

A comparison of the Pilgrims' names with those of their children reveals a startling shift in nomenclature. Biblical and religious names become much more prominent in the second generation than in the first. For instance, the Pilgrims gave their children Old Testament names at three times the rate of their own names.

Of the first generation settlers in Plymouth, the majority of whom were born prior to 1600, 41 percent had traditional Norman or Anglo-Saxon names like William and Katherine. In contrast, in the second generation only 10 percent had such names. Where the old Norman and Anglo-Saxon names do appear in the second generation, usually a father's name has been passed to a son. Except for the Standish family (whose father, Myles Sr., was a soldier, and whose two sons Alexander and Charles were named after kings),[9] children seem not to have been named after political leaders.

In the first generation, only three individuals, or about 4 percent, had descriptive names: Humility, Desire, and Faith. Of the children, fifteen had such names, or about 17 percent of the second generation. Out of all the female children, forty-one total, not one was given a nonbiblical saint's name. This had been the dominant trend for centuries.

Why the dramatic shift in nomenclature? Why the Old Testament names? Why not nonbiblical saints' names? Why the descriptive names? Two factors led to an increase in biblical naming: a readily available translation of the Bible into English and the rise of

Puritanism with its emphasis on the Bible. In 1560 the Geneva Bible was printed. This was the first English Bible widely available to the common people.[10] At the same time, Puritanism became a significant force in England, especially through the efforts of Cambridge University's faculty and students. In keeping with the Protestant Reformation, Puritanism stressed the centrality of the Bible.

Given ready access to the Bible and a Puritan theology that emphasized the Bible, an increase in biblical naming was only natural. Writing in 1565, the English Puritan leader Thomas Cartwright gave guidelines for how Puritans were to name their children:

> They which present unto baptism ought to be persuaded not to give those that are baptized the names of God, or of Christ...nor such as savour of paganism...but chiefly such whereof there are examples in the Holy Scriptures, in the names of those who are reported in them to have been godly and virtuous.[11]

English Protestants took Cartwright's exhortation seriously.

7.3 WHY OLD TESTAMENT NAMES?

Before English translations of the Bible became readily available, Old Testament names were rare. Those who preferred religious nomenclature generally opted for a nonbiblical saint's name or a New Testament name. David Hume, in his monumental *History of England*, evaluated the change in nomenclature that occurred after English Bibles became readily available:

> It was usual for [Christians] at that time to change their names from Henry, Edward, Anthony, William, which they regarded as heathenish, into others more sanctified and godly: even the New Testament names, James, Andrew, John, Peter, were not held in such regard as those which were borrowed from the Old Testament, Hezekiah, Habakkuk, Joshua, Zerobabel.[12]

The names of the *Mayflower* passengers and their children illustrated this trend. Hume, however, did not explain *why* the Old Testament names were preferred over the New Testament ones. The reason can be found in Puritanism's close ties to Judaism:

> Puritanism was akin to Judaism. The idea of that kinship was wonderfully appealing to devout New Englanders. It helped confirm their conviction that they, like the Israelites in the Old Testament, were a chosen people, specially favored by God.[13]

The Plymouth settlers in particular thought of themselves as similar to the ancient Israelites who wandered in search of the Promised Land. William Bradford wrote about the Plymouth settlement in language parallel to that of the Old Testament:

> May not and ought not the children of these fathers rightly say: "Our fathers were Englishmen which came over this great ocean, and were ready to perish in this wilderness; but they cried unto the Lord, and He heard their voice and looked on their adversity."[14]

Just as the Israelites left the oppression of Egypt for the Promised Land of Canaan, so the Pilgrims and later Puritans left the oppression of England for the Promised Land of the

Pilgrims' farewell on the Mayflower

New World. This Old Testament imagery of making a journey to escape oppression and obtain liberty captured the early settlers' imagination. It also affected their nomenclature. George Stewart writes: "The Puritans attempted to establish the Kingdom of God in the New World. Nowhere can we find a better exemplification of this idea than in given names."[15]

7.4 WHY DESCRIPTIVE NAMES?

Besides Old Testament names, the first settlers also used descriptive names, that is, names having a clear English meaning. Consider the names of four children of the colony's spiritual leader, Elder William Brewster: Love, Wrestling, Fear, and Patience. By 1605, Puritans and Separatists were regularly using such names (Separatists were Protestants who, like the Pilgrims, believed in separating from the Church of England).

Although giving children descriptive names may strike us as bizarre, the Puritans and Separatists had a well-defined rationale for this practice. Brewster and several of his colleagues were well educated. They knew the Old Testament, the language it was written in (Hebrew), and the customs described in it. They found that individuals in the Old Testament were given names that had specific meanings in Hebrew (e.g., Adam means "human," Abraham means "father of many," and Joshua means "Yahweh saves").

Because of their affinity for Judaism, the Puritans simply adapted this practice, substituting English for Hebrew. David Hume observes that "sometimes a whole godly sentence was adopted as a name."[16] Old Testament names were often entire Hebrew phrases (e.g., Maher-Shalal-Hash-Baz meant "Hasten-the-spoil-rush-upon-the-prey"). The Puritans imitated Hebrew custom. One writer reports that the name Fight-the-good-fight-of-faith was a common Puritan name.[17]

Sometimes when parents gave their children names with clear descriptive meanings, they did so hoping that the child would grow into the name (e.g., Thankful, Patience, Mercy, Humility, and Faith). Consider, for instance, the sons of William and Susanna White: Resolved and Peregrine. Peregrine is Latin for pilgrim or sojourner. These names suggest that the parents saw their children's lives as a journey requiring determination. Here again is the theology of fugitives from Egypt seeking the Promised Land.

7.5 THE NEW ENGLAND BABY-NAMING BOOK: THE BIBLE

The first settlers were nonconformists who preferred Old Testament heroes to great Norman invaders. Their nomenclature reflected that preference. They came to establish a "Zion in the Wilderness" or a "New Jerusalem," terms referring to the restoration of ancient Israel. They saw God as their ultimate ruler and themselves as God's chosen people. By and large, their name-giving confirms Governor Bradford's claim that "it was religious men that began the work and they came for religious reasons."[18]

Succeeding generations in Massachusetts would take this Bible-based nomenclature to an even greater extreme. Of all the children born in Boston from 1640 to 1649, ninety percent received biblical names! Among the most popular names of the decade were the following Old Testament names:[19]

Boys	Girls
Ebeneezer	Sarah
Samuel	Hannah
Isaac	Abigail
Jonathan	Rebecca
Joseph	Ruth

The New Englanders' rule for naming their children was straightforward: names should either be biblical (especially from the Old Testament) or be descriptive of virtue. The Puritan Samuel Sewall recorded in his diary the criterion he used to choose a name: "I was struggling whether to call her Sarah or Mehetabel; but when I saw Sarah's standing in the Scripture...I resolv'd on that side."[20]

Some Puritans were not as deliberate as Sewall. "The Bible seems to have been opened at random and the first name that was seen was immediately adopted," writes Leslie Dunkling.[21] Puritan birth records confirm this thesis in that they record names of biblical villains like Judas, Jezebel, and Caiaphas.

The names in the following families almost sound fictitious. Nevertheless, these are four typical families of seventeenth-century Massachusetts:

Cornelius Thayer's children[22]	Jonathan Rugg's children[23]
Cornelius	Bathsheba
Moses	Sarah
Gideon	Hepsibah
David	Abraham
Ezekiel	Mehitable
Eliakim	Hannah
Hezekiah	Jonathan
Jeremiah	John
Abigail	Ebeneezer

Nathaniel Wood's children[24]	Samuel Partridge's children[25]
Nathaniel	Hannah
Daniel	Thankful
John	Samuel
Isaac	Ebeneezer
Bathsheba	Abigail
Hannah	Benjamin
Phebe	Silence
Aaron	Mehitable
Moses	Joshua
Reuben	Caleb
Jonathan	

By the turn of the nineteenth century, biblical naming began to diminish in the United States. Even so, it never fully faded away. The early settlers' nomenclature left an indelible mark on American history. No matter what their own religious views may have been, the namesakes of ABRAHAM Lincoln, BENJAMIN Franklin, NOAH Webster, JONATHAN Edwards, SAMUEL Adams, ABIGAIL Adams, AARON Burr, ELIJAH Lovejoy, and NATHANIEL Hawthorne all testify to the Christian ideals of America's Puritan settlers.

AMERICA'S

The highest glory of the American Revolution is this: it connected, in one dissoluble

bond, the principles of civil government with the principles of Christianity.

    - John Quincy Adams

PASSAGE TO

We hold these truths to be sacred and undeniable: that all men are created equal and

independent, that from that equal creation they derive inherent and inalienable rights.

    - Thomas Jefferson, Declaration of Independence (first draft), 1776

LIBERTY

Before any man can be considered as a member of civil society, he must be consid-

ered as a subject of the Governor of the universe.

    - James Madison, <u>The Memorial and Remonstrance</u>, *1785*

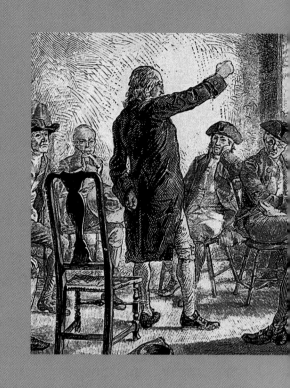

THE AMERICAN REVOLUTION

8.1 BETWEEN PLYMOUTH ROCK AND INDEPENDENCE HALL

In 1673, almost twenty years before the witch crisis at Salem, a young man named John Wise graduated from Harvard and became a Puritan minister. He embraced the Westminster Confession and was thoroughly trained in biblical interpretation and languages.[1] The aspect of Wise's thought that is so important for understanding the development of early America, however, is this: he provided the philosophical justification for the political theory that would give rise to the United States of America.

Using the law of nature as his starting point (see section 1.1), Wise explained the origin and function of government. He argued that people institute governments to promote their interests and to secure their rights and concerns. He noted that liberty, equality, and self-preservation are rights that are "instampt" upon a person's nature "as a Creature which God has made and furnished essentially with many Enobling Immunities."[2] Wise admitted that he was not the originator of these ideas, but that he was drawing from thinkers like Warrington and Pufendorf.[3]

Independence Hall

As we examine the political theories of Jefferson, Adams, and Madison, it will become plain that their views correspond unmistakably with those of Wise. This is not to say that they had Wise in mind when they articulated their ideas; but the similarity does indicate a *conceptual* linkage between Plymouth Rock and Independence Hall. In John Wise we have a philosophical "missing link" between the Puritans and the Founders.[4] Wise was not the only one. Alice Baldwin has studied the influence of the New England ministers on the Founders:

> *For generations the ministers had kept alive the doctrines of the seventeenth century and had presented them to their people.... Most significant was the conviction that fundamental law was the basis of all rights. God ruled over men by a divine constitution. Natural and Christian rights were legal rights because they were a part of the law of God.... The similarity between the political philosophy of the seventeenth century and that of the American Revolution has often been pointed out, but the lines of transmission have never been clearly traced. The teachings of the New England ministers provide one line of*

Plymouth Rock landing

unbroken descent. For two generations and more New Englanders had…been taught that these rights were sacred and came from God and that to preserve them they had a legal right of resistance and, if necessary a right to…alter and abolish governments and by common consent establish new ones.[5]

Although the Puritanism of the seventeenth century continued to flourish in New England in the eighteenth century, in England a new form of Anglicanism emerged that was unwelcome in New England. Anglicanism was the official state-sponsored religion of England and was organized as the Church of England. From the Anglican perspective, since the colonists were English, they ought to be members of the Church of England. The missionary arm of the Anglican Church was called the Society for the Propagation of the Gospel (SPG). The SPG had regularly been sending representatives to America, and Puritan leaders were suspicious of their motives.[6]

Controversy erupted when the Church of England began deliberations about sending an Anglican bishop to New England. Such a bishop would automatically control all church activities and appointments in New England. Jonathan Mayhew, who graduated from Harvard in 1744, was the most outspoken opponent against having an Anglican bishop in New England. Mayhew was a New England minister who embraced the writings of Algernon Sidney (see section 2.6).[7] In 1750, Mayhew used the anniversary of King Charles I's beheading as an opportunity to declare that the people have the right and duty to resist a government that would impose religion on them. His sermon included many principles later adopted by the Founders:

No civil rulers are to be obeyed when they enjoin things that are inconsistent with the commands of God: All such disobedience is lawful and glorious; particularly, if persons refuse to comply with any legal establishment of religion, because it is a gross perversion and corruption of pure and divine religion.… The only reason of the institution of civil government; and the only rational ground for submission to it, is the common safety and utility. If therefore, in any case, the common safety and utility would not be promoted by submission to government, but the contrary, there is no ground or motive for obedience and submission, but, for the contrary, [resistance and revolution].[8]

Here is a clear link between Calvin and the Founders. Mayhew's source for the first part of this quote is Book IV:20 of Calvin's *Institutes*. The second portion, which alludes to the social compact theory, derives from Calvin's heirs in England and America, particularly Rutherford, Sidney, and Wise.

In this sermon Mayhew approves the Puritan Revolution of the 1640s (see section 2.1) and declares that the Puritans were justified in beheading King Charles I: "It may be said that Cromwell and his adherents were not, properly speaking, guilty of rebellion, because he whom they beheaded was not, properly speaking, their king, but a lawless tyrant."[9]

This sermon, which encouraged resistance against English authority, was preached twenty-five years before the Revolutionary War. The royal governor viewed Mayhew as a rabble-rouser who was inciting the colonists toward rebellion.[10] Another loyal follower of the Crown, Peter Oliver, accused Mayhew of fomenting a revolutionary crisis.[11]

Mayhew's sermon gave firm theological and philosophical grounds for resisting unjust intrusions by the Hanover kings of England. Note that in 1750 taxes were not the issue (the Stamp Act crisis, for instance, was still fifteen years in the future). Mayhew's sermon was strictly concerned with the king's legislating the colonists' religious beliefs. Some scholars credit this religious controversy with being the spark that ignited the American Revolution.[12]

This controversy spilled over to Virginia. Despite their official association with the Church of England, Virginians had developed a "de facto congregational religion."[13] They were accustomed to their autonomy and resented the Church of England's interference with any aspect of their local church government.[14] Many Virginians agreed with Mayhew's views rather than with those of their fellow Anglicans back in England.

In the mid-1750s Mayhew and the New England clergy were distracted by the outbreak of the French and Indian War. This war resulted from the common desire of both the American colonists and the English to expand their influence westward across North

George Washington and troops defeating French

America. Since the French were in the way, this meant driving them out. The New England clergy, including Mayhew, actually supported the king in his efforts to defeat the French. This was perhaps the last time the New Englanders and the British Crown saw eye to eye.

After the French were defeated, a new crisis arose. The king had spent a great deal of money providing military forces to drive out the French. Who, then, should pay the debt? In Parliament's view, those who benefited from it, namely, the American colonists. In 1764 Parliament passed the Revenue Act and in 1765 the Stamp Act. These acts imposed taxes on the colonists for "defraying the expenses of defending, protecting, and securing British colonies and plantations in America."[15] The taxes seemed perfectly reasonable and fair to Parliament, but the colonists thought otherwise.

Although the governments of the various colonies had been taxing their own citizens for years, that was in keeping with the English Common Law because those citizens were represented in the colonial assemblies. James Otis, who graduated from Harvard in 1743, articulated the

James Otis

115

colonists' opposition to British taxes. Citing Common Law authorities dating back to the Magna Carta, Otis insisted that the Stamp Act violated the God-given rights of the colonists:

> When the parliament shall think fit to allow the colonists a representation in the House of Commons, the equity of their taxing the colonies will be as clear as their power is at present of doing it without.... It seems plain, that the reason why Ireland and the [American] plantations are not bound...is because they are not represented in the British parliament.[16]

Here is the origin of the slogan that incited the American Revolution: "No taxation without representation."[17]

This new crisis also revived the old controversy about an Anglican bishop in New England and the presence of the SPG. The New England ministers argued that the Stamp Act crisis and the Anglican controversy were two sides of the same coin. Besides Jonathan Mayhew, who died in 1766, Charles Chauncey and Ezra Stiles were leading clergymen who took this tack. Although the king never did impose Anglicanism on the New Englanders, the colonial leaders saw religious coercion and unjust taxation as ever-present threats by the British crown.

affix the STAMP.

This is the Place to

Literature against The Stamp Act

The colonial leaders fused both issues into one. "To long standing religious grievances," writes Carl Bridenbaugh, "fresh civil ones were now added, and it was the conjunction that produced the crisis [of the Revolution]."[18] John Witherspoon, for example, argued that if Americans yield their civil liberties on taxes, then they will next be forced to yield their religious liberties.[19] James Otis, John Hancock, Samuel Adams, and John Adams—all Harvard graduates—saw the conflict as encompassing both political and religious rights.

John Adams noted that the religious aspect of the conflict between America and England greatly contributed to the colonists' revolutionary spirit.[20] A cartoon in the *London Political Register* in 1769 illustrated the religious nature of the conflict. The cartoon depicted an Anglican clergyman being thrown out of America by a mob of colonists; one colonist is holding a book titled *Sidney on Government*.[21]

Conflicts over religion and taxes gave the colonial leaders the opportunity to put the political theories they had been developing into practice.[22] They were already eager to resist the king, to follow in the footsteps of their seventeenth-century forebears, and to complete what Cromwell had started but was unable to maintain.

Religious controversy helped precipitate the American Revolution. Alice Baldwin summarizes how this controversy contributed to American independence as follows:

The arguments used against England were no new ones; on the contrary they had a continuous history running far back into the past. They were the result of long discussions, of traditional belief, of continual re-interpretation of the Bible in the light of new philosophy; they grew out of theology and church polity, out of sharp ecclesiastical controversy.[23]

The alliance of the ministers with the leaders of the agitation against England was one reason for its success. They were organized and could easily communicate with each other. They were able and zealous propagandists with a remarkable opportunity for reaching the people. All through the struggle they used every means at their disposal to present the old arguments with new force.[24]

8.3 SAMUEL ADAMS AND THE SONS OF LIBERTY

Thomas Jefferson described Samuel Adams as the "fountain" of American independence.[25] Why? In 1736, a fourteen-year-old Adams entered Harvard to become a Puritan clergyman.[26] In 1743, at age twenty-one, he stood before the Royal Governor of Massachusetts and argued that it is within a Christian's rights to resist the will of a king when necessary for the good of the people.[27] In his argument he drew on the Protestant resistance theories of Calvin, Beza, Ponet, the *Vindiciae*, Rutherford, Knox, Milton, and Locke (see chapters 1 and 2). From that time forward, Adams dedicated himself to politics, law, and patriotism. Nonetheless, he always remained a Puritan.

Samuel Adams

While at Harvard, Adams befriended a younger fellow-student named James Otis. The two (along with a future Harvard graduate named John Hancock) helped instigate the American Revolution. Together they organized a band of agitators known as the Sons of Liberty. The Sons of Liberty challenged the British crown's right to tax or impose religious standards on the colonies.

For Adams these were two sides of the same coin. He knew the religious sentiments of his fellow Americans, and he knew how to arouse their passions. He therefore made the early settlers' quest for liberty the essence of the conflict. According to Adams, the danger the colonists faced was "the utter loss of those religious Rights, the enjoyment of which our good

117

Sons of Liberty

forefathers had more especially in their intention, when they explored and settled the new world."[28]

In March 1770 a group of youths in Boston badgered a British officer in the town square by throwing snowballs at him. Several other officers came to his aid, and a brawl ensued. A

British officer named Kilroy shot and killed an American named Sam Gray. Crispus Attucks, an African-American, was also shot. By the end of the conflict, five Americans fell victim to the British muskets. Samuel Adams called the event a "massacre."[29] One of his fellow agitators, Paul Revere, quickly manufactured a printed illustration of the incident and circulated numerous copies of it throughout Boston. Propaganda like this kept the revolutionary fires stoked.

Boston Massacre

When Parliament later imposed a tax on tea, Adams again rallied his followers. He called a meeting at the Old South Church in Boston and organized an act of civil disobedience. The plan was to board a ship in Boston Harbor that contained a cargo of East Indian tea and dispose of it. Adams made it clear that innocent civilians were not to be harmed.

The meeting was then dismissed, and thousands of citizens followed Adams and his band down to the wharf. About fifty men colored with face-paint of native warriors and wielding hatchets embarked upon the ship while thousands looked on. Adams declared that this act would "save the country." It certainly ensured further clashes with the British.

Although Jefferson was drawing on Locke when he wrote the Declaration of Independence, Jefferson was also drawing on Samuel Adams. Adams popularized Locke's political principles

Boston Tea Party

and made them America's own. In 1772 Adams delivered an address titled, "The Rights of the Colonists." He wrote:

> Among the natural Rights of the Colonists are these: First, a Right to Life; second, to Liberty; third, to Property;…and in the case of intolerable oppression, civil or religious, to leave the society they belong to, and enter into another. When men enter into society, it is by voluntary consent.[30]

According to Adams, these principles derive from "the first law of nature." Moreover, "the right to freedom being the gift of God Almighty, it is not in the power of man to alienate this gift and voluntarily become a slave."[31] The entire political theory of the Declaration was there in Adams's 1772 document.[32] But unlike Jefferson, who was a Unitarian, Adams was a Bible-believing Puritan.

Samuel Adams was far more than a Harvard theologian or a Lockean philosopher. He was one of the shrewdest political figures in America's history. If not for Samuel Adams in the North and Patrick Henry in the South, the United States may never have been united. In earlier colonial days New Englanders had little respect for Virginians, and vice versa. They had very different worldviews, particularly in their understanding of Christianity and in their way of life.

Citizens of New England were primarily subsistence farmers, merchants, or craftsmen. They also approved of Cromwell and the Puritans who beheaded Charles I Stuart. In the South, the economy revolved around cash crops: tobacco, rice, indigo, and cotton. The people tended to support the British monarchy and ally themselves with the Stuart kings. Both Charleston and Carolina had been named for Charles II Stuart,[33] and the affection he shared with the Virginians led him to designate the colony his "Old Dominion."[34]

Slavery in the South troubled the Northern Puritans and led them to dissociate themselves from the South as much as possible. Likewise, Southerners tended to view the New Englanders as an uncultivated working-class of stodgy do-gooders whose rigid Calvinism deceived them into thinking they were God's chosen people. Although the Great Awakening had been an intercolonial event that eased the

Samuel Adams

provincialism of the colonies, sharp disagreements between North and South remained until the time of Samuel Adams.

Prayer at Continental Congress

Adams initiated "Committees of Correspondence" to promote cooperation among the colonies in dealing with the British Crown. These committees evolved into the Continental Congress, the assembly that produced the Declaration of Independence. When the first Continental Congress convened in Philadelphia in September 1774, the Virginians were cautious about cooperating with "radical Protestants" from New England. Likewise, many Northern Presbyterians saw the Southern Anglicans as enemies.[35] Left unchecked, these tensions could have disrupted the first Continental Congress and ultimately prevented the formation of the United States.

To ease the tension, Samuel Adams (a Puritan) motioned that a Southern minister (an Anglican) invoke God's blessing on the assembly. This was very shrewd. Later, John Adams would write:

[George] Washington was kneeling there, and [Patrick] Henry, [Edmund] Randolph, [John] Rutledge, [Richard Henry] Lee, and [John] Jay, and by their side there stood, bowed in reverence, the Puritan Patriots of New England.... It was enough to melt a heart of stone.[36]

This gesture was returned when Patrick Henry, during his "give me liberty, or give me death" oration in Richmond, Virginia, called the Puritans "Our brethren" who are "already in the [battle]-field."[37] Samuel Adams and Patrick Henry inspired their respective regions of America to join forces with the other.[38]

Samuel Adams and John Hancock were at the home of their pastor, the Rev. Jonas Clark, in Lexington, Massachusetts, on the evening of April 18, 1775,

Patrick Henry

when Paul Revere arrived with the news that General Gage's troops were approaching. When the first shots were fired on April 19, 1775, Adams exclaimed, "Oh! what a glorious morning this is!" Five days before the next major battle at Bunker Hill, the British military offered a pardon to all Americans who would lay down their arms and retire. There were only two exceptions: Samuel Adams and John Hancock. The offer did not extend to them. As leaders of the Sons of Liberty they were unforgivable.[39]

In August 1775, the king of England proclaimed that the colonies were "engaged in open and avowed rebellion," and were thus outside the protection of his government or laws. Shortly thereafter, Parliament passed the Prohibitory Act, which declared that all American ships and their cargoes were forfeit to the British Crown.

In order to solidify Southern support for the war, John Adams urged that the Continental Congress employ a Virginian to lead the Continental forces. The Congress agreed. General George Washington assumed command of the Continental forces in Boston.

On New Year's Day 1776, the king leveled Norfolk, Virginia, with naval artillery. In May 1776, the colonists learned that the king had signed treaties with German states to obtain mercenary soldiers to invade the colonies. The king had not only refused to protect the rights of the colonists, but he was now poised for war.

George Washington

8.4 THE "PRESBYTERIAN REBELLION"

"The Revolution of 1776," according to the celebrated historian George Bancroft, "was a Presbyterian measure. It was the natural outgrowth of the principles which the Presbyterianism of the Old World planted in her sons."[40] What did Bancroft mean?

Those who lived through the American Revolution saw it as a continuation of the seventeenth-century Protestant revolutions in England (i.e., the English Civil War and the Glorious Revolution). In describing the American Revolution of 1776, William Jones told King George III: "This has been a Presbyterian war from the beginning as certainly as that in 1641."[41] Another supporter of King George wrote: "I fix all the blame for these extraordinary proceedings upon the Presbyterians. They have been the chief and principal instruments in all these flaming measures."[42]

The Royal Governor of Georgia wrote that the revolution was based upon "Oliverian principles" (referring to Oliver Cromwell).[43] Several other voices loyal to the king were quick to trace the American endeavor to the politics of the Puritans and Presbyterians of

SAMUEL ADAMS'S
"COMMITTEE OF CORRESPONDENCE"

DECLARES THE RIGHTS OF THE COLONISTS

November, 1772

NATURAL RIGHTS OF THE COLONISTS AS MEN

Among the NATURAL RIGHTS of the colonists are these: first, a right to life; second, to liberty; third, to property; together with the right to support and defend them in the best manner they can. These are evident branches of, rather than deductions from, the duty of self-preservation, commonly called the first law of nature.

All men have a right to remain in a state of nature as long as they please; and in case of intolerable oppression, civil or religious, to leave the society they belong to, and enter into another.

When men enter into society, it is by voluntary consent; and they have a right to demand and insist upon the performance of such conditions and previous limitations as form an equitable original compact.

Every natural right not expressly given up, or, from the nature of a social compact, necessarily ceded, remains.

All positive and civil laws should conform, as far as possible, to the law of natural reason and equity.

As neither reason requires nor religion permits the contrary, every man living in or out of a state of civil society has a right peaceably and quietly to worship God according to the dictates of his conscience.

Just and true liberty, equal and impartial liberty, in matters spiritual and temporal, is a thing that all men are entitled to by the eternal and immutable laws of God and nature, as well as by the law of nations and well-grounded municipal laws, which must have their foundation in the former.

In regard to religion, mutual toleration in the different professions thereof is what good and candid minds in all ages have ever practiced, and, both by precept and example, inculcated on mankind. And it is generally agreed among Christians that this spirit of toleration, in the fullest extent consistent with the being of civil society, is the chief characteristical mark of the church. Insomuch that Mr. Locke has asserted and proved, beyond the possibility of contradiction on any solid ground, that such toleration ought to be extended to all whose doctrines are not subversive of society....

The right to freedom being the gift of God Almighty, it is not in the power of man to alienate this gift and voluntarily become a slave.

THE RIGHTS OF THE COLONISTS AS CHRISTIANS

THESE MAY BE BEST understood by reading and carefully studying the institutes of the great Lawgiver and Head of the Christian Church, which are found clearly written and promulgated in the New Testament.

By the act of the British Parliament, commonly called the toleration act, every subject in England [not seeking to overthrow society] was restored to, and reestablished in, his natural right to worship God according to the dictates of his own conscience. And, by the charter of this province, it is granted, ordained, and established (that is, declared as an original right) that there shall be liberty of conscience allowed in the worship of God to all Christians [except those seeking to overthrow society], inhabiting, or which shall inhabit or be resident within, such province or territory. Magna Charta itself is in substance but a constrained declaration or proclamation and promulgation in the name of the King, Lords,

and Commons, of the sense the [Commoners] had of their original, inherent, indefeasible natural rights as those of free citizens equally perdurable with the other. That great author, that great jurist, and even that court writer, Mr. Justice Blackstone, holds that this recognition was justly obtained of King John, sword in hand. And peradventure it must be one day, sword in hand, again rescued and preserved from total destruction and oblivion.

THE RIGHTS OF THE COLONISTS AS SUBJECTS

All persons born in the British American colonies are, by the laws of God and nature and by the Common Law of England…well entitled, and by acts of the British Parliament declared to be entitled, to all the natural, essential, inherent, and inseparable rights, liberties, and privileges of subjects born in Great Britain or the Realm….

The legislative has no right to absolute, arbitrary power over the lives and fortunes of the people; nor can mortals assume a prerogative not only too high for men, but for angels, and therefore reserved for the exercise of the Deity alone.

the seventeenth century.[44] The historian Edmund Morgan reported that royal officials in the colonies complained that the Presbyterians are "as averse to Kings as they were in the Days of Cromwell, and some begin to cry out, 'No King but King Jesus.'"[45]

Thomas Jefferson adopted as his own motto the cry of the Puritans during the English Civil War: "Resistance to tyranny is obedience to God."[46] A Hessian captain, fighting on behalf of the British during the American Revolution, told a friend in Germany: "Call this war, dearest friend, by whatsoever name you may, only call it not an American Revolution; it is nothing more nor less than an Irish-Scotch Presbyterian Rebellion."[47]

It was not only the opponents of colonial independence who identified the American cause with Presbyterian rebellion. The colonists themselves were fond of that link. Just as we have our national heroes (e.g., Washington, Jefferson, and Lincoln), so did the early American colonists. Their three favorites were Oliver Cromwell, John Hampden, and Algernon Sidney.[48] All three were Puritan leaders associated with the seventeenth century rebellions in England.

Samuel Adams enjoyed being called a "Roundhead."[49] The Sons of Liberty referred to Cromwell as a "glorious fellow" and yearned for a new Cromwell to "espouse their cause."[50] Editorials criticizing the British government in several colonial newspapers were signed with the pseudonym "Oliver Cromwell."[51] In 1774, a Connecticut clergyman described the English Civil War as the "good old days":

England was never more happy before, nor much more since, than after the head of the first Stuart was severed from his body, and while it was under the protectorship of Oliver Cromwell.[52]

A tavern in Boston was named "Cromwell's Head." The sign outside, which featured a likeness of Cromwell, was just high enough to pass under if one ducked a few inches Apparently, those who entered were supposed to bow to Cromwell's image.[53]

As for the colonists who took up arms during the Revolution, the majority were Presbyterians.[54] They understood their struggle as a continuation of the seventeenth-century Protestant revolutions in England. As Page Smith notes:

The Protestant Reformation produced a new kind of consciousness and a new kind of man. The English Colonies in America, in turn, produced a new and unique strain of that consciousness.... It is impossible to understand the intellectual and moral forces behind the American Revolution without understanding the role that Protestant Christianity played in shaping the ideals, principles and institutions of colonial America....

The right of resistance to unlawful authority, so clearly enunciated by the Parliamentary leaders [of the English Civil War] and confirmed by the Glorious Revolution of 1689 was the basis on which the Americans opposed the unlimited authority of Parliament over the British colonies.[55]

TWO FOUNDING DOCUMENTS

9.1 THE DECLARATION OF INDEPENDENCE

The actions of the king and Parliament in the 1770s gradually convinced the colonial leadership in America that the British form of government could not protect the colonists' rights. In late spring 1776, colony after colony began taking steps toward independence. As the new state governments formed, they also began declaring that inalienable, God-given rights were the basis of their new social order. Jefferson's friends in Virginia wrote the following words as the first sentence of the Virginia Bill of Rights, the very first part of the state's constitution:

A declaration of rights made by the representatives of the good people of Virginia, assembled in full and free convention; which rights do pertain to them and their posterity, as the basis and foundation of government.[1]

The American approach far exceeded the British approach. It made inalienable rights truly the basis of government. Those rights could not be vetoed by government. To the contrary, if government violated those rights, the government could be opposed. The Virginia Constitution said, for example:

That all men are by nature equally free and independent, and have certain inherent rights, of which, when they enter into a state of society, they cannot, by any compact, deprive or divest their posterity; namely, the enjoyment of life and liberty, with the means of acquiring and possessing property, and pursuing and obtaining happiness and safety...and that, when any government shall be found inadequate or contrary to these purposes, a majority of the community hath an indubitable, inalienable, and indefeasible right to reform, alter, or abolish it; in such manner as shall be judged most conducive to the public weal.[2]

One month later, the united colonies, calling themselves the United States of America, recited these principles in the Declaration of Independence, proclaiming individual rights—inalienable rights of personhood—as the foundation of their state governments and their national union.

The Declaration of Independence is a literary masterpiece. In it, Jefferson tied together centuries of thinking concerning law, government, and rights. In 1822, reflecting on the philosophy behind the Declaration, Jefferson wrote that the goal of writing it was "not to find out new principles, or new arguments, never before thought of." He continued,

All its [i.e., the Declaration of Independence's] authority rests then on the harmonizing sentiments of the day, whether expressed in conversation, in letters, printed essays, or in the elementary books of public right, as Aristotle, Cicero, Locke, Sidney, etc.[3]

Although Jefferson was the principal author of the Declaration, its ideas did not originate with him. M. Stanton Evans writes:

These ideas were rooted in centuries of British, and American, practice, and by the era of the Declaration were anything but new. Only by neglecting the growth of the English common law, religious-feudal contract doctrine, the covenant theology of the Puritans, and a great deal else, could one arrive at [any alternative] conclusions. Such are the intellectual wages of ignoring history.[4]

128

Thomas Jefferson

Jefferson drew from the Magna Carta, the English Common Law, Medieval and Protestant resistance theories, the English Bill of Rights, and the Petition of Right, as well as a host of colonial political documents. Jefferson was not an innovator but rather a synthesizer who was able to combine these sources and apply them to the American situation.

Even so, it is widely held that the Declaration of Independence is an Enlightenment document that carefully avoids traditional Christian terminology, substituting instead vaguely religious terminology. For example, instead of the "Law of Christ," Jefferson referred to "the law of nature's God." Additionally, although the first draft of the Declaration referred to "sacred truths," the final draft substituted the language of "self-evident truths." For concepts like consent of the governed, self-evident truths, and inalienable rights, was Jefferson essentially looking to the Enlightenment, or was he drawing on Christian sources?

The Declaration is not simply a product of Deism, the Enlightenment, the Renaissance, or Græco-Roman philosophy. This is not to say that these sources did not play a role in America's founding—they did. But if we look closely at the wording and the ideas contained in the Declaration, it becomes clear that the primary influence that shaped the document was the Christian tradition in law and theology.[5]

It is no contradiction to say that Jefferson adopted a Christian view of law and rights even though he himself was not a Christian in the traditional sense. Jefferson was immersed in a Christian culture. Whether he personally acknowledged Christ as Savior matters little to whether his theories were Christian. Jefferson absorbed, by cultural osmosis, the general worldview of his Christian mentors.

Jefferson's cultural context was thoroughly Christian. His education did not occur at the hands of deists in Paris, but at the feet of clergymen in Virginia. Between the ages of nine and sixteen, he was tutored by two orthodox ministers: Rev. James Maury and Rev. William Douglas.[6] When he studied law at the College of William and Mary he was not the pupil of Voltaire. His mentor was George Wythe, a "devout Christian and by no means a deist."[7] Jefferson called Wythe "my second father, my earliest and best friend."[8]

Jefferson embraced the creator-redeemer distinction. He also embraced the basic principles of law and rights common to Catholics, Puritans, Presbyterians, Baptists, and other Christian groups. One historian summed up the influence of Christianity on Jefferson as follows:

Jefferson and other secular-minded Americans subscribed to certain propositions about law and authority that had their roots in the Protestant Reformation. It is a scholarly commonplace to point out how much Jefferson (and his fellow delegates to the Continental Congress) were influenced by Locke. Without disputing this we would simply add that an older and deeper influence—John Calvin—was of more profound importance (or that Locke's consciousness, like Jefferson's, was a consequence in large part of the Reformation).[9]

9.2 THE LAW OF NATURE AND NATURE'S GOD

In the opening sentence of the Declaration, an appeal to "the law of nature and nature's God" appears. This is often regarded as a conscious attempt by Jefferson to describe God in deistic terms. A more thorough study, however, reveals that this terminology had for centuries been part of the canon law of the Roman Catholic Church. From there it passed to Christians more generally in England and became squarely implanted in the English Common Law of the thirteenth century.[10]

One of Jefferson's most influential sources was Sir Edward Coke (see chapter 4). Coke was a Puritan whose writings on the Common Law served as the central textbook for legal studies at the College of William and Mary, where Jefferson received his formal training.[11] Writing in 1610, Coke explained the meaning of the phrase "law of nature":

The law of nature is that which God at the time of creation of the nature of man infused into his heart, for his preservation and direction; and this is lex æterna [the eternal law], the moral law, called also the law of nature... And by the law, written with the finger of God in the heart of man, were the people of God a long time governed, before the law was written by Moses, who was the first reporter or writer of law in the world. The Apostle, in the Second Chapter to the Romans saith, Cum enim gentes quae legem non habent naturaliter ea quae legis sunt faciant [While the gentiles who do not have the law do naturally the things of the law].... This law of nature, which indeed is the eternal law of the creator, infused into the heart of the creature at the time of his creation, was [before any written laws], and before any judicial or municipal laws.[12]

THE UNANIMOUS DECLARATION OF THE THIRTEEN UNITED STATES OF AMERICA

IN CONGRESS JULY 4, 1776

When, in the course of human events, it becomes necessary for one people to dissolve the political bands which have connected them with another, and to assume among the powers of the earth, the separate and equal station to which the laws of nature and of nature's God entitle them, a decent respect to the opinions of mankind requires that they should declare the causes which impel them to the separation.

We hold these truths to be self-evident, that all men are created equal, that they are endowed by their Creator with certain unalienable rights, that among these are life, liberty and the pursuit of happiness. That to secure these rights, governments are instituted among men, deriving their just powers from the consent of the governed. That whenever any form of government becomes destructive to these ends, it is the right of the people to alter or to abolish it, and to institute new government, laying its foundation on such principles and organizing its powers in such form, as to them shall seem most likely to effect their safety and happiness.

Prudence, indeed, will dictate that governments long established should not be changed for light and transient causes; and accordingly all experience hath shown, that mankind are more disposed to suffer, while evils are sufferable, than to right themselves by abolishing the forms to which they are accustomed. But when a long train of abuses and usurpations, pursuing invariably the same object evinces a design to reduce them under absolute despotism, it is their right, it is their duty, to throw off such government, and to provide new guards for their future security. Such has been the patient sufferance of these colonies; and such is now the necessity which constrains them to alter their former systems of government.

The history of the present King of Great Britain is a history of repeated injuries and usurpations, all having in direct object the establishment of an absolute tyranny over these states. To prove this, let facts be submitted to a candid world:

- He has refused his assent to laws, the most wholesome and necessary for the public good.
- He has forbidden his governors to pass laws of immediate and pressing importance, unless suspended in their operation till his assent should be obtained; and when so suspended, he has utterly neglected to attend to them.
- He has refused to pass other laws for the accommodation of large districts of people, unless those people would relinquish the right of representation in the legislature, a right inestimable to them and formidable to tyrants only.
- He has called together legislative bodies at places unusual, uncomfortable, and distant from the depository of their public records, for the sole purpose of fatiguing them into compliance with his measures.
- He has dissolved representative houses repeatedly, for opposing with manly firmness his invasions on the rights of the people.
- He has refused for a long time, after such dissolutions, to cause others to be elected; whereby the legislative powers, incapable of annihilation, have returned to the people at large for their exercise; the state remaining in the meantime exposed to all the dangers of invasion from without, and convulsions within.
- He has endeavored to prevent the population of these states; for that purpose obstructing the laws for naturalization of foreigners; refusing to pass others to encourage their migration hither, and raising the conditions of new appropriations of lands.
- He has obstructed the administration of justice, by refusing his assent to laws for establishing judiciary powers.
- He has made judges dependent on his will alone, for the tenure of their offices, and the amount and payment of their salaries.
- He has erected a multitude of new offices, and sent hither swarms of officers to harass our people, and eat out their substance.
- He has kept among us, in times of peace, standing armies without the consent of our legislatures.
- He has affected to render the military independent of and superior to the civil power.
- He has combined with others to subject us to a jurisdiction foreign to our constitution, and unacknowledged by

our laws; giving his assent to their acts of pretended legislation:

- For quartering large bodies of armed troops among us:
- For protecting them, by a mock trial, from punishment for any murders which they should commit on the inhabitants of these states:
- For cutting off our trade with all parts of the world:
- For imposing taxes on us without our consent:
- For depriving us in many cases, of the benefits of trial by jury:
- For transporting us beyond seas to be tried for pretended offences:
- For abolishing the free system of English laws in a neighbouring province, establishing therein an arbitrary government, and enlarging its boundaries so as to render it at once an example and fit instrument for introducing the same absolute rule in these colonies:
- For taking away our charters, abolishing our most valuable laws, and altering fundamentally the forms of our governments:
- For suspending our own legislatures, and declaring themselves invested with power to legislate for us in all cases whatsoever.
- He has abdicated government here, by declaring us out of his protection and waging war against us.
- He has plundered our seas, ravaged our coasts, burnt our towns, and

destroyed the lives of our people.

- He is at this time transporting large armies of foreign mercenaries to compleat the works of death, desolation and tyranny, already begun with circumstances of cruelty and perfidy scarcely paralleled in the most barbarous ages, and totally unworthy the head of a civilized nation.
- He has constrained our fellow citizens taken captive on the high seas to bear arms against their country, to become the executioners of their friends and brethren, or to fall themselves by their hands.
- He has excited domestic insurrections amongst us, and has endeavoured to bring on the inhabitants of our frontiers, the merciless Indian savages, whose known rule of warfare, is an undistinguished destruction of all ages, sexes and conditions.

In every stage of these oppressions we have petitioned for redress in the most humble terms: our repeated petitions have been answered only by repeated injury. A prince, whose character is thus marked by every act which may define a tyrant, is unfit to be the ruler of a free people.

Nor have we been wanting in attentions to our British brethren. We have warned them from time to time of attempts by their legislature to extend an unwarrantable jurisdiction over us. We have reminded them of the circumstances of our emigration and settlement here. We have appealed to their native justice and magnanimity, and we have conjured them by the ties of our common kindred to disavow these usurpations, which, would inevitably interrupt our connections and correspondence. They too have been deaf to the voice of justice and of consanguinity. We must, therefore, acquiesce in the necessity, which denounces our separation, and hold them, as we hold the rest of mankind, enemies in war, in peace friends.

We, therefore, the representatives of the United States of America, in General Congress, assembled, appealing to the Supreme Judge of the world for the rectitude of our intentions, do, in the name, and by the authority of the good people of these colonies, solemnly publish and declare, that these united colonies are, and of right ought to be, free and independent states; that they are absolved from all allegiance to the British Crown, and that all political connection between them and the state of Great Britain, is and ought to be totally dissolved; and that as free and independent states, they have full power to levy war, conclude peace, contract alliances, establish commerce, and to do all other acts and things which independent states may of right do. And for the support of this declaration, with a firm reliance on the protection of divine Providence, we mutually pledge to each other our lives, our fortunes and our sacred honor.

Coke grounded the law of nature squarely in the Christian doctrine of creation. Coke's conception of the law of nature or natural law cannot therefore be attributed to the Stoic philosophy of the ancient Greeks and Romans. Nor for that matter can it be attributed to the Renaissance and Enlightenment philosophies that took their understanding of natural law from Stoicism.

According to Stoic philosophy, the world and everything in it (including ourselves) are indeed governed by natural laws. Unlike Coke, however, the Stoics had no doctrine of creation. Within Stoicism, natural law was a brute given that could work to our benefit or detriment depending on fate. Within Christianity, on the other hand, God implanted the law of nature at creation specifically for our benefit. The Stoic conception of natural law was impersonal. The Christian conception of natural law was personal—God instituted natural law because he was looking out for us. The conception of natural law in the Declaration hinges on a beneficent creator and is therefore specifically Christian.

Coke's understanding of the law of nature as *prior to* written laws was crucial to American independence. According to the law of King George III, Jefferson and his compatriots were outlaws. To legitimate American independence, Jefferson therefore needed to appeal to a law *that was before* the written law, a law written not in books, but "infused into the heart of the creature at the time of his creation."

Jefferson also drew heavily on Sir William Blackstone (see chapter 4).[13] Blackstone followed directly in Coke's footsteps in explaining the law of nature. In his *Commentaries*,

Declaration of Independence

which were among Jefferson's favorite books, Blackstone devoted seven pages to defining the "law of nature." Blackstone writes as an orthodox Christian within a long tradition of orthodox Christians: "As man depends absolutely upon his maker for every thing, it is necessary that he should in all points conform to his maker's will. This will of his maker is called the law of nature."[14] According to Blackstone, all human laws depended either upon that unwritten law (the law of nature) or upon the Bible: "Upon these two foundations, the law of nature and the law of revelation, depend all human laws."[15]

The concept of natural law appeared in virtually all the key writings that influenced the Founders. The key document of English Calvinists, the Westminster Confession, used the term "law of nature." Calvin himself had employed the concept: "The law of God which we call moral [law], is nothing else than the testimony of the natural law, and of that conscience which God has engraven on the minds of men."[16] In *Lex Rex* Samuel Rutherford cited the "law of nature" as grounds for political dissent. Richard Hooker, the preeminent theologian and political theorist of the Anglican Church, also championed the "law of nature." Locke in turn drew upon Rutherford and Hooker. By citing the law of nature at the outset of the Declaration, Jefferson was therefore simply reflecting a long tradition of Christian political and legal theory.[17]

Jefferson invoked the "law of nature's God" to remind the king that the power of government is divinely ordained *through the consent of the people*. This was the position of Rutherford, Sidney, and Locke, as well as that of the New England Protestants. One Harvard Puritan had argued "the voice of the people is the voice of God." The American struggle for independence can therefore be understood as a conflict between natural law versus written law, or, correspondingly, as a conflict between religious dissent versus religious conformity.[18]

9.3 Self-Evident Truths, Inalienable Rights, and Slavery

History has left us an important clue for understanding what was in Jefferson's mind as he wrote the Declaration. We still have Jefferson's *first draft*. When Jefferson wrote the first draft of the Declaration, he penned the following words: "We hold these truths to be *sacred and undeniable*: that all men are created equal and independent, that *from that equal creation they derive inherent and inalienable rights [emphasis added]*."[19] Since Jefferson initially wrote that basic human rights are "sacred," why does the final draft substitute "self-evident" for "sacred"?

The concept of "self-evident truths" had appeared in Locke's *Essay on Human Understanding*. Locke characterized the truth of a proposition as self-evident if its truth was immediately apparent upon reflection. Propositions that are self-evidently true therefore do not require proof or the assistance of other propositions to establish their truth.[20] An example of a self-evident truth is that a part cannot exceed the whole. Once we reflect on what it means for something to be a part and to be a whole, the truth of this proposition is immediately apparent. Self-evidence does not deny the divine origin of a truth; it simply makes a truth universally apparent.

Consider next what it means for a truth to be "sacred." Christian theology recognizes at least two kinds of sacred truths: (1) those which God has made known only to certain people through special revelation, and (2) those which God has made evident to the whole world by giving every person the power to see their truth immediately upon reflection.[21] Now it's clear that the truths in this second category are self-evident truths.

By changing "sacred" to "self-evident," the editor who modified Jefferson's first draft of the Declaration did not deny that our basic human rights constitute a sacred truth. Rather, the editor was making the argument of the first draft more precise. A self-evident truth is a sacred truth which no one, regardless of religious or ideological preference, can deny. All self-evident truths are sacred truths, but not vice versa.

The difference between "sacred" and "self-evident" has nothing to do with one truth having religious significance and the other having none. The change from "sacred" to "self-evident" was simply to clarify that these rights not only derive from God, but also derive from God in such a way that all people are compelled to acknowledge them. Except for that clarification, the two terms are synonymous, and the difference in their meanings—at least in the mind of any eighteenth-century thinker—is negligible.

In the early published copies of the Declaration of Independence we find the phrase "unalienable rights."[22] In modern English we call them inalienable rights. In 1776, at a time when dictionaries were only beginning to standardize the spellings of words, "unalienable" and "inalienable" were interchangeable. There was no difference in meaning between the two spellings. Both spellings were used by members of the Continental Congress.

What did Jefferson and the Founders mean by the term "inalienable rights"? The term was drawn from the English Common Law of property. When people own land or other kinds of property, they may sell it, give it away, rent or lease it, or transfer it to others. In the Common Law, to sell or transfer one's rights to property was to "alienate" them.[23]

Inalienable rights are rights that are so essential to our identity as humans that no one can sell them or give them away without denying one's own personhood. They are higher than ordinary property rights. Ordinary rights can be bartered, sold, or traded. Inalienable rights cannot. The creator endows people with these inalienable rights, attaching them to human nature. Since inalienable rights are part of the definition of humanity, to take them away is to attack humanity itself.

The distinction is a simple one. Some rights can be "alienated," such as ownership rights over a particular piece of land. Those rights can be bartered, sold, or traded. Other rights, however, cannot be alienated—such as the right to own property in the first place.

Inalienable rights were God's gift to humanity at creation. Jefferson and his colleagues inherited this idea from Christianity:

When the Patriot leaders were pressed to make an axiomatic case for freedom, they routinely did so on a religious basis…. Sam Adams and James Otis, for example, put it that, "the right of freedom being the gift of God almighty, it is not in the power of man to alienate this gift." John Adams

Jefferson's first draft of the Declaration of Independence

likewise contended that human freedom was founded in the ordinance of the Creator…. John Dickinson, for instance, said of American freedoms: "We claim them from a higher source, from the King of Kings and Lord of all the earth."… Hamilton's version was "The sacred rights of mankind are not to be rummaged for among parchments and musty records. They are written …by the Hand of the Divinity… The Supreme Being…invested [mankind] with an inviolable right to personal liberty." Jay asserted that "we are…entitled by the bounty of an indulgent Creator to freedom."[24]

Because Jefferson believed the right to liberty flowed from the fact of creation, it comes as no surprise that, later in the first draft of the

Committee writing Declaration of Independence

Declaration, Jefferson harshly attacked the institution of slavery, complaining:

> He [King George III] has waged cruel war against human nature itself, violating its most sacred rights of life & liberty in the persons of distant people who never offended him, captivating & carrying them into slavery in another hemisphere, or to incur miserable death in their transportation thither.[25]

Jefferson's argument against slavery is really an argument against tyranny and parallels Samuel Rutherford's argument against tyranny in *Lex Rex*. Though composed 130 years before the Declaration, Rutherford's argument has the same structure as Jefferson's. According to Rutherford, the king is subject to the laws of nature. The laws of nature assign inherent rights to every individual. And if the king becomes a tyrant by criminally violating the laws of nature and the people's God-given rights, the king can be dethroned.

On page 1 of *Lex Rex*, Rutherford insisted that there is a law of nature, given by God, to which all human beings are subject—even the king. On page 2 he insisted that this means that all people are *"born equally free."*[26] From the equality of persons he argued that people possess inalienable rights. These inalienable rights in turn derive from God's having "endowed [each] person with a sort of royalty, of a divine image, that his life cannot be taken."[27] What defines our humanity is that we are "endued with God's image."[28] Being "born equally free" or "born free and equal" is ours automatically at birth. It is unconditional.

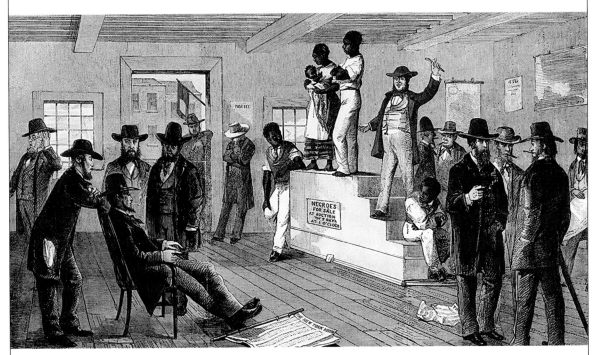

Virginia slave auction

What, then, to do with slavery? Rutherford explained that differences in position do not indicate differences in personhood: "All are born alike and equal."[29] In another place he writes: "Man by nature is born free."[30] Since differences in position do not imply unequal personhood, children have the same personhood rights that adults have. Rutherford explained that adults clearly have inalienable rights, which they cannot surrender or give away.[31] Since their posterity, meaning their unborn children, have the same rights, parents cannot give away the rights of their posterity either.[32] People are not free to make themselves slaves, and they are forbidden to take any action that would make their children slaves. Hereditary slavery is forbidden by the laws of nature.[33]

Slavery clearly undercut the equality of personhood. Nonetheless, slavery, like divorce, had been permitted in the Old Testament. Some people therefore saw a justification for slavery in the Bible. Maybe slavery was all right. If their argument was sound, this would make liberty an alienable right and would make inequality natural, just as Aristotle had said. Rutherford answered this way:

Slavery of servants to lords or masters, such as were of old amongst the Jews, is not natural, but against nature. Because slavery is malum naturae [bad by nature, or evil in and of

Slaves gathering cotton

138

itself], a penal evil and contrary to nature, and a punishment of sin. A man being created according to God's image, he is res sacra, a sacred thing, and can no more, by nature's law, be sold and bought, than a religious and sacred thing dedicated to God.[34]

Rutherford's statement here is crucial. The key to overturning slavery is that people are created in the image of God. Slavery, war, inequality, tyranny and the like are not part of the law of nature. They are a curse. They are contrary to nature. They violate God's original design for creation.[35] Slavery denies and degrades the image of God in humanity. The only justification for enduring slavery is to save one's life.[36]

Rutherford was unmoved at slavery's being practiced and allowed in Israel under the Old Testament law. Polygamy had also been practiced and allowed, but it violated God's original plan. Slavery was no more the norm for society than divorce was the goal for marriage. Slavery existed in the Old Testament as a consequence of humanity's sinfulness. Slavery resulted from social injustice mixed with unfortunate circumstances. These circumstances could not be allowed to dictate Christian principle. Christian teaching, Rutherford insisted, must adhere to God's original plan, which rejected slavery.

Jefferson also rejected the legitimacy of slavery, and this despite its practice in the colonies as well as on his own plantation. Against Jefferson's wishes, criticism of slavery was removed from the Declaration. The pro-slavery element in the middle and Southern colonies was too politically powerful.

Jefferson had previously denounced slavery in his *Summary View of the Rights of British America* in 1774. According to Jefferson, slaves must be freed and treated like other human beings. They must also be enfranchised, meaning that they should be made full citizens, enjoying both personhood rights and citizenship rights:

The abolition of domestic slavery is the great object of desire in those colonies, where it was unhappily introduced in their infant state. But previous to the enfranchisement of the slaves we have, it is necessary to exclude all further importations from Africa… The God who gave us life gave us liberty at the same time; the hand of force may destroy, but cannot disjoin them.[37]

9.4 CONSENT OF THE GOVERNED

Where did Jefferson acquire his concept of "government by consent of the governed"? To answer this question, compare the following statements:

It is clearly agreed, by all, that the care of safety and wellfare was the original cause or occasion of common weales and of many familyes subjecting themselves to rulers and laws… From the premises will arise these conclusions: No common weale can be founded but by free consent.[38]

We hold these truths to be self-evident… That to secure these rights [life, liberty, & the pursuit of happiness], governments are instituted among men, deriving their just powers from the consent of the governed.[39]

The two statements are essentially identical. Jefferson wrote the second. John Winthrop, a prominent New England theologian, wrote the first. Winthrop wrote this statement 140 years prior to the Declaration. John Locke, who is generally credited with being the original source of Jefferson's political theories, was only five years old at the time.

Government by the consent of the people did not originate with Jefferson or Locke. It was characteristic of *Puritan* political theory.[40] There were an abundance of seventeenth-century Puritan scholars, both English and American, who developed this theory.[41] This philosophical contribution by the Puritans to the founding of the United States is often overlooked. Nonetheless, it is easily identified and documented in the original sources. In discussing the concept of "consent of the governed," M. Stanton Evans writes:

> *These notions were obviously not of secular or Enlightenment provenance, and in particular were not derived from Locke. Again, the chronological factor is decisive; the evidence cited here not only predates the Second Treatise [i.e., Locke's <u>Second Treatise on Government</u>], most of it predates the existence of Locke himself. <u>The Mayflower Compact</u> was written in 1620; Massachusetts and its elections date from 1630.[42]*

9.5 RELYING ON DIVINE PROVIDENCE

The final line of the Declaration invokes "the protection of Divine Providence." The Founders understood Divine Providence as God's care for and control of the world. God, for the Founders, was actively involved not only with the universe as a whole, but also with their personal affairs—especially their conflict with England. Providence for the Founders was not a deistic notion where God winds up the universe and then lets it run on its own.[43]

The Declaration appeals to a deity who intervenes in human affairs. Jefferson wrote the Declaration with Patrick Henry's speech in his ears: "An appeal to arms and to the God of hosts is all that is left us…. We shall not fight our battles alone. There is a just God who presides over the destinies of nations, and who will raise up friends to fight our battles for us."[44]

In 1775, a year before writing the Declaration, Jefferson had authored with John Dickinson *The Necessity for Taking Up Arms*. There they wrote:

> *Our cause is just… We gratefully acknowledge, as signal instances of the divine favor toward us, that His Providence would not permit us to be called into this severe controversy until we were grown up to our present strength… With a humble confidence in the mercies of the Supreme and impartial Judge and Ruler of the Universe, we most devoutly implore his divine goodness to protect us happily through this great conflict.[45]*

Earlier that year Joseph Warren, a New England patriot who was killed at Bunker Hill, had written concerning the beginning of the war:

> *To the persecution and tyranny of [King George's] cruel Ministry we will not tamely submit—appealing to Heaven for the justice of our cause, we determine to die or be free…*
> *We sincerely hope that the Great Sovereign of the universe, who has so often appeared for the English nation, will support you in every rational and many exertion with these*

colonies for saving it from ruin.[46]

Warren wrote this after delivering a passionate speech in which he linked God's providence to the righteousness of the American cause: "If you perform your part, you must have the strongest confidence that the same Almighty Being who protected your pious and venerable forefathers…will still be mindful of you, their offspring."[47]

The Founders appealed to Divine Providence because they were convinced that their cause was just. The Founders "repeatedly reassured themselves that God would champion their endeavors because they were championing the rights which the Lord had bestowed upon humanity."[48] For the Founders, Divine Providence was not an impersonal force. The God who governed the world through Divine Providence was a personal being, committed to justice and opposed to injustice.

The concept of Divine Providence was part of the Founders' Protestant heritage. God's providential care and control of the world had been a huge theme for the Protestant Reformers, especially for John Calvin. It's hard to overemphasize the importance of Divine Providence for the Founders.[49] Because their cause was just and because Divine Providence was on their side, they could be fearless in their conflict with the British.

9.6 THE FEDERAL CONSTITUTION

The writing of the United States Constitution completed the union of American states that began eleven years earlier at the Second Continental Congress. The Second Continental Congress had met at the Pennsylvania State House in Philadelphia, now known as Independence Hall. In the summer of 1787 the colonial leaders returned to Philadelphia to establish the principles upon which the United States would rest.

Signing of the Declaration of Independence

The chief architect of the United States Constitution was James Madison. Although Madison's early training is often ignored, it significantly influenced his writing of the Constitution.[50] As a youth, he had studied under a Scottish Presbyterian, Donald Robertson, to whom Madison gave the credit for "all that I have been in life."[51] Later he was trained in theology at Princeton under the Rev. John Witherspoon. Witherspoon's Calvinism was an important source for Madison's political ideas.[52]

The key idea of the new Constitution was contained in the word *federal*, a term based in Calvinist theology. In the American colonies, the words *federal* and *federal head* were widely known and generally understood because of the widespread influence of Calvinist Christianity. In the 1780s, to say that America was a *federal* government with a *federal* constitution immediately implied that Calvinist principles were being employed in forming the new union.

PATRICK HENRY'S SPEECH

RICHMOND, VIRGINIA, MARCH 23, 1775

If we wish to be free—if we mean to preserve inviolate those inestimable privileges for which we have been so long contending—if we mean not basely to abandon the noble struggle in which we have been so long engaged, and which we have pledged ourselves never to abandon until the glorious object of our contest shall be obtained—we must fight! I repeat it, sir, we must fight! An appeal to arms and to the God of hosts is all that is left us!

They tell us, sir, that we are weak; unable to cope

Patrick Henry's speech

with so formidable an adversary. But when shall we be stronger? Will it be the next week, or the next year? Will it be when we are totally disarmed, and when a British guard shall be stationed in every house? Shall we gather strength by irresolution and inaction? Shall we acquire the means of effectual resistance by lying supinely on our backs and hugging the delusive phantom of hope, until our enemies shall have bound us hand and foot? Sir, we are not weak if we make a proper use of those means which the God of nature hath placed in our power. The millions of people, armed in the holy cause of liberty, and in such a country as that which we possess, are invincible by any force which our enemy can send against us.

Besides, sir, we shall not fight our battles alone. There is a just God who presides over the destinies of nations, and who will raise up friends to fight our battles for us. The battle, sir, is not to the strong alone; it is to the vigilant, the active, the brave. Besides, sir, we have no election [choice]. If we were base enough to desire it, it is now too late to retire from the contest. There is no retreat but in submission and slavery! Our chains are forged! Their clanking may be heard on the plains of Boston! The war is inevitable—and let it come! I repeat it, sir, let it come.

It is in vain, sir, to extenuate the matter. Gentlemen may cry, Peace, Peace—but there is no peace. The war is actually begun! The next gale that sweeps from the north will bring to our ears the clash of resounding arms! Our brethren are already in the field! Why stand we here idle? What is it that gentlemen wish? What would they have? Is life so dear, or peace so sweet, as to be purchased at the price of chains and slavery? Forbid it, Almighty God! I know not what course others may take; but as for me, give me liberty or give me death!

143

The English word *federal* comes from the Latin word *fœdus*, which means a permanent bond or union. *Fœdus* was often used in the Latin Bible to translate the Hebrew word for "covenant." The Puritans and other Calvinists affirmed a "federal" or covenant theology. The word *federal* in American culture was widely linked to the Puritans and to the Westminster Confession and Catechism (1646). In the New England states where Calvinism was particularly strong, many Christians viewed the Constitution through Calvinist lenses.

By 1787, federal political principles had been prevalent for some time, particularly in New England, due to the influence of the Puritans. There was a close connection between the political federalism of the New England and the covenant theology of the Puritans. As historian Robert Alley observed: "One can trace a direct movement from biblical covenant to church covenant to constitutions, whether state or federal."[53]

When applied to the Constitution, the word *federal* signified two things. First, it referred to the nature of the new union. Second, it referred to the new way that the government was organized, and particularly to the relationship between the individual states and the whole American nation. The Founders called their new government a "federal government" and the constitution a "federal constitution."

In Calvinist theology, Adam was called the "federal head," or covenantal head of the human race. Adam's fall into sin was said to bring guilt and death to the human race. School children in the colonies routinely learned to recite the phrase "In Adam's fall, we sinned all" (see section 6.1). They were taught to view themselves as federally or covenantally linked to him as their ancestor and federally united with his sin.

Calvinist theology also applied the term *federal head* to Noah. According to the Puritans and other Calvinists, after the Great Flood, Noah became Adam's replacement as the new "federal head" of the human race. All human beings were thus subject to the laws of nature because God reinstituted those laws through his covenant with Noah and all of Noah's descendants.

Nonetheless, within Calvinist theology the term *federal head* was applied preeminently to Jesus Christ. He is the "last Adam" and the new "federal head" of those he has redeemed. Through Christ's death on the cross, there is now a new covenant in his blood, a covenant of redemption. Therefore, Christ is the federal or covenantal head of the church, which is regarded as his body.

In Calvinist theology, because Christ replaces Adam as the federal head, Christians are no longer federally linked to Adam's sin and guilt. Through the new covenant in Christ's blood, Christians are federally linked to Christ's righteousness. The new covenant in Christ's blood breaks the link to Adam's sin and guilt. It is in this federal link to Christ that the Christian finds forgiveness, salvation, and redemption.

The Puritan view of Christ as federal head implied that the covenant between Christ and Christian believers could never be broken. This meant that one's salvation was eternal and could never be lost. The believer was permanently and unbreakably united to Christ. The union between Christ and the believer was indivisible.

In Calvinist theology, therefore, a federal union was an unbreakable union based on a sacred covenantal agreement. Even when used in secular contexts, the word *federal* came to refer to a permanent and practically unbreakable bond. This secular use of the word reflected its Protestant, and especially Calvinist, background.

For Calvinists in the founding era, therefore, a federal union was permanent and unbreakable. It united the peoples of the several states into one American people. It made them one civil body politic. As one body politic they had a common national government, the "federal government." Just as in the covenant of marriage the husband and wife are two persons but "one flesh," so in the covenant of federal union there were many states but

144

James Madison

one nation. On this view, the American nation was now a "federal nation," with a written covenant—the "Federal Constitution."

In sum, the states and their peoples had entered into a new federal bond with each other that was similar to marriage. It was a permanent bond that could only be broken by death. This form of union was so strong that to end it would require the death of the United States as a nation.

In our day, the significance of our federal union is rarely discussed. When people hear the word *federal*, they do not think about the nature of the union. They focus instead on the relationship between the states and the national government, or "political federalism." To do so is to see only half the picture, however. By focusing only on the political side of federalism, we overlook the essence of the "more perfect union."

9.8 THE FEDERALIST PAPERS

James Madison, John Jay, and Alexander Hamilton wrote the most famous defense of the Constitution. Madison was known as the "Father of the Constitution." John Jay later became the first Chief Justice of the United States Supreme Court. Alexander Hamilton was a military hero of the Revolutionary War and one of the delegates to the Constitutional Convention in 1787.[54]

Hamilton, Madison, and Jay had each studied Calvinist theology. They explained their support for the new constitution in a series of newspaper articles originally titled "The Federalist." Later these articles were published in book form under the title *The Federalist Papers*. In *The Federalist Papers*, Hamilton, Madison, and Jay adopted principles drawn from Calvinist theology, but then applied them as

John Jay

Alexander Hamilton

American constitutional principles. This fact is often overlooked but should really come as no surprise. The basic premise throughout *The Federalist Papers* is the principle of permanent union.

In their eyes, *the American union was no longer a simple and flimsy alliance between state governments. It was a sacred covenant that united all the various peoples of the various states into one political body.* It was a permanent bond of union, just as certainly as the marriage covenant transforms a man and a woman into one flesh. The goal of *The Federalist Papers* was to sell this concept to the states.

There was a large faction of politicians, called anti-federalists, who had serious reservations about the union. They noted that, in spite of the intercolonial success of the Revolution, very serious differences between the states remained, particularly in their worldviews, their religious practices, and their ways of life. They stressed the sovereignty and rights of the individual states. They feared that too much central power might return them to the same situation they faced with King George III prior to the Revolution.

The authors of *The Federalist Papers* were persuasive. In addition to their well-constructed arguments, they had a political giant on their side: George Washington. It is difficult to convey just how revered Washington was in America after the Revolution. Americans all but worshiped him. His endorsement of federalism was tantamount to divine approval.

Even so, the anti-federalists' influence was strong enough to prevent the Constitution from being ratified unless it included the Bill of Rights. The Bill of Rights was drafted in 1791. It guaranteed the states a great deal of latitude to govern themselves and to protect themselves from undue federal intrusions.

9.9 THE CONSTITUTION AND RELIGIOUS LANGUAGE

It has been said that the United States Constitution is not a Christian document because nowhere does it explicitly acknowledge "our Lord and Savior Jesus Christ." Over the years there have been repeated efforts to make the Constitution "Christian" by amending the preamble to refer to "our Lord and Savior Jesus Christ." This cosmetic change would add ecclesiastical language merely as a decoration. It would have no material effect on any of the concepts in the document.

For the Puritans, ecclesiastical language was never the key. The content and the underlying concepts were the key. Terms like *due process of law* had an explicitly Christian heritage. The entire Constitution rested on a Puritan view of human sinfulness, which

T H E

FEDERALIST:

ADDRESSED TO THE

PEOPLE OF THE STATE OF NEW-YORK.

NUMBER I.

Introduction.

AFTER an unequivocal experience of the ineffi-
cacy of the subsisting federal government, you
are called upon to deliberate on a new constitution for
the United States of America. The subject speaks its
own importance; comprehending in its consequences,
nothing less than the existence of the UNION, the
safety and welfare of the parts of which it is composed, the fate of an empire, in many respects, the
most interesting in the world. It has been frequently
remarked, that it seems to have been reserved to the
people of this country, by their conduct and example,
to decide the important question, whether societies of
men are really capable or not, of establishing good
government from reflection and choice, or whether
they are forever destined to depend, for their political
constitutions, on accident and force. If there be any
truth in the remark, the crisis, at which we are arrived,
may with propriety be regarded as the æra in which

A   that

Title page from The Federalist Papers

needed to be kept in check through a balance of governmental powers. For the Puritans, that was the kind
of evidence that was relevant to showing the Christian
impact on the Constitution.[55]

By 1776, the Puritans were fully convinced that
equality of all human beings, individual inalienable
rights, liberty of conscience, and government by the
consent of the governed derived from Christian principles and ideals. Thanks largely to the Puritans,
these concepts became foundational to the American
colonial outlook at the time of independence.

These were not Enlightenment concepts. They
were Puritan concepts. Even so, they were more than
just Puritan concepts. They were part of that broader
stream of Christian thought in which the Puritans
stood. The colonists saw these concepts as Puritan
because for decades the Puritans had preached, written, and fought about them, and because prior to
1776 the Puritans were the acknowledged intellectual leaders of the colonies.

Equality of all human beings, individual inalienable rights, liberty of conscience, and government by
the consent of the governed were Christian concepts
even though they were expressed in ordinary lan-
guage. What's more, from the Puritan perspective, ordinary language was the *right* language
for expressing them. Ordinary language was the language of creation and applied to all peoples. These concepts, though they derived from Christianity, were for all people, regardless
of their faith.

The Federalist Papers, No. 39
The Conformity of the Plan to Republican Principles

For the Independent Journal.

James Madison

To the People of the State of New York:

THE last paper having concluded the observations which were meant to introduce a candid survey of the plan of government reported by the convention, we now proceed to the execution of that part of our undertaking.

The first question that offers itself is, whether the general form and aspect of the government be strictly republican. It is evident that no other form would be reconcilable with the genius of the people of America; with the fundamental principles of the Revolution; or with that honorable determination which animates every votary of freedom, to rest all our political experiments on the capacity of mankind for self-government. If the plan of the convention, therefore, be found to depart from the republican character, its advocates must abandon it as no longer defensible.

What, then, are the distinctive characters of the republican form?...

First. In order to ascertain the real character of the government, it may be considered in relation to the foundation on which it is to be established; to the sources from which its ordinary powers are to be drawn; to the operation of those powers; to the extent of them; and to the authority by which future changes in the government are to be introduced.

On examining the first relation, it appears, on one hand, that the Constitution is to be founded on the assent and ratification of the people of America, given by deputies elected for the special purpose; but, on the other, that this assent and ratification is to be given by the people, not as individuals composing one entire nation, but as composing the distinct and independent States to which they respectively belong. It is to be the assent and ratification of the several States, derived from the supreme authority in each State, the authority of the people themselves. The act, therefore, establishing the Constitution, will not be a NATIONAL, but a FEDERAL act.

That it will be a federal and not a national act, as these terms are understood by the objectors; the act of the people, as forming so many independent States, not as forming one aggregate nation, is obvious from this single consideration, that it is to result neither from the decision of a MAJORITY of the people of the Union, nor from that of a MAJORITY of the States. It must result from the UNANIMOUS assent of the several States that are parties to it, differing no otherwise from their ordinary assent than in its being expressed, not by the legislative authority, but by that of the people themselves. Were the people regarded in this transaction as forming one nation, the will of the majority of the whole people of the United States would bind the minority, in the same manner as the majority in each State must bind the minority; and the will of the majority must be determined either by a comparison of the individual votes, or by considering the will of the majority of the States as evidence of the will of a majority of the people of the United States. Neither of these rules have been adopted. Each State, in ratifying the Constitution, is considered as a sovereign body, independent of all others, and only to be bound by its own voluntary act. In this relation, then, the new Constitution will, if established, be a FEDERAL, and not a NATIONAL constitution.

The next relation is, to the sources from which the ordinary powers of government are to be derived. The House of Representatives will derive its powers from the people of America; and the people will be represented in the same proportion, and on the same principle, as they are in the legislature of a particular State. So far the government is NATIONAL, not FEDERAL. The Senate, on the other hand, will derive its powers from the States, as political and coequal societies; and these will be represented on the principle of equality in the Senate, as they now are in the existing Congress. So far the government is FEDERAL, not NATIONAL. The executive power will be derived from a very compound source. The immediate election of the President is to be made by the States in their political characters. The votes allotted to them are in a compound ratio, which considers them partly as distinct and coequal societies, partly as unequal members of the same society. The eventual election, again, is to be made by that branch of the legislature which consists of the national representatives; but in this particular act they are to be thrown into the form of individual delegations, from so many distinct and coequal bodies politic. From this aspect of the government it appears to be of a mixed character, presenting at least as many FEDERAL as NATIONAL features.

The difference between a federal and national government, as it relates to the OPERATION OF THE GOVERNMENT, is supposed to consist in this, that in the former the powers operate on the political bodies composing the Confederacy, in their political capacities; in the latter, on the individual citizens composing the nation, in their individual capacities. On trying the Constitution by this criterion, it falls under the NATIONAL, not the FEDERAL character; though perhaps not so completely as has been understood. In several cases, and particularly in the trial of controversies to which States may be parties, they must be viewed and proceeded against in their collective and political capacities only. So far the national countenance of the government on this side seems to be disfigured by a few federal features. But this blemish is perhaps unavoidable in any plan; and the operation of the government on the people, in their individual capacities, in its ordinary and most essential proceedings, may, on the whole, designate it, in this relation, a NATIONAL government.

But if the government be national with regard to the OPERATION of its powers, it changes its aspect again when we contemplate it in relation to the EXTENT of its powers. The idea of a national government involves in it, not only an authority over the individual citizens, but an indefinite supremacy over all persons and things, so far as they are objects of lawful government. Among a people consolidated into one nation, this supremacy is completely vested in the national legislature.

Among communities united for particular purposes, it is vested partly in the general and partly in the municipal legislatures. In the former case, all local authorities are subordinate to the supreme; and may be controlled, directed, or abolished by it at pleasure. In the latter, the local or municipal authorities form distinct and independent portions of the supremacy, no more subject, within their respective spheres, to the general authority, than the general authority is subject to them, within its own sphere. In this relation, then, the proposed government cannot be deemed a NATIONAL one; since its jurisdiction extends to certain enumerated objects only, and leaves to the several States a residuary and inviolable sovereignty over all other objects. It is true that in controversies relating to the boundary between the two jurisdictions, the tribunal which is ultimately to decide, is to be established under the general government. But this does not change the principle of the case. The decision is to be impartially made, according to the rules of the Constitution; and all the usual and most effectual precautions are taken to secure this impartiality. Some such tribunal is clearly essential to prevent an appeal to the sword and a dissolution of the compact; and that it ought to be established under the general rather than under the local governments, or, to speak more properly, that it could be safely established under the first alone, is a position not likely to be combated.

If we try the Constitution by its last relation to the authority by which amendments are to be made, we find it neither wholly NATIONAL nor wholly FEDERAL. Were it wholly national, the supreme and ultimate authority would reside in the MAJORITY of the people of the Union; and this authority would be competent at all times, like that of a majority of every national society, to alter or abolish its established government. Were it wholly federal, on the other hand, the concurrence of each State in the Union would be essential to every alteration that would be binding on all. The mode provided by the plan of the convention is not founded on either of these principles. In requiring more than a majority, and particularly in computing the proportion by STATES, not by CITIZENS, it departs from the NATIONAL and advances towards the FEDERAL character; in rendering the concurrence of less than the whole number of States sufficient, it loses again the FEDERAL and partakes of the NATIONAL character.

The proposed Constitution, therefore, is, in strictness, neither a national nor a federal Constitution, but a composition of both. In its foundation it is federal, not national; in the sources from which the ordinary powers of the government are drawn, it is partly federal and partly national; in the operation of these powers, it is national, not federal; in the extent of them, again, it is federal, not national; and, finally, in the authoritative mode of introducing amendments, it is neither wholly federal nor wholly national.

PUBLIUS

SEPARATION OF CHURCH AND STATE

The American colonies declared independence from England in July 1776. That event marked the start of a great upheaval in America's social order. First there was the military war with England, fought with muskets, guns, and cannons. Perhaps even more significant, however, was the contest of ideas that took place simultaneously.

That contest took place among the Americans themselves. The outcome was a new social order called the United States of America. The Founders finished their work in 1791 when the Bill of Rights was added to the United States Constitution. In fifteen short years, they had devised a new kind of nation, the likes of which had never been seen.

One distinctive of the new nation was its emphasis on religious liberty and separation of church and state. For previous generations and even centuries, people throughout Europe had tried to achieve religious liberty. At best, they succeeded only in part.

The Americans were successful, however. How they did it is an intriguing subject. What was special about the American experience that enabled the Founders to succeed where Europe had failed? How were American ideas different? What role did religion play in bringing about the new social order? What did the Founders mean by religious liberty and separation of church and state? In defining these terms did the Founders draw from Christian principles and ideals? This chapter addresses these questions.

From 1607 to 1776, Virginia was an English colony. In England, the government controlled religion. There was no such thing as full religious liberty or separation of church and state. Virginia was not alone in wrestling with the questions of religious liberty, separation of church and state, and religious taxes and assessments.

The contest over religious liberty had been going on ever since the first settlers landed in America in the early 1600s. In Virginia, the contest primarily involved Anglicans, Baptists, and Presbyterians. In other colonies it involved Puritans, Quakers, Lutherans, Mennonites, Catholics, and many other groups as well.

Trade, travel, and communication between the colonies meant that there were many shared ideas between Virginians and New Englanders. Puritans, Presbyterians, Quakers, and Baptists would often borrow each other's best arguments, where such arguments did not clash with their own core beliefs. These shared ideas welded the American colonies into one people. They also eroded the barriers between the various religious groups.

As one of England's colonies, Virginia was directly controlled by the king. The king was in charge of the civil government and was also in charge of the church. The king had established the Anglican Church as the official, government-supported church for the colony. Because the church was supported through tax money, all Virginia taxpayers were forced to support the Anglican Church, whether they were members of that church or not.

English kings demanded to be honored as God's chosen instruments and often used force to get their way. They claimed to rule by divine right, meaning that they were God's direct representatives on earth. They could imprison, torture, and even execute people who disagreed with the government's view of "right religion."

From time to time, the king and Parliament granted toleration to religious groups who were not Anglicans. This was particularly true after 1688, when William and Mary took the throne in England as a result of the Glorious Revolution. They promised to be more lenient in the area of religion than previous monarchs had been. In 1689, England passed a law declaring that several persecuted religious groups would now be tolerated by the English government.[1]

Even in the very concept of toleration, however, there was an implied threat. The government could withdraw such toleration at any time. Although religious toleration diminished persecution, the state still dominated the church. They were not really separate.

Consequently, even though many religious denominations thrived in Virginia, they were never truly free. They existed by government's permission and grace. As late as 1774, no Baptist minister could preach in Virginia unless the colonial legislature granted him a license.

Amidst this backdrop two very important Virginians were born and raised: Thomas Jefferson and James Madison. After being involved with the relation between church and state in Virginia, they greatly influenced how the same issues were handled later at the national level. They honed their arguments and perfected their theories in Virginia before taking them to the national stage. Thus, the contest in Virginia for religious liberty pre-figures the larger struggle for religious liberty in the founding of the United States.

As a young man, Madison had determined to become a minister. He had the words of the Westminster Confession memorized at a very early age. He attended the College of New Jersey (Princeton) intending to be ordained a minister of the gospel. Madison's principal philosophical influence came from John Witherspoon, Madison's professor at Princeton. Witherspoon was an ordained Calvinist minister with very traditional Christian views.

John Witherspoon

Witherspoon also strongly supported religious liberty. Arguing from the Westminster Confession and other Puritan sources, Witherspoon convinced Madison that the only correct principle upon which to establish a Christian republic was liberty of conscience. During his studies at Princeton, Madison reconsidered his professional goals and decided to put his energy toward a legal profession rather than the ministry. He felt he could serve the nation better in that forum. Nevertheless, his religious training continued to permeate all of his work. James Smylie has convincingly argued that Witherspoon's Calvinism was the "source of [Madison's] political presuppositions."[2]

Madison's place in the founding of the United States is central. Madison was one of the main architects of the United States Constitution. His work earned him the title "Father of the Constitution." To complete the Constitution, a Bill of Rights was added in 1791. The Bill of Rights contained ten amendments[3] to the Constitution. The First Amendment declared, "Congress shall make no law respecting an establishment of religion, or pro-hibiting the Free Exercise thereof." Madison was one of the principal writers of the First Amendment, the source of our present religious liberties.

Jefferson's contribution to America's founding and to religious liberty was no less impor-tant than Madison's. Jefferson himself regarded his writings on religious liberty as among his three most important achievements. When he wrote his epitaph, he judged his Statute for Religious Liberty a higher achievement than his founding of the University of Virginia. Only one thing did he place above his Statute for Religious Liberty: his authoring of the Declaration of Independence.

Besides being the principal author of the Declaration of Independence, Jefferson is widely regarded as the official interpreter of the First Amendment to the United States Constitution. The phrase "separation of church and state" can be traced to Jefferson. It is in his 1802 letter to the Danbury Baptist Association that Jefferson said the First

155

Amendment erected a "wall of separation" between church and state.

Jefferson was particularly fond of Baptists. He assured his Baptist friends in Connecticut that the First Amendment stopped the federal government from interfering with religion. Jefferson's phrase, "wall of separation," has been cited ever since as being fundamental to understanding the First Amendment. Jefferson, however, did not establish this principle to contain religion. Instead, he believed, as did John Milton and John Locke, that true religion flourishes best when the civil authorities practice a hands-off policy.

In taking this position, Jefferson and the other Founders were not discarding Christian views in favor of Enlightenment views.[4] As previous chapters have shown, the legal theory used by the Founders derived from Christianity. Moreover, it was already at least six hundred years old at the time of the founding. Its principles had been a permanent fixture for centuries in the writings of the English Common Law.

In practical terms, it makes no difference whether the Founders learned their ideas about law and rights in church, or whether they learned them from studying law books or the books of political philosophers. We are dealing here with a question of roots. It is fair to conclude that in fundamentally important ways, their basic view of law and rights arose in large part from the direct impact of Western Christianity.

10.3 THE VIRGINIA BILL OF RIGHTS

In May 1776, in a time of great crisis, Virginia's colonial representatives met at Williamsburg. The king of England had already leveled the city of Norfolk, Virginia, with naval artillery. The colonists had also learned that the king intended further military actions against them. He was waging war on his own subjects and had declared them outside of his protection.

As a result, the Virginia representatives declared that Virginia was no longer a colony of England but was now an independent state. On June 12, 1776, they published the first part of the new state constitution. It was a bill of rights consisting of sixteen articles. The rest of the state's constitution, which defined the powers and structure of Virginia's new government, was completed about a month later.

A number of Virginia leaders, including George Mason, Patrick Henry, and James Madison, helped draft the Virginia Bill of Rights. Section 16 struck directly at the British practice of merging church and state. It reads:

Section 16. That religion, or the duty which we owe to our Creator, and the manner of discharging it, can

VIRGINIA BILL *of* RIGHTS

DRAWN ORIGINALLY BY GEORGE MASON AND
ADOPTED BY THE CONVENTION OF DELEGATES

June 12, 1776.

A Declaration of Rights made by the Representatives of the good People of Virginia, assembled in full and free Convention; which Rights do pertain to them, and their Posterity, as the Basis and Foundation of Government.

I.

That all Men are by Nature equally free and independent, and have certain inherent Rights, of which, when they enter into a State of Society, they cannot, by any Compact, deprive or divest their Posterity; namely, the Enjoyment of Life and Liberty, with the Means of acquiring and possessing Property, and pursuing and obtaining Happiness and Safety.

II.

That all Power is vested in, and consequently derived from, the People; that Magistrates are their Trustees and Servants, and at all Times amenable to them.

III.

That Government is, or ought to be, instituted for the common Benefit, Protection, and Security, of the People, Nation, or Community; of all the various Modes and Forms of Government that is best, which is capable of producing the greatest Degree of Happiness and Safety, and is most effectually secured against the Danger of Mal-administration; and that, whenever any Government shall be found inadequate or contrary to these Purposes, a Majority of the Community

hath an indubitable, unalienable, and indefeasible Right, to reform, alter, or abolish it, in such Manner as shall be judged most conducive to the public Weal.

IV.

That no Man, or Set of Men, are entitled to exclusive or separate Emoluments or Privileges from the Community, but in Consideration of public Services; which, not being descendible, neither ought the Offices of Magistrate, Legislator, or Judge, to be hereditary.

V.

That the legislative and executive Powers of the State should be separate and distinct from the Judicative; and, that the Members of the two first may be restrained from Oppression, by feeling and participating the Burthens of the People, they should, at fixed Periods, be reduced to a private Station, return into that Body from which they were originally taken, and the Vacancies be supplied by frequent, certain, and regular Elections, in which all, or any Part of the former Members, to be again eligible, or ineligible, as the Laws shall direct.

That

Virginia Bill of Rights

be directed only by reason and conviction, not by force or violence; and therefore, all men are equally entitled to the free exercise of religion, according to the dictates of conscience; and that it is the mutual duty of all to practise Christian forbearance, love, and charity towards each other.

Section 16 completely reversed the centuries-old British practice of government control of religion. It proclaimed that religion is outside the power of government. The Virginia Constitution made religion a matter between an individual and God. According to Section 16, religion is a matter of "reason and conviction," meaning that religion is a matter of the heart and mind.

Section 16 proclaimed that the authority of civil government extends only to outward deeds—and then only if those deeds are harmful. Civil government has no authority over ideas or beliefs. It cannot punish people for what is in their hearts and minds. It can only punish bad deeds and harmful conduct. Section 16 insisted that religion and its practice were outside the scope of government power.

10.4 Taxes and the Use of Force

Governments use force to collect unpaid taxes. A tax is only as effective as the government's authority to use force to collect it. In colonial Virginia, taxes funded the Anglican Church. When Baptists, Presbyterians, or other religious people in Virginia refused to pay those taxes, they encountered governmental force and violence.

But Section 16 said that governmental force and violence had no place in religious matters. This meant that government had no right to impose such taxes. If Virginia was going to be free of religious coercion, the church in Virginia had to be independent from the state. New laws were therefore needed to implement the changes called for by Section 16.

When the Virginia legislature convened in October 1776, it was overwhelmed by the size of its task. All the old laws were *colonial* laws, which had to be revised now that Virginia was a state rather than a colony. In particular, although the new constitution provided for religious liberty, the old laws did not.

The legislators were faced with a grim fact. Every able-bodied man was needed to fight the British. This included Baptists, Presbyterians, Lutherans and others, all of which were treated as second-class citizens under the old laws. The time was right to make everyone equal since they would all be fighting a common enemy.

Consequently, the legislature canceled every law that "renders criminal the maintaining any opinion in matters of religion" or "the exercising any mode of worship" different from the Anglican Church.[5] The legislature also exempted dissenting churches and individuals from paying taxes or assessments that funded the Anglican Church. [6]

This was not the end of the tax issue, however. The convention that drafted Virginia's constitution was not the ordinary legislature. Technically, the two bodies were separate.[7] The constitutional convention was elected mainly by dissenters, voters who were mostly

Baptists, Presbyterians, and others opposed to a state church. The members of the legislature, on the other hand, were mostly Anglicans, who had strong ties to the old regime.

Many in the legislature were not yet ready to discard the British approach. Despite the language of Virginia's constitution, the legislature hesitated to implement the new principles. They refused to do away with the state-established church. Moreover, they were ready to pass new taxes to fund their preferred religious causes as soon as the war crisis eased.

Between 1777 and 1779, debate raged throughout Virginia over taxation and the state-established church. Edmund Pendleton and Robert Carter Nicholas were staunch Anglicans and politically powerful legislators. They wanted to keep the established church and raise new taxes for it. The majority of the voters, however, wanted an end to the merger of church and state—and thus an end to religious taxes.[8]

10.5 JEFFERSON'S STATUTE FOR RELIGIOUS LIBERTY

In 1779, when Thomas Jefferson was elected governor of Virginia, he decided to use his position to force the issue of religious liberty with the legislature. He therefore wrote a bill promoting religious liberty—the Statute for Religious Liberty.[9] This was the statute noted on Jefferson's grave as second of the three most important achievements in his life. He introduced it into the legislature through a friendly delegate named John Harvie, who was from Jefferson's home county of Albemarle.

The Statute for Religious Liberty provided concrete means for enforcing Section 16 of the Virginia Bill of Rights. It would establish religious liberty and disestablish the Anglican Church. It would outlaw religious taxes and assessments. The bill sparked intense debate and did not become law in Virginia until 1786—nearly ten years after the Virginia Constitution called for separation of church and state. Jefferson wrote the bill in 1779, only three years after the Declaration of Independence, while the war with England was still underway.

Jefferson's bill brought the issue of religious liberty to the forefront of Virginia politics. If the bill became law, it would mandate religious liberty for every person in Virginia. It would stop the government from interfering with religion. And it would forbid state-spon-

Jefferson's Tombstone

158

sored churches, funded with tax money. The law would give teeth to Virginia's new constitution, which declared religious liberty an inalienable right, beyond the reach of government.

Jefferson's bill for religious liberty is just as remarkable as Section 16 of the Virginia Bill of Rights. Both bills rejected the British and medieval approaches to religion that combined church and state. Instead, drawing from the stream of Christian thought that included the English Common Law and the Protestant Reformation, these bills stressed the creator-redeemer distinction as well as the liberty of conscience inherent in this distinction.

VIRGINIA STATUTE FOR RELIGIOUS FREEDOM (1786)

THOMAS JEFFERSON

I. Well aware:
- that Almighty God has created the mind free;
- that all attempts to influence it by temporal [civil] punishments or burdens or by civil incapacitations [lack of fitness for office], tend only to…[produce] habits of hypocrisy and meanness and are a departure from the plan of the Holy Author of our religion, who, being Lord both of body and mind, yet chose not to propagate [spread] it by coercions [force] on either, as was in his Almighty power to do;
- that the impious presumption of legislators and rulers, civil as well as ecclesiastical [religious], who, being themselves but fallible and uninspired men, have assumed dominion [rule] over the faith of others, setting up their own opinions and modes of thinking as the only true and infallible [ones], and, such, endeavoring to impose them on others, have established and maintained false religions over the greatest part of the world and through all time;
- that to compel a man to furnish contributions of money for the propagation of opinions which he disbelieves is sinful and tyrannical;
- that even…forcing him to support this or that teacher of his own religious persuasion is depriving him of the comfortable liberty of giving his contributions to the particular pastor whose morals he would make his pattern and whose powers he feels most persuasive to righteousness…;
- that our civil rights have no dependence on our religious opinions any more than [on] our opinions in physics or geometry;

• that therefore the proscribing [of] any citizen as unworthy [of] the public confidence by laying upon him an incapacity of being called to offices of trust and emolument unless he profess or renounce this or that religious opinion is depriving him injuriously of those privileges and advantages to which in common with his fellow citizens he has a natural right;…

• that to suffer the civil magistrate to intrude his powers into the field of opinion and to restrain the profession or propagation of principles on supposition of their ill tendency is a dangerous fallacy which at once destroys all religious liberty, because he [the magistrate], being, of course, judge of that tendency, will make his opinions the rule of judgment and approve or condemn the sentiments of others only as they shall square with, or differ from, his own;

• that it is time enough for the rightful purposes of civil government for its officers to interfere when principles break out into overt [open, or public] acts against peace and good order; and, finally,

• that truth is great and will prevail if left to herself, that she is the proper and sufficient antagonist to error and has nothing to fear from the conflict, unless by human interposition disarmed of her natural weapons, free argument and debate, [for] errors [cease] to be dangerous when it is permitted freely to contradict them.

II. Be it enacted by the General Assembly that no man shall be compelled to frequent or support any religious worship, place, or ministry whatsoever, nor shall otherwise suffer on account of his religious opinions or belief; but that all men shall be free to profess, and by argument to maintain, their opinion in matters of religion, and that the same shall in no wise diminish, enlarge, or affect their civil capacities.

III. And though we well know that this assembly, elected by the people for the ordinary purposes of legislation only, [has] no power to restrain the acts of succeeding assemblies, constituted with powers equal to her own, and that therefore to declare this act to be irrevocable would be of no effect in law; yet, as we are free to declare, and do declare, that the rights hereby asserted are of the natural rights of mankind, and that if any act shall hereafter be passed to repeal the present or to narrow its operation, such act will be an infringement [violation] of natural rights.

In Albemarle County where Jefferson lived, many of his voting neighbors were Baptists or other opponents of religious establishment. Like them, Jefferson too was a dissenter. His personal religious views differed from those supported by the government.[10]

Jefferson spent much time conferring with Baptist leaders to hear their views about separation of church and state. He became familiar with the Baptist struggle for religious liberty, which had been going on for over a century. Where religious liberty was concerned, he adopted both their arguments and their biblical citations as his own.

In 1776, Jefferson was a member of the Committee on Religion in the House of Delegates. It was his job to review the hundreds of petitions and memorials that flooded in from all over Virginia. These came primarily from Baptist and Presbyterian churches, religious associations and individuals who opposed the government's control of religion. Despite a busy schedule, it appears that Jefferson not only read many of these petitions, but also met with representatives from various counties who explained their petitions to him.

When Jefferson was in Philadelphia in 1776, the famed Baptist activist from Massachusetts, Isaac Backus, placed his views on church-state separation before the entire Continental Congress. Like Virginia, Massachusetts and the rest of the colonies were still working to solve the tough questions about what the right approach to church and state should be.

In 1777, the Baptist General Association began drafting a religious liberty law. They submitted their work to Jefferson and Madison. From 1777 to 1779, Jefferson conferred with the Baptists on this matter. One of the Baptist leaders was Jeremiah Walker. He was the clerk for the Baptist General Association and was the association's delegate from Goochland County to the Virginia legislature. As soon as Jefferson's bill was made public in 1779, the Baptist General Association voted its full support for the measure.[11] Their views and Jefferson's coincided, as did their reasons and arguments. In essence, Jefferson's bill simply framed the Baptist approach to church-state relations in legal language.

The Baptists unanimously opposed merging church and state. Their petitions and memorials used arguments that were virtually identical to the ones used by Jefferson in his bill for religious liberty.[12] Virginia Presbyterians who supported religious liberty used similar arguments. It is from these Baptist and Presbyterian petitions that Jefferson derived the framework of his argument. Although Jefferson authored Virginia's laws regarding religious liberty, it was the Baptists and Presbyterians who provided the underlying theory and inspiration.

In the bill's preamble, Jefferson began by saying that "Almighty God hath created the mind free…." He started with the premise that God is the creator, and since the creator made the mind free, the mind is not under the state's control. If government uses force to coerce people's minds, it is "a departure from the plan of the Holy Author of our religion, who, being Lord both of body and mind, yet chose not to propagate it by coercions on either, as was in his Almighty power to do."[13]

There is no question to whom Jefferson is referring here. He is speaking of Jesus of Nazareth, who during his earthly ministry refused to force people to follow him.[14] Jefferson calls him the "Holy Author of our religion," the "Lord both of body and mind," and "Almighty." These are not the descriptions of an ordinary mortal. The preamble deliberately refers to Jesus in standard Christian terms, setting him apart from ordinary men and identifying him as the divine redeemer.[15]

How was Jesus relevant to Jefferson's view of religious liberty? Given Jefferson's familiarity with Baptist and Presbyterian thinking on this issue, he may have had a specific incident in mind from the life of Jesus. In the Gospel of Luke, when Jesus was rejected in a certain village, his disciples asked whether they should call down fire from heaven to punish the villagers. Jesus rebuked his disciples for even thinking that way, telling them that they had the wrong spirit. Jesus explained that he did not come to destroy but to save people.[16]

Whether Jefferson had that specific incident in mind or not, throughout the bill he tacitly commends Jesus for never forcing people to believe the gospel. Jesus' example sets the standard of piety. According to Jefferson, rulers who act differently and coerce their subjects are "impious."[17] It does not matter whether they are civil rulers or religious rulers. Neither have the right to impose their beliefs on others. For Jefferson, neither church nor state can use physical punishments, torture, or other forms of coercion to enforce belief.

Next Jefferson argued that taxes to support any religious denomination were a form of coercion. He called such taxes "sinful and tyrannical," still using Christian language to explain the foundation of religious liberty and the separation of church and state.[18] The Baptist petitions and memorials had also called such taxes sinful and tyrannical.

Jefferson explained that the civil government should only use its power to punish "overt acts against peace and good order." It should never punish ideas, beliefs, or opinion. Civil government can deal only with outward conduct, not with hearts and minds. This is the strain of thought which evolved out of the Protestant Reformation. Jefferson also insisted that people should not lose their civil rights simply because their religious views are out of step with the government's.[19]

When we look for the roots of religious liberty in Virginia, we find that they are Christian, though differing sharply from the British and medieval tradition. The political activism that led to religious liberty was initiated by Christians, and the arguments and principles were Christian as well. In light of these facts, it is completely reasonable to conclude that Virginia's very first law declaring religious liberty was founded on Christian core beliefs and supported by an explicitly Christian rationale.

10.8 RELIGIOUS TAXES

For religious liberty to become a reality in Virginia, the struggle against religious taxes and assessments had to be won. Jefferson's bill became the rallying cry of dissenters opposed to religious taxes. His opponents, however, stymied the bill in the legislature. Legislators refused to put the bill to a vote. This encouraged voters to elect more delegates who supported religious liberty. As a result, the makeup of the legislature began to change.

Finally, Jefferson's opponents decided to force the issue by proposing a new law instituting religious taxes and assessments. Passing such a law would have contradicted the Virginia Constitution, nullifying the clear meaning of Section 16. The following bill was

Newly established United States

proposed on November 11, 1784:

That the people of this Commonwealth according to their respective abilities, ought to pay a moderate tax or contribution annually for the support of the Christian religion, or of some Christian church, denomination, or communion of Christians, or of some form of Christian worship.

All eyes were on Virginia to see how events would unfold. Would Virginia break with the customs and traditions of its royalist past? British culture, traditions, customs, and outlook were strongest in Virginia. Even after independence, Virginia was more thoroughly British in culture and outlook than the other states. It was not at all clear that Virginia would take a firm stand for religious liberty.

How Virginia decided this issue would profoundly affect the rest of the nation. Virginia was the largest state in America. At the time, West Virginia, Kentucky, and the Northwest Territories were still part of Virginia. Five states were later carved from the Northwest Territories. When Jefferson was governor of Virginia in 1799, he ruled a state whose territory was one and a half times the size of California. New York was only one-fifth the size of Virginia. Massachusetts, New Jersey, and New Hampshire were each slightly larger than three percent of the size of Virginia. Rhode Island was only slightly larger than some Virginia counties.

The controversy in Virginia over religious taxes did not happen in a vacuum. The years between 1768 and 1774 were a time of religious persecution in Virginia. The king of England was furious after the Stamp Act crisis of 1765. He believed that religious dissenters in the colonies, particularly the Presbyterians, were most responsible for the colonies' resistance to his policies.

The king retaliated by implementing measures that led to religious persecution in Virginia. Despite British laws about toleration, even Presbyterians were persecuted for not conforming to the state-established religion. From 1768 to 1776, therefore, Presbyterian dissenters were just as vocal as the Baptists in calling for complete religious liberty. Both were extremely pleased when the Virginia Constitution of 1776 called for religious liberty.

By the early 1780s, however, the persecution had stopped and the colonies had gained the upper hand over England. Instead of siding with Jefferson's bill, many of Virginia's Presbyterians flip-flopped. They stopped demanding complete religious liberty. Now they wanted the state to fund the Presbyterian Church with tax money just as it had funded the Anglican Church. The coalition of Baptists and Presbyterians collapsed.

After 1779, a number of Presbyterians began sending petitions and memorials to the legislature that supported religious taxes. They wanted to disestablish the Anglican Church so that it was no longer Virginia's official church. In its place they wanted the Presbyterian Church to become the established church. The Religious Assessments bill, which called for raising taxes to support Christian churches in Virginia, diametrically opposed Jefferson's bill. It is ironic that an obscure contest over a tax bill should mark such an important milestone for religious liberty.

Madison did not wait for his Baptist friends to ask for his help. He was ready to fight the Religious Assessments bill as soon as he learned that it had been introduced.[20] Madison conceived a brilliant strategy. He would write an anonymous tract against the bill. Then he would work through his dissenting friends to conduct a statewide petition drive against the bill and in favor of Jefferson's bill, which was still tabled. If he succeeded, he would not only defeat the tax bill, but also obtain the passage of Jefferson's bill.

While the tax bill was being distributed in the counties, Madison wrote *A Memorial and Remonstrance on the Religious Rights of Man*. It immediately took its place with the most important documents ever written on religious liberty. Its effect was phenomenal. Madison's argument was so compelling, especially when read side by side with the tax bill, that even Anglicans began writing the legislature demanding that the tax bill be withdrawn. The Virginia Presbyterians also swung behind Jefferson's bill. They wrote the legislature demanding that Jefferson's bill be passed instead of the tax bill.

The Baptists, of course, were elated. Enshrined in Madison's *Memorial and Remonstrance* were the very arguments that Baptist dissenters had been making since they first fled English persecution in 1593.[21] Madison's principles were the same ones that had cost the lives of the Baptist movement's founders. These were the principles for which the Baptists had suffered 170 years of persecution.

Madison's principles were identical, for example, with those of the Rev. John Smyth, one of the first Baptists. Smyth was expelled from the Anglican clergy for asserting that King James I had no authority over religion, the church, or people's hearts and minds. Smyth started an "illegal" church of separatists. In 1608 he and his church fled to Amsterdam, Holland. There he published his Baptist views about separating church and state. Smyth's writings are among the first in the English language advocating *full* religious liberty.[22]

Smyth died of consumption in 1612. His replacement, Thomas Helwys, returned to England to spread the Baptist message. He wrote a book explaining his views on the separation of church and state. When he gave a copy to the king, he was immediately arrested and placed in the notorious Newgate prison, where he died in 1616.

Helwys's death began a string of martyrdoms for the Baptist cause. He died for preaching and believing what was the cornerstone of the 1612 London Confession:

That the magistrate is not by virtue of his office to meddle with religion or with matters of conscience, to force or compel men to this or that form of religion, or doctrine: but to leave the Christian religion free to every man's conscience, and to handle only civil transgressions,…injuries and wrongs against men…for Christ only is the King and lawgiver of the Church and conscience.[23]

Madison began his Remonstrance by citing Section 16 of the Virginia Constitution. Since the Virginia Constitution was the highest law of the state, any legislation contrary to it would be unconstitutional. According to Madison, the Virginia Constitution recognized God's claims on people and the people's duties toward God. Since the religious tax bill violated both God's claims on people and the state's constitution, it was doubly wrong.

Madison defined religion as "a duty owed to our creator." Religion was therefore not a duty owed to the government. This meant that if the government passed laws to control religion, government was putting itself in the place of God and committing idolatry. The supporters of the tax bill thought that they were promoting Christianity. According to Madison they were really violating the first commandment, which said: Thou shalt have no other gods before me.

This duty to God, Madison argued, existed before government existed and was therefore higher than any duty to the state. Sincere religious people were duty-bound to disobey the government if it made itself higher than God. For Madison, people must always view themselves first and foremost as "subject[s] of the Governor of the universe." This meant that a person's earthly citizenship and civil duties are always secondary to God's requirements.

It also meant that when a government came into existence, there were certain claims that it could not make on anyone. Government was barred from making any claim to control religion. According to Madison, religion belonged completely to God and was completely outside of any earthly authority: "We maintain therefore that in matters of religion, no man's right is abridged by the institution of Civil Society and that Religion is wholly exempt from its cognizance."

Society could not control a person's religion because religion was a personal duty between an individual and God. The community had nothing to do with it. Therefore religion was "wholly exempt" from society's cognizance.

Madison went on to explain that since religion was exempt from society at large, it was also exempt from government, because governments were formed by society. But if "religion be exempt from the authority of the Society at large, still less can it be subject to that of the Legislative Body. The latter are but the creatures and viceregents of the former. Their jurisdiction is both derivative and limited."

Madison then insisted that Christianity as originally conceived did not include the merger of church and state. Authentic Christianity had no place for government involvement in religion. He urged that if a law about religion must be passed, it should "propose a restoration of this primitive State in which its [Christianity's] Teachers depended on the voluntary rewards of their flocks." Reflecting on the history of Christianity, Madison wrote:

During almost fifteen centuries has the legal establishment of Christianity been on trial. What have been its fruits? More or less in all places, pride and indolence in the Clergy, ignorance and servility in the laity, in both, superstition, bigotry and persecution. Enquire of the Teachers of Christianity for the ages in which it appeared in its greatest lustre; those of every sect point to the ages prior to its incorporation with Civil policy.

Madison concluded that authentic Christianity forbids merging church and state. Madison's point was not lost on his predominantly Protestant audience. Protestants were accustomed to arguing that the Catholic Church had been wrong for mixing government and religion. In the *Remonstrance* Madison scolded Protestants for doing the same thing.

MEMORIAL AND REMONSTRANCE

JAMES MADISON

To the Honorable the General Assembly of the Commonwealth of Virginia:

We the subscribers, citizens of the said Commonwealth, having taken into serious consideration, a Bill printed by order of the last Session of General Assembly, entitled "A Bill establishing a provision for Teachers of the Christian Religion," and conceiving that the same if finally armed with the sanctions of a law, will be a dangerous abuse of power, are bound as faithful members of a free State to remonstrate against it, and to declare the reasons by which we are determined. We remonstrate against the said Bill,

1. Because we hold it for a fundamental and undeniable truth, "that religion or the duty which we owe to our Creator and the manner of discharging it, can be directed only by reason and conviction, not by force or violence." The Religion then of every man must be left to the conviction and conscience of every man; and it is the right of every man to exercise it as these may dictate.

This right is in its nature an unalienable right. It is unalienable, because the opinions of men, depending only on the evidence contemplated by their own minds cannot follow the dictates of other men: It is unalienable also, because what is here a right towards men, is a duty towards the Creator.

It is the duty of every man to render to the Creator such homage and such only as he believes to be acceptable to him. This duty is precedent, both in order of time and in degree of obligation, to the claims of Civil Society. Before any man can be considered as a member of Civil Society, he must be considered as a subject of the Governor of the Universe: And if a member of Civil Society, do it with a saving of his allegiance to the Universal Sovereign.

We maintain therefore that in matters of Religion, no man's right is abridged by the institution of Civil Society and that Religion is wholly exempt from its cognizance. True it is, that no other rule exists, by which any question which may divide a Society, can be ultimately determined, but the will of the majority; but it is also true that the majority may trespass on the rights of the minority.

2. Because Religion be exempt from the authority of the Society at large, still less can it be subject to that of the Legislative Body. The latter are but the creatures and viceregents of the former. Their jurisdiction is both derivative and

limited: it is limited with regard to the co-ordinate departments, more necessarily is it limited with regard to the constituents.

The preservation of a free Government requires not merely, that the metes and bounds which separate each department of power be invariably maintained; but more especially that neither of them be suffered to overleap the great Barrier which defends the rights of the people. The Rulers who are guilty of such an encroachment, exceed the commission from which they derive their authority, and are Tyrants. The People who submit to it are governed by laws made neither by themselves nor by an authority derived from them, and are slaves.

3. Because it is proper to take alarm at the first experiment on our liberties. We hold this prudent jealousy to be the first duty of Citizens, and one of the noblest characteristics of the late Revolution. The free men of America did not wait till usurped power had strengthened itself by exercise, and entangled the question in precedents. They saw all the consequences in the principle, and they avoided the consequences by denying the principle. We revere this lesson too much soon to forget it.

Who does not see that the same authority which can establish Christianity, in exclusion of all other Religions, may establish with the same ease any particular sect of Christians, in exclusion of all other Sects? that the same authority which can force a citizen to contribute three pence only of his property for the support of any one establishment, may force him to conform to any other establishment in all cases whatsoever?

4. Because the Bill violates the equality which ought to be the basis of every law, and which is more indispensable, in proportion as the validity or expediency of any law is more liable to be impeached. If "all men are by nature equally free and independent," all men are to be considered as entering into Society on equal conditions; as relinquishing no more, and therefore retaining no less, one than another, of their natural rights.

Above all are they to be considered as retaining an "equal title to the free exercise of Religion according to the dictates of Conscience." Whilst we assert for ourselves a freedom to embrace, to profess and to observe the Religion which we believe to be of divine origin, we cannot deny an equal freedom to those whose minds have not yet yielded to the evidence which has convinced us.

If this freedom be abused, it is an offence against God, not against man: To God, therefore, not to man, must an account of it be rendered. As the Bill violates equality by subjecting some to peculiar burdens, so it violates the same principle, by granting to others peculiar exemptions. Are the Quakers and Menonists the only sects who think a compulsive support of their Religions unnecessary and unwarrantable? Can their piety alone be entrusted with the care of public worship? Ought their Religions to be endowed above all others with extraordinary privileges by which proselytes may be enticed from all others?

We think too favorably of the justice and good sense of these denominations to believe that they either covet preeminences over their fellow citizens or that they will be seduced by them from the common opposition to the measure.

5. Because the Bill implies either that the Civil Magistrate is a competent Judge of Religious Truth; or that he may employ Religion as an engine of Civil policy. The first is an arrogant pretension falsified by the contradictory opinions of Rulers in all ages, and throughout the world: the second an unhallowed perversion of the means of salvation.

6. Because the establishment proposed by the Bill is not requisite for the support of the Christian Religion. To say that it is, is a contradiction to the Christian Religion itself, for every page of it disavows a dependence on the powers of this world: it is a contradiction to fact; for it is known that this Religion both existed and flourished, not only without the support of human laws, but in spite of every opposition from them, and not only during the period of miraculous aid, but long after it had been left to its own evidence and the ordinary care of Providence.

Nay, it is a contradiction in terms; for a Religion not invented by human policy, must have pre-existed and been supported, before it was established by human policy. It is moreover to weaken in those who profess this Religion a pious confidence in its innate excellence and the patronage of its Author; and to foster in those who still reject it, a suspicion that its friends are too conscious of its fallacies to trust it to its own merits.

7. Because experience witnesseth that ecclesiastical establishments, instead of maintaining the purity and efficacy of Religion, have had a contrary operation.

During almost fifteen centuries has the legal establishment of Christianity been on trial. What have been its fruits? More or less in all places, pride and indolence in the Clergy, ignorance and servility in the laity, in both, superstition, bigotry and persecution. Enquire of the Teachers of Christianity for the ages in which it appeared in its greatest lustre; those of every sect point to the ages prior to its incorporation with Civil policy.

Propose a restoration of this primitive State in which its Teachers depended on the voluntary rewards of their flocks, many of them predict its downfall. On which Side ought their testimony to have greatest weight, when for or when against their interest?...

11. Because it will destroy that moderation and harmony which the forbearance of our laws to intermeddle with Religion has produced among its several sects. Torrents of blood have been spilt in the old world, by vain attempts of the secular arm, to extinguish Religious dis-

cord, by proscribing all difference in Religious opinion. Time has at length revealed the true remedy. Every relaxation of narrow and rigorous policy, wherever it has been tried, has been found to assuage the disease....

15. Because finally, "the equal right of every citizen to the free exercise of his Religion according to the dictates of conscience" is held by the same tenure with all our other rights.

According to Madison, the Baptists, Quakers, moderate Presbyterians, and other dissenters had been right all along about not merging church and state. Religious liberty was the only correct principle, and it alone was authentically Christian. Now was the time for the people of Virginia and the legislature to recognize that they had not been following Christianity as it was originally conceived.

10.10 MADISON'S IMPACT

The impact of Madison's *Remonstrance* in the counties was staggering. When the legislature convened, the volume of petitions had grown so large that the tax bill was not even put to a vote.[24]

One of the activists who had gathered signatures in the petition drive was Jeremiah Moore, a Baptist pastor who had been imprisoned for preaching. He and others put at least 10,000 signatures into Jefferson's hands.[25] Some place the number as high as 15,000.[26] Such numbers were huge in a day when the entire colonial population was only around 2 million.

The legislature, which was still largely dominated by Anglicans, convened on October 17, 1785. When the tax bill came up for consideration it failed in the Committee of the Whole by only three votes. Without Madison's *Remonstrance* and the signatures it generated, the tax bill would surely have passed in the committee. Most likely it would then have passed in the assembly as well.

Instead, the tax bill was defeated. After its defeat, Madison reintroduced Jefferson's bill for religious liberty. That bill finally passed on December 17, 1785. Jefferson's bill for religious liberty, written in 1779, was not signed into law until January 1786. It remains law in Virginia today, and Madison's Section 16 is still part of the Virginia Constitution. The defeat of the tax bill marked a turning point not only for Virginia but also for America as a whole.

10.11 CONTEMPORARY VIEWS

It has become popular recently to argue that Christianity had little to do with America's founding. Many believe, for instance, that Jefferson's and Madison's views on separation were based on a personal hostility toward Christianity. In other words, the purpose of separating church and state was to keep religious people out of politics. Many have also begun to doubt that there was ever a Christian rationale for separating church and state, to say nothing of Jefferson and Madison adopting such a rationale.

This chapter has examined three turning-point documents in the history of religious liberty and the separation of church and state. First we looked at Section 16 of the Virginia Constitution, which Madison helped to write. Next we looked at Jefferson's bill for religious liberty, which provided concrete means for enforcing Section 16. Finally, we examined Madison's *Memorial and Remonstrance*, which argued for religious liberty and against government control of religion. In all three instances, we found that Madison and Jefferson argued from explicitly Christian premises to defend religious liberty and deny the government control over religion.

This fact is particularly striking where Jefferson is concerned. Personally, he was a Unitarian and did not believe that Jesus was divine. In his religious liberty bill, however, his arguments were completely in harmony with the Baptist and moderate Presbyterian view of religious liberty. In fact, it appears that he drew his arguments directly from those sources. Rather than arguing as an opponent of Christianity, Jefferson openly adopted the legal arguments of dissenting Protestants.

There is a simple reason why Jefferson could comfortably use the term "wall of separation" when writing to the Danbury Baptists in 1802. The term was not an attack on Christianity or Christian principles.[27] Indeed, Jefferson knew that his Baptist friends would immediately recognize that the term was consistent with Baptist principles. Their denom-

THE BILL OF RIGHTS

Passed by Congress September 25, 1789.
Ratified December 15, 1791.

AMENDMENT I

Congress shall make no law respecting an establishment of religion, or prohibiting the free exercise thereof; or abridging the freedom of speech, or of the press; or the right of the people peaceably to assemble, and to petition the government for a redress of grievances.

AMENDMENT II

A well-regulated militia being necessary to the security of a free State, the right of the people to keep and bear arms shall not be infringed.

AMENDMENT III

No soldier shall, in time of peace, be quartered in any house without the consent of the owner; nor in time of war but in a manner to be prescribed by law.

AMENDMENT IV

The right of the people to be secure in their persons, houses, papers and effects, against unreasonable searches and seizures, shall not be violated, and no warrants shall issue but upon probable cause, supported by oath or affirmation, and particularly describing the place to be searched, and the persons or things to be seized.

AMENDMENT V

No person shall be held to answer for a capital or otherwise infamous crime, unless on a presentment or indictment of a grand jury, except in cases arising in the land or naval forces, or in the militia, when in actual service in time of war or public danger; nor shall any person be subject for the same offense to be twice put in jeopardy of life or limb; nor shall be compelled in any criminal case to be a witness against himself, nor be deprived of life, liberty, or property, without due process of law; nor shall private property be taken for public use, without just compensation.

AMENDMENT VI

In all criminal prosecutions the accused shall enjoy the right to a speedy and public trial, by an impartial jury of the State and district wherein the crime shall have been committed, which district shall have been previously ascertained by law, and to be informed of the nature and cause of the accusation; to be confronted with the witnesses against him; to have compulsory process for obtaining witnesses in his favor, and to have the assistance of counsel for his defense.

AMENDMENT VII

In suits at common law, where the value in controversy shall exceed twenty dollars, the right of trial by jury shall be preserved, and no fact tried by a jury shall be otherwise reexamined in any court of the United States than according to the rules of the common law.

AMENDMENT VIII

Excessive bail shall not be required, nor excessive fines imposed, nor cruel and unusual punishments inflicted.

AMENDMENT IX

The enumeration in the Constitution of certain rights shall not be construed to deny or disparage others retained by the people.

AMENDMENT X

The powers not delegated to the United States by the Constitution, nor prohibited by it to the States, are reserved to the States respectively, or to the people.

ination had been preaching the separation of church and state for two hundred years. Baptists were demanding such a separation long before Jefferson and Madison were born. Now their hard-fought principle was in the Virginia Constitution. From there it entered the federal Constitution as the First Amendment.

10.12 CONCLUSION

Separating church and state in Virginia, and subsequently in the United States, was a remarkable achievement. Thomas Jefferson and James Madison displayed exceptional leadership. Without them, success would have been unlikely. It is important to recognize, however, that separation of church and state was not new with them. They were in the right place, at the right time, with the right training, tools, and support to make religious liberty a reality.

Moreover, they drew their ideas about religious liberty and separation of church and state from Christian sources. Martin Luther had called for religious liberty and for separation of church and state at the very start of the Protestant Reformation. Dissenting Puritans, calling themselves Baptists, made it a centerpiece of their movement in England and America beginning in the early 1600s.

It was in the American colonies that the dangers of allowing government to control religion came fully to light. All Christian groups in America agreed that the Jewish government had been wrong to punish Jesus of Nazareth for teaching ideas that the government disapproved. All agreed that the Roman Empire was wrong to persecute, punish, and kill the early Christians for their unpopular religious views.

Jefferson and Madison demonstrated that government's control of religion, so familiar because it had gone on for so long, was fundamentally wrong. Both based their arguments for religious liberty and separation of church and state on Christian principles and ideals. In place of the old merger between church and state, they and the other Founders hammered out a new social order guaranteeing full civil and religious liberty to its citizens. That social order is the authentic legacy of our founding. It is a legacy rooted in Christian principles and ideals.

Absolutism. A political theory which accords unlimited powers to the government, usually a monarchy. Embraced by several of the Stuart kings of England.

Adams, Samuel. Harvard-trained Boston politician. He entered Harvard with the intention of becoming a clergyman and argued as his graduation thesis on political resistance to tyrants. He was one of the earliest and loudest voices protesting the policies of King George III toward the American colonists.

Anglican. The denomination of Christians officially endorsed by the English monarchy.

Apprentice. A person studying a craft or trade by assisting a skilled practitioner of that trade.

Baptist. A denomination of Christians emphasizing the voluntary character of Christian faith and thus refusing to baptize anyone who has not made a conscious decision to follow Christ.

Blackstone, Sir William. An eighteenth-century English legal scholar whose writings provided the foundation and guidelines for most legal principles established in the United States.

174

Blue Laws. Laws forbidding "Offenses Against God and Religion," enacted throughout America during the seventeenth and eighteenth centuries.

Boston Massacre. An act of violence that took place in Boston in 1770 involving a group of colonists and British military patrolling the streets. The colonists agitated the soldiers, who then opened fire, killing several. Paul Revere mass-produced a picture depicting this event from the colonists' perspective, thereby furthering rebellious sentiments in New England.

Boston Tea Party. Organized by Samuel Adams and the Sons of Liberty, this event took place in 1773 as colonists boarded a British cargo vessel in Boston Harbor and disposed of its contents (tea) by throwing it overboard.

Catechism. A manual for religious instruction, usually composed of a series of questions and answers.

Cavaliers. Persons sympathetic to the cause of King Charles I during the English Civil War.

Committees of Correspondence. An intercolonial system of political interest groups who shared common causes and sentiments. Initiated by Samuel Adams, these groups evolved into the Continental Congresses.

Common Law. The body of laws that evolved over time by the accumulation of past judicial deliberations.

Commonwealth. An independent state or community, especially a democratic republic, united by a social contract or tacit agreement of the people for the common good.

Consent of the Governed. In social contract theory this is where the government's power is grounded.

Covenant. A solemn agreement or bond between two parties. A covenant can extend until the death of the parties or even to future generations. For example, the covenant of marriage ends at the death of a spouse; the covenant of a last will and testament, on the other hand, extends to future generations.

Creator-redeemer distinction. A theological distinction differentiating the role of God as (1) the Lord and governor of all the universe (creator), and (2) the Lord and Savior of individual souls (redeemer). According to classic Christian teaching, the government must ensure that the people honor God as creator but must not legislate how the people respond to God as redeemer.

Deism. Belief in a supreme being who created the universe but does not intervene in it. A deistic universe is a clockwork universe.

Divine right of kings. A political theory that vests all authority, both civil and ecclesiastical, in the monarch and is justified by supposing that God has specifically appointed the monarch.

Doctrine. A teaching or principle, typically of religious significance (e.g., the doctrine of the Trinity).

Ecclesiastic/ecclesiastical. Pertaining to church affairs.

Enlightenment. European intellectual movement of the seventeenth and eighteenth centuries, embracing science and reason, and rejecting superstition and religious intolerance.

Excommunication. An official act of terminating someone's membership in a church because of unacceptable beliefs or practices.

Federalism. The union of separate sovereign governments or individuals into a bond which does not terminate their individual identities.

The Federalist Papers. Newspaper articles written by James Madison, John Jay, and Alexander Hamilton defending the plan for a federal constitution.

The Glorious Revolution. The bloodless overthrow of King James II by the Parliament in 1688 at which William and Mary replaced James as monarchs in England.

Hanovers. The family of monarchs that ruled England for the greater part of the eighteenth century.

Henry, Patrick. A Virginia politician who became famous for urging his fellow Virginians to join the New Englanders' war against the British.

Heresy. Belief or practice that seriously contradicts accepted orthodox teaching.

Jacobite. A person remaining loyal to the Stuart family after the Glorious Revolution.

Jefferson, Thomas. Graduate of William and Mary College; author of the Declaration of Independence; politician, philosopher, lawyer, and theologian; third president of the United States.

Latin. The common language of Western scholars up until the nineteenth century; during the early years of this country, Latin was regarded as an essential part of a person's education.

Liberty of conscience. The view that religious beliefs must be embraced voluntarily and that government has no authority to impose religious beliefs.

Madison, James. A divinity student and graduate of College of New Jersey (Princeton); chief architect of the U.S. Constitution and Bill of Rights.

Magna Carta. A document signed in 1215 by King John of England, guaranteeing ecclesiastical and political rights to the English people. This document became the chief political weapon used by the American colonists against George III in the years preceding the American Revolution.

Memorial and Remonstrance. Madison's most famous work that argues the case for liberty of conscience.

Mundus Novus. Latin for "New World;" the North and South American continents.

Natural law/law of nature. The laws by which God orders the creation. Natural law includes both physical laws, like the laws of physics and chemistry, and moral laws that govern human interaction.

Nomenclature. The practice of selecting names.

Orthodox. Embracing beliefs and practices that conform to mainstream traditional teachings. When capitalized this term refers to the federation of Christian churches that acknowledge the authority of the patriarch of Constantinople.

Papacy. The office of the Roman Catholic pope.

Patriarchy. Social arrangement where authority is generally vested in the male members of the society.

Presbyterian. A Protestant who follows the teachings of John Calvin regarding that form of church government in which central authority is vested in elders (*presbyters*) called senator and corresponding to the political system of republicanism. Used in colonial times to designate anyone who followed Calvin's teachings, this term now denotes the American Protestant denomination that adopted the label "Presbyterian" in the late eighteenth century.

Primer. A very basic textbook.

Protestant Reformation. The movement beginning in the early sixteenth century which sought to reform abuses in the Roman Catholic Church. The three most significant issues were: (1) the authority of the Bible vs. the authority of the church in defining Christian doctrine, (2) the role of God's grace vs. the role of human effort in salvation, (3) the role of every individual as a priest vs. the role of church officers alone as priests.

Providence. God's preservation, protection, and sustenance of his people and the creation generally. During the colonial era, striking coincidences were often regarded as the providence of God.

Puritanism. An English Protestant movement that endorsed the principles of the Reformation (especially those laid out by John Calvin) and sought to "purify" the English church of all elements contrary to these principles.

Renaissance. Fourteenth- to sixteenth-century European intellectual movement that stressed art and learning, and revived interest in classical antiquity.

The Restoration. The era ushered in after the death of Oliver Cromwell, in which the Stuart monarchy under Charles II was reestablished in England.

Roundhead. An individual sympathetic to Parliament during the English Civil War.

Sabbath. From the Hebrew word meaning to rest. This term was used in the colonial period synonymously with Sunday and was most commonly designated "the Lord's Day." Keeping the Sabbath (i.e., not working on the Sabbath) was required by law throughout the colonial period.

Secular. Pertaining to temporal and worldly matters rather than to the church and spiritual matters.

Self-evident. A philosophical term describing statements whose truth becomes immediately apparent upon reflection. For instance, that the whole cannot be smaller than any part becomes immediately apparent once we reflect on what it means for something to be a whole and a part.

Seminary. A school dedicated to the theological training of ministers.

Separatism. An English Protestant movement that endorsed the principles of the Reformation (especially those laid out by John Calvin), but unlike Puritanism sought to separate itself from the English church. The Pilgrims were Separatists.

Social contract theory. A political theory in which the people form a government by common consent and thereafter cooperate for social benefits. On this view the function of government is not to be served but rather to serve the interests of the governed. As soon as government no longer fulfills this function, it ceases to be legitimate.

Sons of Liberty. A group of Bostonian men who resisted the colonial policies of George III.

SPG (Society for the Propagation of the Gospel). The agency of the Anglican Church that sought to bring the New England churches under Anglican control. This intrusion into colonial affairs sparked the first discussions about a possible American revolution in the 1750s.

The Stamp Act. A policy implemented by George III to recover revenues that were expended on behalf of the colonists during the French and Indian War. This policy taxed numerous colonial goods.

Stoicism. An ancient Greek school of philosophy emphasizing virtue and equating wisdom with living in harmony with natural law. Since the Stoics had no doctrine of creation, they conceived of natural law as intrinsic to the universe, and not as something given by a creator God.

Stuarts. The English royal family that reigned during the greater part of the seventeenth century. Their absolutism brought them into conflict with the Puritans.

Toleration. A governmental policy that permits diverse religious groups to worship as they please.

Tories. Forces in England that supported James II just prior to the Glorious Revolution. Later, during the American Revolution, the term was used to designate those sympathetic to George III.

Tudors. The English royal family that reigned during the sixteenth century. Members of this family varied in their religious sympathies from a strict Protestantism (Edward VI) to a strict Roman Catholicism (Mary I).

Virginia's Statute for Religious Freedom. Jefferson's second most treasured piece of writing (the Declaration of Independence being the first). This law sets forth Jefferson's case for liberty of conscience.

Vocatio. Latin for vocation or calling. A person's path in life, determined through inclinations and talents.

Whigs. Forces in Parliament that successfully removed James II from the throne of England in the Glorious Revolution of 1688. Later, during the American Revolution, the term was used to designate those hostile to George III.

1. Francis Fitzgerald, *America Revised: History Schoolbooks in the Twentieth Century* (New York: Vintage, 1980).

2. The first comprehensive American history text was Cotton Mather's *Magnalia Christi Americana* (originally published in 1702; reprint, Edinburgh: Banner of Truth Trust, 1979). Translated from Latin into English, the title reads *The Great Works of Christ in America.* Soon after America's Founding, the standard text was Frederick Butler's *A History of the United States of America* (Buffalo, N.Y.: Lazell & Francis, 1826). Butler claimed that "the principles of civil and religious liberty" are the product of America's Christian roots. George Bancroft's, *History of the United States, from the Discovery of the American Continent* (New York: Appleton, 1883), became the standard text in the mid-nineteenth century. Bancroft similarly viewed the United States as the offspring of Christianity. See especially I:604-613.

3. For a historical account of how Christianity became identified with fideism, see Donald Fuller and Richard Gardiner, "Reformed Theology at Princeton and Amsterdam in the Late Nineteenth Century," *Presbyterion*, Fall 1995, 21(2):89-117, especially 103ff.

1. Isaac Kramnick and R. Laurence Moore, *The Godless Constitution: The Case against Religious Correctness* (New York: Norton, 1996).

2. *Edwards v. Aguillard*, 482 U.S. 578 (1987).

3. Samuel Cooper, *A Sermon* (1780), in Ellis Sandoz, ed., *Political Sermons of the Founding Era, 1730-1805* (Indianapolis: Liberty Press, 1991), 637, quoting Acts 17:26.

4. Alexander Hamilton, *The Farmer Refuted* (1775), in Harold C. Syrett, ed., *Papers of Alexander Hamilton* (New York: Columbia University Press, 1961-79), I:122.

UNIT ONE / CHAPTER ONE

1. Harold Berman, *Law and Revolution: The Formation of the Western Legal Tradition* (Cambridge, Mass.: Harvard University Press, 1983), 115.

2. Richard L. Perry, *Sources of Our Liberties: Documentary Origins of Individual Liberties in the United States Constitution and Bill of Rights*, rev. ed. (Chicago: American Bar Foundation, 1978), 11.

3. Martin Luther, *Secular Authority: To What Extent it Should be Obeyed*, in John Dillenberger, ed., *Martin Luther: Selections From His Writings* (New York: Doubleday, 1962), 383.

4. Martin Luther, *Dass Eine Christliche Versammlung Oder Gemeinde Recht und Macht Habe*, cited in Ewald M. Plass, ed., *What Luther Says: An Anthology* (St. Louis: Concordia, 1959), 295-296.

5. Luther, *Secular Authority*, 383.

6. Martin Luther, *Epistel S. Petri Gepredigt und Ausgelegt*, cited in Plass, *What Luther Says*, 601.

7. Martin Luther, *Sermon on Luke 2:1-14, December 25, 1531*, cited in Plass, *What Luther Says*, 294.

8. Luther, *Secular Authority*, 383.

9. John Calvin, *Institutes of the Christian Religion*, 2 volumes, John T. McNeill, ed. (Philadelphia: Westminster, 1960). Hereafter, Calvin's *Institutes*.

10. At a young age most of the Founders had memorized a document called the Westminster Catechism, which was a brief summary of Calvin's theology. See section 2.2.

11. See John Eidsmoe, *Christianity and the Constitution: The Faith of our Founding Fathers* (Grand Rapids, Mich.: Baker, 1987) for a general treatment of Calvin's influence on the Founders. See also Loraine Boettner's, *The Reformed Doctrine of Predestination* (Philadelphia: Presbyterian and Reformed, 1972), 382ff. Hamilton was a Calvinist and a student of a Presbyterian clergyman Hugh Knox, who was a Princeton graduate. See Broadus Mitchell, *Alexander Hamilton: Youth to Maturity 1755-1788* (New York: Macmillan, 1957), 32-33. See also Roger Sherman Boardman, *Roger Sherman: Signer and Statesman* (New York: De Capo Press, 1971), 16-19; Herbert S. Allan, *John Hancock: Patriot in Purple* (New York: MacMillan, 1948), 39; Harriet O'Brien, *Paul Revere's Own Story* (Boston: Perry Walton, 1929), 25; and Elbridge Henry Goss, *The Life of Colonel Paul Revere*, reprint (Freeport, N.Y.: Books for Libraries Press, 1971 [1891]), 17.

12. Eidsmoe, *Christianity and the Constitution*, 60-67. Althusius, Grotius, Pufendorf, Sidney, and Rutherford were explicitly orthodox Protestants. Locke's early immersion in Calvin's theology is well documented. See Maurice Cranston, *John Locke: A Biography* (London: Longmans, 1957), 1-28; John Marshall, *John Locke: Resistance, Religion, and Responsibility* (Cambridge: Cambridge University Press, 1994), 3-4; Winthrop Hudson, "John Locke: Heir of Puritan Political Theorists," in George L. Hunt, ed., *Calvinism and the Political Order* (Philadelphia: Westminster Press, 1965), 108-129; and H. R. Fox Bourne, *Life of John Locke* (London: H. S. King, 1876), I:35ff.

13. Donald S. Lutz, "The Relative Importance of European Writers on Late Eighteenth Century American Political Thought," *American Political Science Review*, 1984, 78:189-197.

14. Calvin, *Institutes*, IV:XX:1.

15. Ibid., III:XIX:15.

16. Ibid., IV:X:27.

17. Ibid., IV:XX:1.

18. Ibid., IV:X:8.

19. Ibid., IV:X:5. This passage from Calvin profoundly affected the Westminster Confession, the influential document written about one hundred years later as a synopsis of Calvin's theology. See section 2.2.

20. Ibid., IV:XX:1.

21. Daniel 6:10,22-23. Daniel refused to follow the king's order forbidding him to pray to his God.

22. Calvin, *Institutes*, IV:XX:32.

23. Ibid., IV:XX:31.

24. There are several scholarly works that elucidate this fact. One of the best is Keith L. Griffin, *Revolution and Religion: American Revolutionary War and the Reformed Clergy* (New York: Paragon House, 1994).

25. Theodore Beza, "The Right of Magistrates," in Julian Franklin, ed. and trans., *Constitutionalism and Resistance in the Sixteenth Century* (New York: Pegasus, 1969).

26. John Adams, *Defence of the Constitutions of Government of the United States of America* (London: Dilly, 1787), in Charles Francis Adams, ed., *The Works of John Adams, Second President of the United States: With A Life of the Author*, 10 vols. (Freeport, N.Y.: Books for Libraries Press, 1969), VI:3-4. See also Roger Schultz, "A Celebration of Infidels: The American Enlightenment in the Revolutionary Era," *Contra Mundum*, Fall 1991, 1:19-33.

27. *Vindiciae Contra Tyrannos*, Harold Laski, ed. (Gloucester, Mass.: Peter Smith, 1963 [1579]).

28. For a clear discussion of this connection see David W. Hall, "The Reformation Roots of Social Contract," *Premise*, October 1997, 4(3), on-line journal: http://capo.org/premise/current/p971009.htm

29. John Knox, *The Works of John Knox*, David Laing, ed. (Edinburgh: James Thin, 1895), IV:415-416.

30. John Ponet, *A Shorte Treatise of Politike Power, and of the True Obedience which Subjects owe to Kynges and other Civil Governours*, reprint (New York: De Capo Press, 1972 [1556]).

31. C. F. Adams, ed., *Works of John Adams*, VI:3-4.

32. Christopher Goodman, *How Superior Powers Ought to be Obeyed, and Wherein they may Lawfully by God's word be Disobeyed and Resisted*, reprint (New York: Facsimile Text Society, 1931 [1558]).

33. Johannes Althusius, *The Politics of Johannes Althusius*, Frederick Carney, trans. (Boston: Beacon Press, 1964 [1618]).

34. John Milton, "The Tenure of Kings and Magistrates," in Merritt Y. Hughes, ed., *Complete Poems and Major Prose* (Indianapolis: Bobbs-Merrill, 1957 [1650]).

35. Westminster Confession, XXIII:2, in John H. Leith, ed., *Creeds of the Churches*, 3rd ed. (Atlanta: John Knox Press, 1982), 192-230.

36. John P. Mackay, Bennett Hill, and John Buckler, *A History of World Societies* (New York: Houghton-Mifflin, 1992), 550-551.

37. Ibid., 552.

38. Ibid., 553.

39. Ibid.

40. Ibid., 643.

41. "The True Lawe of Free Monarchs," in *Minor Works of King James VI and I* (Edinburgh: Scottish Text Society, 1982), 57ff.

42. Mackay et al., *History of World Societies*, 645.

43. For the Christian background of the Magna Carta and the Common Law see chapter 7.

1. See section 8.4, "The Presbyterian Rebellion." In *Religious Origins of the American Revolution* (Missoula, Mont.: Scholar's Press, 1976), 6, Page Smith writes, "The right of resistance to unlawful authority, so clearly enunciated by the Parliamentary leaders [of the English Civil War] and confirmed by the Glorious Revolution of 1689 was the basis on which the Americans opposed the unlimited authority of Parliament over the British colonies." See also Jonathan Clark, *The Language of Liberty* (Cambridge: Cambridge University Press, 1994); and Alan Heimert, *Religion and the American Mind* (Cambridge, Mass.: Harvard University Press, 1966), 357-359.

2. John P. Mackay, Bennett Hill, and John Buckler, *A History of World Societies* (New York: Houghton-Mifflin, 1992), 645.

3. John Milton, "Of Reformation Touching Church Discipline in England" (London: Thomas Underhill, 1641), 69.

4. Mackay et al., *History of World Societies*, 645.

5. "It is false that the people doth or can by the law of nature, resign their whole liberty in the hand of a king: 1. They cannot resign to others that which they have not in themselves.... [B]ut the people hath not an absolute power in themselves to destroy themselves, or to exercise those tyrannous acts spoken of, 1 Sam. viii. 11-15, &c.; for neither God nor nature's law hath given any such power. 2. He who constituteth himself a slave is supposed to be compelled [by violence, constraint, or extreme necessity] to that unnatural act of alienation of that liberty which he hath from his Maker from the womb,..." Samuel Rutherford, *Lex Rex: or, The Law and the Prince* (London: John Field, 7 October 1644; reprinted Harrisonburg, Va.: Sprinkle Publications, 1982), 81-82.

6. Winthrop Hudson, "John Locke: Heir of Puritan Political Theorists," in George L. Hunt, ed., *Calvinism and the Political Order* (Philadelphia: Westminster Press, 1965), 108-129.

7. Leith points out that the Westminster Confession was "adopted by Presbyterians in Scotland and England and became the dominant standards of Presbyterianism in the English-speaking world. The Confession was adopted with modifications by Congregationalists [i.e., Puritans] in England and New England, and it was the basis of the Baptist creeds, the London Confession, 1677, 1688, and the Philadelphia Confession of Faith, 1742." In John H. Leith, ed., *Creeds of the Churches*, 3rd ed. (Atlanta: John Knox Press, 1982), 192-193.

8. Benjamin B. Warfield, "The Westminster Assembly and its Work," *Princeton Theological Review*, 1908, 6:177-210.

9. Westminster Confession, XX, in Leith, *Creeds of the Churches*, 215-216.

10. James H. Smylie, "Madison and Witherspoon: Theological Roots of American Political Thought," *American Presbyterians*, 1995, 73(3):155-163.

11. George McMichael, ed., *Anthology of American Literature*, 5th ed. (New York: Macmillan, 1993), 120.

12. Alice Morse Earle, *Child Life in Colonial Days* (New York: MacMillan, 1922), 132.

13. Ibid., 244.

183

14. Mary Latimer Gambrell, *Ministerial Training in Eighteenth Century New England* (New York: Columbia University Press, 1937), 58. Also Richard Warch, *School of the Prophets: Yale College, 1701-1740* (New Haven, Conn.: Yale University Press, 1973), 36, 38. At Princeton Seminary, assent to it was required well into the twentieth century.

15. Herbert S. Allan, *John Hancock: Patriot in Purple* (New York: MacMillan, 1948), 39. Samuel Sewall, one of Yale's founders insisted that the school's charter "oblige the President to ... ground the Students in the Principles of Religion by ... making them recite the Assemblys Confession of Faith." In Franklin B. Dexter, ed., *Documentary History of Yale University under the Original Charter of the Collegiate School of Connecticut, 1701-1745* (New Haven, Conn.: Yale University Press, 1916), 8, 32.

16. Benjamin B. Warfield, *The Works of Benjamin B. Warfield* (Oxford: Oxford University Press, 1931), VI:369.

17. Franklin to Catherine Ray, October 16, 1775, in Leonard Labaree, ed., *The Papers of Benjamin Franklin* (New Haven: Yale University Press, 1963), VI:225.

18. Warfield, *Works*, VI:337-338.

19. *The Trial and Execution of King Charles I: Facsimiles of the Contemporary Official Accounts* (Missoula, Mont.: Scholar's Press, 1966), 6.

20. Ibid., 33, 39.

21. Cotton Mather, *Magnalia Christi Americana*, 2 volumes, reprint (Edinburgh: Banner of Truth Trust, 1979 [1702]), I:79.

22. Mackay et al., *History of World Societies*, 646.

23. Stuart E. Prall, ed., *The Puritan Revolution; a Documentary History*, (Garden City, N.Y., Anchor Books, 1968), 261.

24. Quoted in Prall, *The Puritan Revolution*, 261.

25. Mackay et al., *History of World Societies*, 646.

26. Paul S. Boyer, Clifford E. Clark Jr., Joseph F. Kett, Neal Salisbury, Harvard Sitkoff, and Nancy Wolloch, *The Enduring Vision: A History of the American People* (Lexington, Mass.: D.C. Heath, 1993), 92ff.

27. Maurice Cranston, *John Locke: A Biography* (London: Longmans, 1957), 1-28.

28. H. R. Fox Bourne, *Life of John Locke* (London: H. S. King, 1876), I:243.

29. Constitution of Carolina (1669), in Bourne, *Life of John Locke*, I:241-242.

30. Ibid.

31. Ibid.

32. James Gordon Clap, "John Locke," in Paul Edwards, ed., *The Encyclopedia of Philosophy* (New York: MacMillan, 1967), IV:502.

33. John Locke, *An Essay Concerning Human Understanding* (New York: Dover, 1959), I:prolegomena.

34. John Locke, *The Reasonableness of Christianity* (Stanford: Stanford University Press, 1958), sec. 227.

35. John Locke, *The Second Treatise of Government* (New York: Liberal Arts Press, 1956), sec. 92.

36. Locke, *The Reasonableness of Christianity*, secs. 28-29, 31, 33-34, 73, 143.

37. Clap, "John Locke," IV:501.

38. John Milton, *Areopagitica: A Speech for the Liberty of Unlicensed Printing. To the Parliament of England*, in Alexander Witherspoon, ed., *Seventeenth Century Prose and Poetry* (New York: Harcourt Brace Jovanovich, 1982 [1644]), 415.

39. Bourne, *Life of John Locke*, I:243.

40. John Locke, *The Works of John Locke* (London: 1823), VI:64.

41. Thomas Jefferson valued Locke's and Milton's religious writings. See Thomas Jefferson to Robert Skipwith, August 3, 1771, in Thomas Jefferson, *The Papers of Thomas Jefferson* (Princeton: Princeton University Press), 1:374-81. Jefferson was not opposed to Christianity, but thought it was a good thing. What he opposed was coercing Christianity. See chapter 11.

42. Ronald A. Wells and Thomas Askew, eds., *Liberty and Law: Reflections on the Constitution in American Life and Thought* (Grand Rapids, Mich.: Eerdmans, 1987), 27.

43. Stanley Jaki, *The Savior of Science* (Edinburgh: Scottish Academic Press, 1990) traces the Christian foundations of the Copernican Revolution, which sparked the Enlightenment. See also Ernst Cassirer, *The Philosophy of the Enlightenment* (Princeton University Press, 1951).

44. See Eidsmoe, *Christianity and the Constitution*, 48-49. Bacon's ideas developed alongside those of his Puritan colleagues at Cambridge. Compare Bacon's method to that suggested by the Puritan leader William Ames in his *Alia Technometriae Delineatio* (1598). In vindicating the Biblical accounts of miracles, Bacon argued that God, because he is supernatural, is not bound to any laws of science. Bacon firmly believed in the authority of the Bible. Newton, the premier scientist of his age and by some accounts of all time (see Michael Hart, *The 100: A Ranking of the Most Influential Persons in History* [New York: Citadel Press, 1992]), set out to prove that Biblical prophecies validate the divine inspiration of the Bible. Locke believed in the divine origin of the Bible and argued that the various theological debates of his day should be replaced by a return to the Bible. See James Clap, "John Locke," IV: 501-502.

45. Eidsmoe, *Christianity and the Constitution*, 65-67. Calvinist professors in Laussane were lecturing on Pufendorf's principles as early as 1684. In America, Puritans embraced his theories as early as the 1710s.

46. See Edmund Burke, *Reflections on the Revolution in France*, J. G. A. Pocock, ed. (Indianapolis: Hackett, 1987 [1790]).

47. See chapter 4. By and large, American professors were careful to avoid endorsing European philosophers who were not proponents of orthodox Christian views (e.g., Hobbes, Spinoza, Hume, and Voltaire).

48. Benjamin Franklin, *The Autobiography of Benjamin Franklin*, in Charles W. Eliot, ed., *The Harvard Classics*, vol. 1 (New York: Collier, 1909), 77.

49. The standard work explaining how the Enlightenment impacted America is Henry May, *The Enlightenment in America* (Oxford: Oxford University Press, 1976).

50. Scott A. Nelson, *The Discourses of Algernon Sidney* (Madison: Associated University Press, 1993), 21.

51. David Hume, *The History of England: From the Invasion of Julius Cæsar to the Abdication of James the Second, 1688* (Boston: Philips, Sampson, and Company, 1856), 5:325ff.

52. Nelson, *Discourses of Algernon Sidney*, 116.

53. Jonathan Scott, *Algernon Sidney and the English Republic, 1623-1677* (Cambridge: Cambridge Univeristy Press, 1988), 5. Also Nelson, *Discourses of Algernon Sidney*, 8.

54. Caroline Robbins, "Algernon Sidney's *Discourses Concerning Government*: Textbook of Revolution," *William and Mary Quarterly*, 1947, 3rd series, 4:266-296.

55. Peter Karsten, *Patriot Heroes in England and America: Political Symbolism and Changing Values over Three Centuries* (Madison, Wis.: University of Wisconsin Press, 1978), 51.

56. Thomas Jefferson, *Life and Sacred Writings of Thomas Jefferson* (New York: Modern Library, 1944), 719.

57. Nelson, *Discourses of Algernon Sidney*, 7.

58. David Hume, *History of England*, 5:331ff.

59. Nelson, *Discourses of Algernon Sidney*, 136.

60. H. Trevor Colbourn, *The Lamp of Experience: Whig History and the Intellectual Origins of the American Revolution* (Chapel Hill, N.C.: University of North Carolina Press, 1965).

61. Loraine Boettner, *The Reformed Doctrine of Predestination* (Philadelphia: Presbyterian and Reformed, 1972), 373.

62. The town of Princeton, which gives its name to another prominent American University, was also named for "Prince" William. The original college building is called Nassau Hall. Nassau was Prince William's home in Holland.

63. Richard Ashcraft, *Revolutionary Politics and Locke's Two Treatises of Government* (Princeton, N.J.: Princeton University Press, 1986).

64. Winthrop S. Hudson, *Religion in America* (New York: Scribner's, 1981), 94. See also Winthrop S. Hudson, "John Locke: Heir of Puritan Political Theorists," in George L. Hunt, ed., *Calvinism and the Political Order* (Philadelphia: Westminster Press, 1965), 108-129.

65. See Smith, *Religious Origins of the American Revolution*, 6. John Wingate Thornton, *The Pulpit of the American Revolution* (Boston: Gould and Lincoln, 1860) writes, "New England shared in the English Revolution of 1640,... reaffirmed the same maxims of liberty in the revolution of 1688, and stood right on the record for the third revolution of 1776." See also Jonathan Clark, *The Language of Liberty* (Cambridge: Cambridge University Press, 1994); and *Religion and the American Mind* (Cambridge, Mass.: Harvard University Press, 1966), 357-59.

UNIT ONE / CHAPTER THREE

1. Cotton Mather, *Magnalia Christi Americana*, 2 vols., reprint (Edinburgh: Banner of Truth Trust, 1979 [1702]), I:67.

2. Ibid., I:86.

3. William Bradford, *Of Plymouth Plantation, 1620-1647*, Samuel Eliot Morison, ed. (New York: Knopf, 1952), 73.

4. Perry Miller and Thomas H. Johnson, eds., *The Puritans* (New York: Harper & Row, 1963), 199.

5. John Cotton, quoted by Keith L. Griffin, *Religion and Revolution* (New York: Paragon House, 1994), 26.

6. Hooker, quoted by Miller and Johnson, *Puritans*, 188.

7. Winthrop, quoted in Miller and Johnson, *Puritans*, 199.

8. Miller and Johnson, *Puritans*, 188.

9. M. Stanton Evans, *The Theme is Freedom* (Washington, D.C.: Regnery, 1994), 202.

10. James I (Stuart), R. 1603-1625.

11. This idea would eventually come to full fruition in 1787 when the Founders wrote: ARTICLE 6:2 "This Constitution, and the laws of the United States which shall be made in pursuance thereof ... shall be the supreme law of the land."

12. Benjamin Hart, *Faith and Freedom: The Christian Roots of American Liberty* (Dallas: Lewis and Stanley, 1988), 98.

13. The interference by British monarchs in the lives of the New England Puritans was almost nil until the reign of George III in 1760.

14. John Adams, *Novanglus*, no. VII, in Mortimer Adler, ed., *The Annals of America* (Chicago: Encyclopedia Brittanica, 1968), II:309.

15. John Calvin, *Institutes of the Christian Religion*, 2 volumes, John T. McNeill, ed. (Philadelphia: Westminster, 1960), IV:XX:3. Hereafter, Calvin's *Institutes*.

16. Sir William Blackstone, *Commentaries on the Laws of England*, 4 vols. (Oxford: Clarendon Press, 1765; reprinted Buntingford, England: Layton Press, 1966).

17. See the Epilogue for a thorough discussion of this point.

18. Roger Williams, *The Bloody Tenet of Persecution*, 1644, in Page Smith, *Religious Origins of the American Revolution* (Missoula, Mont.: Scholar's Press, 1976), 122.

19. Ibid.

20. Luke 9:52-56 (KJV): "And they went, and entered into a village of the Samaritans, to make ready for him. And they did not receive him.... And when his disciples James and John saw this, they said, 'Lord, wilt thou that we command fire to come down from heaven, and consume them, even as Elias did?' But he turned, and rebuked them, and said, 'Ye know not what manner of spirit ye are of. For the Son of man is not come to destroy men's lives, but to save them.'"

21. Williams, *The Bloody Tenet of Persecution*, 123.

22. See David D. Hall, ed., *The Antinomian Controversy* (Middletown, Conn.: Wesleyan University Press, 1968).

23. David A. Hollinger, ed., *The American Intellectual Tradition* (Oxford: Oxford University Press, 1989), 39.

24. Ibid., 40.

25. Paul Boyer, ed., *The Salem Witchcraft Papers: Verbatim Transcripts of the Legal Documents of the Salem Witchcraft Outbreak of 1692* (New York: Da Capo Press, 1977).

26. The economic policy the British employed is known as "mercantilism."

27. "Jacob" is the Greek translation of "James." James II was the Stuart king who was dethroned by Parliament in 1688.

28. John Calvin, *Works*, in Benjamin B. Warfield, trans., *The Works of Benjamin B. Warfield* (Oxford: Oxford University Press, 1931), VI:381.

29. Gilbert Tennent, *The Danger of an Unconverted Ministry* (Philadelphia, Pa.: B. Franklin, 1740).

30. George William Pilcher, *Samuel Davies: Apostle of Dissent in Colonial Virginia* (Knoxville, Tenn.: University of Tennessee Press, 1971), 20.

31. Archibald Alexander, *The Log College: Biographical Sketches of William Tennent and His Students, Together with an Account of the Revivals under Their Ministries*, reprint (London: Banner of Truth Trust, 1968 [1851]), 216.

32. Benjamin Franklin, *The Autobiography of Benjamin Franklin*, in Charles W. Eliot, ed., *The Harvard Classics*, vol. 1 (New York: Collier, 1909), 103.

33. Ibid., 101-102.

34. Pilcher, *Samuel Davies*, 119.

35. Ibid.

36. Samuel Davies, quoted in Mark A. Beliles and Stephen K. McDowell, *America's Providential History* (Charlottesville, Va.: Providence Foundation, 1996), 118.

37. Benjamin Rush, *Autobiography of Benjamin Rush*, G. W. Corner, ed. (Princeton: Princeton University Press, 1948), 23-37. See also, John M. Kloos, *A Sense of Deity: The Republican Spirituality of Dr. Benjamin Rush* (New York: Carlson, 1991), 14.

38. Robert R. Howison, *A History of Virginia, from its Discovery and Settlement by Europeans to the Present Time* (Philadelphia: Carey & Hart, 1846), II:180.

39. John Eidsmoe, *Christianity and the Constitution: The Faith of our Founding Fathers* (Grand Rapids, Mich.: Baker, 1987), 248-249.

40. Alan Heimert, *Religion and the American Mind* (Cambridge, Mass.: Harvard University Press, 1966), 156.

41. See Heimert, *Religion and the American Mind*.

42. Keith L. Griffin, *Revolution and Religion: American Revolutionary War and the Reformed Clergy* (New York: Paragon House, 1994), 47-48.

43. Heimert, *Religion and the American Mind*, 144.

UNIT TWO / CHAPTER FOUR

1. Henry de Bracton, *De Legibus et Consuetudinibus Angliae*, English and Latin, with revisions and notes, Samuel E. Thorne, trans. (Cambridge, Mass.: Harvard University Press, 1968-1977).

2. E.g., Leviticus 19:9-10; Matthew 25:35ff.

3. "The Common law, in its modified form, constitutes, therefore, the basis of the laws of all the original members of the Union; and the Constitution of the United States, as well as the Constitutions of the several States, were made in reference to the pre-existing validity of that system, both under the Colonial and State Government." William A. Duer, *Outlines of the Constitutional Jurisprudence of the United States* (New York: Collins and Hannay, 1833), 32-33.

4. For example, the *Wisconsin State Statutes* (1848-1871) state: "No person shall keep open his shop, ware-house or work-house, or shall do any other manner of labor or business, or work, except only works of necessity and charity, or be present at any dancing, or any public diversion, show or entertainment, or take part in any sport, game or play on the Lord's day, (commonly called Sunday;) and every person so offending shall be punished by a fine not exceeding two dollars for each offence.

"That for the purposes of the provisions of the above action, the Lord's day shall be understood to include the time between the midnight preceding, and the midnight following the said day.

"That no person who conscientiously believes that the seventh, or any other day of the week ought to be observed as the Sabbath, and who actually refrains from secular business and labor on that day, shall be liable to the penalties of the above act, for performing secular business or labor on the Lord's day, or first day of the week, unless he willfully disturbs some other person.

"Every person who, on the Lord's day, or at any other time, shall willfully interrupt or disturb any assembly of the people met for the worship of God, within the place of such meeting, or out of it, shall be punished by a fine not exceeding twenty dollars, nor less than five dollars."

5. Harold Berman, *Law and Revolution: The Formation of the Western Legal Tradition* (Cambridge, Mass.: Harvard University Press, 1983), 39, 197-198.

6. For the text and an account of the background of the writing of the Magna Carta see Richard L. Perry, *Sources of Our Liberties: Documentary Origins of Individual Liberties in the United States Constitution and Bill of Rights*, rev. ed. (Chicago: American Bar Foundation, 1978), 1-22.

7. While teaching theology at Paris, Langton was the first to divide the Bible into chapters. His chapter divisions, with a few changes, are still used today. See Bruce Metzger, *Manuscripts of the Greek Bible: An Introduction to Greek Paleography* (New York: Oxford University Press, 1981), 41.

8. Medford Stanton Evans, *The Theme is Freedom* (Washington, D.C.: Regnery, 1994), 150ff.

9. Ibid., 151-152.

10. Perry, *Sources of Our Liberties*, 11.

11. Evans, *The Theme is Freedom*, 151-154.

12. Richard Tuck, *Natural Rights Theories: Their Origin and Development* (New York: Cambridge University Press, 1979), 15.

13. Perry, *Sources of Our Liberties*, 5.

14. On February 17, 1826 Jefferson wrote to Madison: "You will recollect that before the revolution, Coke was the universal elementary book of law students." See also Medford Stanton Evans, *The Theme is Freedom* (Washington, D.C.: Regnery, 1994), 85.

15. Beverly Zweiben, *How Blackstone Lost the Colonies: English Law, Colonial Lawyers, and the American Revolution* (New York: Garland, 1990).

16. Donald S. Lutz, "The Relative Importance of European Writers on Late Eighteenth Century American Political Thought," *American Political Science Review*, 1984, 78:189-197.

17. Sir William Blackstone, *Commentaries on the Laws of England*, 4 vols. (Oxford: Clarendon Press, 1765; reprinted Buntingford, England: Layton Press, 1966), I:117-141, section titled "Of the Absolute Rights of Individuals." Hereafter Blackstone's *Commentaries*.

18. Blackstone, *Commentaries*, I:54.

19. Blackstone's *Commentaries*, I:118.

20. Blackstone's *Commentaries*, I:119.

21. Blackstone's *Commentaries*, I:121.

22. The five members of the committee were John Adams (Massachusetts), Roger Sherman (Connecticut), Benjamin Franklin (Pennsylvania), Robert Livingston (New York), and Thomas Jefferson (Virginia).

23. Evans, *The Theme is Freedom*, 85.

24. In a letter dated May 8, 1825 to Henry Lee, Jefferson reminisced that his early views were not original with him, but were conclusions drawn from comparing various sources such as "elementary books of public right, as Aristotle, Cicero, Locke, Sidney, etc." Cited in Thomas Jefferson, *Life and Sacred Writings of Thomas Jefferson* (New York: Modern Library, 1944), 719.

25. In Adler, *The Annals of America*, vol. II.

26. In the early published copies of the Declaration of Independence, we find the words "unalienable rights." In modern English we call them inalienable rights. In 1776, at a time when dictionaries were only beginning to standardize the spellings of various words, "unalienable" and "inalienable" were interchangeable. There was no difference in meaning between the two spellings. Both spellings were used by members of the Continental Congress. For the present purposes we will use the more modern spelling of "inalienable rights."

1. Edmund S. Morgan, *The Puritan Family: Religion and Domestic Relations in Seventeenth Century New England* (New York: Harper and Row, 1944), 89.

2. Nathaniel B. Shurtleff, ed., *Records of the Governor and Company of the Massachusetts Bay in New England*, in Mortimer Adler, ed., *The Annals of America* (Chicago: Encyclopedia Britannica, 1968 [1853]), I:184.

3. George McMichael, ed., *Anthology of American Literature*, 5th ed. (New York: Macmillan, 1993), 120.

4. Morgan, *Puritan Family*, 89.

5. Alice Morse Earl, *Child Life in Colonial Days* (New York: Macmillan, 1922), 132.

6. All editions of the *New England Primer* published after 1737 contain this prayer.

7. Martin Luther, *Commentary on Galatians* (Grand Rapids: Kregel, 1979), 216.

8. Cotton Mather, *Help for Distressed Parents* (Boston: John Allen, 1695), 28.

9. Page Smith, *Jefferson: A Revealing Biography* (New York: McGraw-Hill, 1976), 23.

10. Morgan, *Puritan Family*, 68

11. Earle, *Child Life in Colonial Days*, 133.

12. Samuel Eliot Morison, *Three Centuries of Harvard* (Cambridge, Mass.: Harvard University Press, 1936), 136.

13. Arthur M. Schlesinger, *The Birth of A Nation* (New York: Knopf, 1968), 184.

14. Louis Leonard Tucker, *Connecticut's Seminary of Sedition: Yale College* (Chester, Conn.: Pequot Press, 1974), 14.

15. Ibid.

16. Samuel Eliot Morison, *The Founding of Harvard College* (Cambridge, Mass.: Harvard University Press, 1935), 359. This is a very high percentage of the total.

17. *New England's Firstfruits* (1643), reprinted in Morison, *Founding of Harvard College*, 420ff.

18. Morison, *Founding of Harvard College*, 194, 264. For an in-depth discussion of this library see Joe Walker Kraus, *Book Collections of Five Colonial College Libraries: A Subject Analysis* (Ph.D. Dissertation, University of Illinois at Urbana, 1960).

19. *New England's Firstfruits*, in Morison, *Founding of Harvard College*, 434.

20. Mary Latimer Gambrell, *Ministerial Training in Eighteenth Century New England* (New York: Columbia University Press, 1937), 58.

21. Kraus, *Five Colonial College Libraries*, 228. Kraus catalogues the written material available at five of the most important colleges in America before the Revolution: Harvard, William & Mary, Yale, Princeton, and Brown.

22. Ibid., 246.

23. Morison, *Three Centuries of Harvard*, 135.

24. Ibid.

25. Seymour Lipsent and David Riesman, *Education and Politics at Harvard* (New York: McGraw-Hill, 1975), 35.

26. Ibid.

27. An *supremo Magistratui resistere liceat, si aliter servari Respublica nequit? Affirmat respondens Samuel Adams.* See William Wells, *The Life and Public Services of Samuel Adams* (Boston: Little, Brown, and Company, 1865), I:10n.

28. Lipsent and Riesman, *Education and Politics at Harvard*, 37.

29. Josiah Quincy, *The History of Harvard University* (Boston: Crosby, Nichols, and Lee, 1860), II:244.

30. These laws and statutes were originally in Latin. This English translation was provided by Lucius F. Robinson and appears in Cotton Mather, *Magnalia Christi Americana*, 2 vols., reprint (Edinburgh: Banner of Truth Trust, 1979 [1702]), II:23. See also the *Statutes of the College of William and Mary* in Adler, *Annals of America*, I:369-372; and *Regulations at Yale College, 1745*, in Adler, *Annals of America*, I:464-467.

31. W. W. Hening, ed., *The Statutes at Large: Being a Collection of all the Laws of Virginia* (Richmond, Va.: Samuel Pleasants Jr., 1809-1823), I:359.

32. Colyer Meriwether, *Our Colonial Curriculum* (Washington, D.C.: Capital Publishing Co., 1907), 42. The Statutes of 1727 indicate that William and Mary "should be a constant seminary" for supplying Virginia with good ministers. See Adler, *Annals of America*, I:371.

33. Lyon B. Tyler, "Original Records of the Phi Beta Kappa Society," in *William and Mary Quarterly*, 1895-1896, I:4:216.

34. J. E. Morpurgo, *Their Majesties' Royall Colledge: William and Mary in the Seventeenth and Eighteenth Centuries* (Williamsburg, Va.: College of William and Mary, 1976), 106.

35. Imogene E. Brown, *American Aristides: A Biography of George Wythe* (Rutherford, N.J.: Fairleigh Dickinson University Press, 1981), 87.

36. Ibid.

37. Franklin B. Dexter, ed., *Documentary History of Yale University under the Original Charter of the Collegiate School of Connecticut, 1701-1745* (New Haven, Conn.: Yale University Press, 1916), 27-28.

38. Richard Warch, *School of the Prophets: Yale College, 1701-1740* (New Haven, Conn.: Yale University Press, 1973), 278.

39. Warch, *School of the Prophets*, 278n. According to James A. Freeman, *Manners and Customs of the Bible* (Plainfield, N.J.: Logos International, 1972), 326: "The disciples of the prophets were called sons, as the teachers are sometimes called father (2 Kings 2:12, 6:21). They were not a monastic order, as some suppose, nor were they merely theological students, though they probably studied the law and the history of God's people, together with sacred poetry and music. The schools of the prophets in which these sons were trained are supposed to have been founded by the prophet Samuel, though their history and origin are involved in obscurity. They were located not only in Bethel, as appears from the text, but also in Rama (1 Sam 14:19,20), in Jericho (2 Kings 2:5), in Gilgal (2 Kings 4:38) and probably in other places. See I Sam. 10:5,10 and 2 Kings 4:1. Their members were numerous, a hundred are spoken of in Gilgal (2 Kings 4:43) and at least fifty in Jericho (2 Kings 2:7). How long the school of the prophets lasted is not definitely known. They seemed to have flourished most in the time of Samuel, Elijah and Elisha. Fifty years after Elisha's death Amos prophesied; and, according to his statement, he had no training in a prophetic school, though it does not follow that none existed in his day. See Amos 6:14."

40. Dexter, *Documentary History of Yale*, 32.

41. Warch, *School of the Prophets*, 271.

42. Henry P. Johnston, *Yale and Her Honor Roll in the American Revolution, 1775-1783* (New York: Harper & Brothers, 1888).

43. Tucker, *Connecticut's Seminary of Sedition*, 6.

44. Ibid., 21.

45. Thomas Jones, *History of New York during the Revolutionary War* (New York: New York Historical Society, 1879), I:3,5.

46. Edmund S. Morgan, *The Gentle Puritan: A Life of Ezra Stiles* (New Haven, Conn.: Yale University Press, 1962), 64.

47. Tucker, *Connecticut's Seminary of Sedition*, 24.

48. Johnston, *Yale and Her Honor Roll*, 7.

49. James Kent, *An Address Delivered at New Haven before the Phi Beta Society* (1831), cited in Tucker, *Connecticut's Seminary of Sedition*, 35.

50. Tucker, *Connecticut's Seminary of Sedition*, 47.

51. Ibid., 11.

52. Warch, *School of the Prophets*, 276n.

53. *A Petition of the Synod of New York to the Churches of Great Britain*, in Lefferts Loetscher, Maurice Armstrong, and Charles Anderson, eds., *The Presbyterian Enterprise* (Philadelphia: Westminster Press, 1956), 57.

54. Thomas J. Wertenbaker, *Princeton: 1746-1896* (Princeton: Princeton University Press, 1946), 85.

55. Richard Gardiner, *Princeton and Paris: An Early Nineteenth Century Bond of Mission* (Unpublished Thesis, Speer Library, Princeton Theological Seminary, 1994).

56. Marvin Olasky, *Fighting for Liberty and Virtue* (Wheaton, Ill.: Crossway, 1995), 119.

57. John Eidsmoe, *Christianity and the Constitution: The Faith of our Founding Fathers* (Grand Rapids, Mich.: Baker, 1987), 81-92.

58. James H. Smylie, "Madison and Witherspoon: Theological Roots of American Political Thought," *American Presbyterians*, 1995, 73(3):155-163. See also Roger Schultz, "Covenanting in America: The Political Theology of John Witherspoon" (Master's Thesis, Trinity Divinity School, 1985).

59. Jonathan Clark, *The Language of Liberty* (Cambridge: Cambridge University Press, 1994), 357.

60. Clark, *The Language of Liberty*, 357.

61. Olasky, *Fighting for Liberty and Virtue*, 129.

62. Varnum Collins, *President Witherspoon* (Princeton: Princeton University Press, 1925), 112.

63. Alexander Leitch, *A Princeton Companion* (Princeton: Princeton University Press, 1978). Five of the college alumni at the convention had attended William and Mary, five Yale, three Harvard, three Columbia, two the University of Pennsylvania, one Oxford, one Glasgow, and one had studied at three universities in Scotland.

1. Edmund S. Morgan, *The Puritan Family: Religion and Domestic Relations in Seventeenth Century New England* (New York: Harper and Row, 1944), 133.

2. James Savage, *Genealogical Dictionary of the First Settlers of New England* (Baltimore: Genealogical Publishing Co., 1986).

3. George McMichael, ed., *Anthology of American Literature* (New York: Macmillan, 1989), 9.

4. Morgan, *Puritan Family*, 39.

5. Thomas Hooker, *A Survey of the Summe of Church Discipline* (London: J. Bellamy, 1648), I:69, "A man is allowed freely to make choice of his wife, and she of her husband, before they need or should perform the duties of husband and wife towards one another." John Winthrop, *Speech to the General Court*, July 3, 1645, said "The woman's own choice makes such a man her husband." In Perry Miller and Thomas H. Johnson, eds., *The Puritans* (New York: Harper & Row, 1963), 205-207.

6. Morgan, *Puritan Family*, 54.

7. Cf. Paul Jehle, *Courtship vs. Dating* (Marlborough, N.H.: Plymouth Rock Foundation, 1998).

8. Morgan, *Puritan Family*, 41. Likewise homosexuality and bestiality were capital offenses.

9. William Ames, *Conscience, with the Power and Causes Thereof* (London: I. Rothwell, T. Slater, and L. Blacklock, 1643), V:204.

10. Morgan, *Puritan Family*, 60-61.

11. Anne Bradstreet, in McMichael, *Anthology of American Literature*, 141.

12. Morgan, *Puritan Family*, 60-61.

13. Thomas Hooker, *The Application of Redemption* (London: Peter Cole, 1659), 137.

14. Morgan, *Puritan Family*, 63-64.

15. John Cotton, *A Meet Help: A Wedding Sermon*, June 19, 1694. In Morgan, *Puritan Family*.

16. Sir William Blackstone, *Commentaries on the Laws of England*, 4 vols. (Oxford: Clarendon Press, 1765; reprinted Buntingford, England: Layton Press, 1966), I:XV.

17. Thomas Hooker, *A Comment Upon Christ's Last Prayer* (London: Peter Cole, 1656), 187.

18. John Winthrop, *Speech to the General Court*, July 3, 1645. In Miller and Johnson, *The Puritans*, 205-207.

19. Ann Taves, ed., *Religion and Domestic Violence in Early New England* (X: Indiana University Press, 1989).

20. Thomas G. West, *Vindicating the Founders: Race, Sex, Class, and Justice in the Origins of America* (New York: Rowman & Littlefield, 1997), 92.

21. Morgan, *Puritan Family*, 39-40. Contrary to myth, "The Puritan wife of New England occupied a relatively enviable position.... Her husband's authority was strictly limited. He could not lawfully strike her." Ibid., 45.

22. Samuel Sewall, *Diary* (New York: Arno Press, 1972), II:93.

23. Morgan, *Puritan Family*, 43.

24. Cotton Mather, *Ornaments for the Daughters of Zion* (Boston: Samuel Phillips, 1692).

25. Patricia U. Bonomi, *Under The Cope of Heaven: Religion, Society, and Politics in Colonial America* (New York: Oxford University Press, 1986), 111.

26. Morgan, *Puritan Family*, 65ff.

27. Ibid., 68.

28. John Cotton, quoted in Morgan, *Puritan Family*, 72. Apparently he had no internal confirmation of his brother's recommendation. He became a school teacher.

29. Morgan, *Puritan Family*, 67.

30. Ibid.

UNIT TWO / CHAPTER SEVEN

1. Elsdon C. Smith, *The Story of Our Names* (Detroit: Gale Research Co., 1970), 7.

2. Ibid.

3. George Rippey Stewart, *American Given Names* (New York: Oxford University Press, 1979), 4.

4. George Rippey Stewart analyzed a thirteenth century English family to identify the motives for naming their children. Of ten children in the family, he found that two of the boys were named after Norman rulers: William and Richard. Richard was named after Richard Strongbow, the Norman conqueror who invaded Ireland. William was named after William the Conqueror. Stewart found that two other boys in the family were also given names of famous Normans. He speculates that the last son, Anselm, which is an English Catholic saint's name, was "the mother's doing, for Anselm was born in Ireland at one of the family's castles, when the father was in England on the king's business." All the girls in the family were given Catholic saints' names, except one, Matilda, who was named

for a queen of Norman descent. This may suggest that fathers generally wished to give their sons names of great Normans, whereas mothers, especially in naming their female children, were more apt to express religious sentiments in their nomenclature. See Stewart, *American Given Names*, 6-7.

5. Frederick Lewis Weis, *Ancestral Roots of Sixty Colonists Who Came to New England Between 1623 and 1650* (Baltimore: Genealogical Publishing Co., 1985), 2, 86.

6. Stewart has collated the birth lists of five London parishes for the decade 1540-1549, which is about one generation after the beginning of the Reformation. He reports that about 50 percent of the men's names came from the New Testament, with John and Thomas the most popular. Only 5 percent of the men's names could be traced to the Old Testament. About 40 percent of the women's names were New Testament names, while only 4 percent were taken from the Old Testament. A large percentage of the non-Biblical names can be traced to Roman Catholic Saints. See Stewart, *American Given Names*, 8-9.

7. William Bradford, *Of Plymouth Plantation, 1620-1647*, Samuel Eliot Morison, ed. (New York: Knopf, 1952), 441-448.

8. James Savage, *Genealogical Dictionary of the First Settlers of New England* (Baltimore: Genealogical Publishing Co., 1986).

9. Myles Standish was not sympathetic to the Separatists' cause. He was from a well-to-do English family, and had always considered himself loyal to the king and the established church.

10. Tim Dowley, ed., *Eerdmans' Handbook to the History of Christianity* (Grand Rapids, Mich.: Eerdmans, 1988), 19.

11. Thomas Cartwright, *Perkins and Cartwright*, Keith Sprunger, ed. (Wichita, Kans.: Bethel Press, 1982), 20.

12. David Hume, *The History of England* (Boston: Philips, Sampson, and Co., 1856), V:442-443.

13. "The Literature of Colonial America," in George McMichael, ed., *Anthology of American Literature* (New York: Macmillan, 1989), 7-8.

14. Bradford, *Of Plymouth Plantation*, 63. Compare the twenty-sixth chapter of Deuteronomy: "A wandering Aramean was my father and he went down into Egypt and sojourned there.... Then we cried to the Lord, the God of our fathers, and the Lord heard our voice and saw our affliction."

15. Stewart, *American Given Names*, 14.

16. Hume, *History of England*, 442. There was a Puritan in London, according to Hume, named If-Christ-had-not-died-for-thee-thou-would-have-been-damned Barebones. Hume quips that he was probably nicknamed "Damned" Barebones.

17. Lesley Ann Dunkling, *First Names First* (London: J.M. Dent and Sons, 1977), 69.

18. Bradford, *Of Plymouth Plantation*, 321.

19. Stewart, *American Given Names*, 9ff.

20. Samuel Sewall, *Diary* (New York: Arno Press, 1972), I:394.

21. Dunkling, *First Names First*, 70.

22. Savage, *Genealogical Dictionary*, IV:275.

23. Ibid., III:585.

24. Ibid., IV:628.

25. Ibid., II:366.

1. George Allan Cook, *John Wise: Early American Democrat* (New York: Columbia University Press, 1952), ch. 2, "Years at Harvard."

2. John Wise, *Vindication of the Government of the New England Churches* (1717), in Perry Miller, ed., *The Puritans* (New York: Harper and Row, 1938), 257ff.

3. Ibid. See Samuel Pufendorf, *De Jure Naturæ et Gentium Libri Octo*, C. H. Oldfather and W. A. Oldfather, joint trans. (Oxford: The Clarendon Press, 1934). The Warrington to which Wise refers is probably Archibald Johnston, Lord Warrington, Scottish judge and statesman.

4. "John Wise's *Vindication* is a landmark in the movement of American thought from Winthrop's *Model of Christian Charity* to Jefferson's *Declaration of Independence*." Page Smith, *Religious Origins of the American Revolution* (Missoula, Mont.: Scholar's Press, 1976), 143.

5. Alice M. Baldwin, *The New England Clergy and the American Revolution* (Durham: Duke University Press, 1928), 168.

6. Mark Noll, Nathan Hatch, George Marsden, David Wells, and John Woodbridge, eds., *Eerdmans' Handbook to Christianity in America* (Grand Rapids, Mich.: Eerdmans, 1983), 133.

7. Peter Karsten, *Patriot Heroes in England and America: Political Symbolism and Changing Values over Three Centuries* (Madison, Wis.: University of Wisconsin Press, 1978), 55.

8. Jonathan Mayhew, *A Discourse Concerning Unlimited Submission* (1750), in Peter N. Carroll, *Religion and the Coming of the American Revolution* (Waltham, Mass.: Ginn-Blaisdell, 1970), 40.

9. Ibid., 47.

10. Smith, *Religious Origins*, 154.

11. Carroll, *Religion*, xi.

12. Carl Bridenbaugh, *Mitre and Sceptre, Transatlantic Faiths, Ideas, Personalities, and Politics, 1689-1775* (New York: Oxford University Press, 1962).

13. Carroll, *Religion*, 28.

14. Ibid.

15. "The Stamp Act," March 22, 1765, in Mortimer Adler, ed., *The Annals of America* (Chicago: Encyclopedia Britannica, 1968), II:143.

16. James Otis, *Rights of the British Colonists* (1764), in Smith, *Religious Origins*, 172-173.

17. Adler, *Annals*, II:158.

18. Bridenbaugh, *Mitre and Sceptre*, 230.

19. Varnum Collins, *President Witherspoon* (Princeton: Princeton University Press, 1925).

20. Adams to Jedediah Morse, December 2, 1815, in Charles Francis Adams, ed., *The Works of John Adams, Second President of the United States: With A Life of the Author*, 10 vols. (Freeport, N.Y.: Books for Libraries Press, 1969), X:185.

21. Karsten, *Patriot Heroes*, 42.

22. Bridenbaugh, *Mitre and Sceptre*. See also Bernard Bailyn, *The Ideological Origins of the American Revolution* (Cambridge, Mass.: Harvard University Press, 1967).

23. Baldwin, *New England Clergy*, 168.

24. Ibid., 171.

25. Thomas Jefferson made this claim toward the end of his life in response to Benjamin Waterhouse's query about who were the key figures responsible for American independence.

26. William Wells, *The Life and Public Services of Samuel Adams* (Boston: Little, Brown, and Company, 1865), I:10.

27. The title of his commencement thesis at Harvard was *An supremo Magistratui resistere liceat, si aliter servari Respublica nequit? Affirmat respondens Samuel Adams.* See E. L. Magoon, *Orators of the American Revolution* (New York: Scribner's, 1848), 97-98.

28. Samuel Adams, *Boston Gazette*, April 4, 1768.

29. Benjamin Hart, *Faith and Freedom: The Christian Roots of American Liberty* (Dallas: Lewis and Stanley, 1988), 254.

30. Samuel Adams, "The Rights of the Colonists" (Boston, 1772), in Adler, *Annals*, II:217.

31. Adler, *Annals*, II:218.

32. Ibid, II:217.

33. *Carolus* is Latin for Charles.

34. To this day Virginians call themselves "Cavaliers" and enjoy referring to their state as the "Old Dominion" state.

35. Benjamin Hart, *Faith and Freedom*, 261.

36. John Adams to Abigail Adams, September 16, 1774.

37. Patrick Henry, March 23, 1775, in Adler, *Annals*, II:323.

38. On the other hand, both of these men opposed a powerful federal government in 1787.

39. Magoon, *Orators of the American Revolution*, 111. The battle of Bunker Hill actually took place on Breed's Hill.

40. George Bancroft, *History of the United States, from the Discovery of the American Continent* (Boston: Little, Brown, 1857-1874).

41. William Jones, "An Address to the British Government on a Subject of Present Concern" (1776), in *The Theological, Philosophical and Miscellaneous Works of the Rev. William Jones*, 12 vols. (London: F., C., and J. Rivington, 1810), XII:356.

42. W. P. Breed, *Presbyterians and the Revolution* (Philadelphia: Presbyterian Board of Education, 1876), 49.

43. Quoted in Arthur M. Schlesinger, *The Colonial Merchants and the American Revolution, 1763-1776* (New York: Columbia University Press, 1918), 380n.

44. E.g., Joseph Galloway, *Historical and Political Reflections on the Rise and Progress of the American Rebellion*, reprint (New York: Johnson Reprint Corp., 1972 [1780]), 20. Alan Heimert, *Religion and the American Mind* (Cambridge, Mass.: Harvard University Press, 1966), 357, indicates that a handful of other Tories made the same connection.

45. Edmund S. Morgan, *The Stamp Act Crisis: Prologue to Revolution* (Chapel Hill, N.C.: University of North Carolina Press, 1953), 254.

46. Stephen Foster suggests that this quote was first uttered by John Bradshaw, the Puritan responsible for executing Charles I in 1649. See Stephen Foster, *Their Solitary Way* (New Haven, Conn.: Yale University Press, 1971), 165. Rutherford, Milton, and Sidney all expressed the same view toward tyranny as in this quote. It is often attributed to William Penn.

47. Heinrichs to Herr H. (January 18, 1778), in "Extracts from the Letter Book of Captain Johann Heinrichs of the Hessian Jager Corps, 1778-1780," *Pennsylvania Magazine of History and Biography*, 1898, 22:137.

48. Karsten, *Patriot Heroes*, 51. In Boston in 1780, one could by a portrait of "four patriots": Cromwell, Hampden, Sidney, and Hancock.

49. Heimert, *Religion and the American Mind*, 358. Cf. section 2.1.

50. Karsten, *Patriot Heroes*, 54.

51. Ibid.

52. Daniel Foster, "A Short Essay on Civil Government" (October 1774), in Heimert, *Religion and the American Mind*, 357.

53. Karsten, *Patriot Heroes*, 54.

54. Loraine Boettner, *The Reformed Doctrine of Predestination* (Philadelphia: Presbyterian and Reformed, 1972), 384.

55. Smith, *Religious Origins*, 1-2, 6. Emphasis added.

Unit Three / Chapter Nine

1. Mortimer Adler, ed., *The Annals of America* (Chicago: Encyclopedia Britannica, 1968), II:103.

2. Ibid.

3. Thomas Jefferson, *Life and Sacred Writings of Thomas Jefferson* (New York: Modern Library, 1944), 719.

4. Medford Stanton Evans, *The Theme is Freedom* (Washington, D.C.: Regnery, 1994), 228.

5. Baldwin concurs: "There is not a right asserted in the Declaration of Independence which had not been discussed by the New England Clergy before 1763." Alice M. Baldwin, *The New England Clergy and the American Revolution* (Durham: Duke University Press, 1928), 168.

6. Page Smith, *Jefferson: A Revealing Biography* (New York: McGraw-Hill, 1976), 23.

7. Imogene E. Brown, *American Aristides: A Biography of George Wythe* (Rutherford, N.J.: Fairleigh Dickinson University Press, 1981), 87.

8. Smith, *Jefferson*, 24.

9. Page Smith, *Religious Origins of the American Revolution* (Missoula, Mont.: Scholar's Press, 1976), 185.

10. Marvin Olasky, *Fighting for Liberty and Virtue: Political and Culture Wars in Eighteenth Century America* (Wheaton, Ill.: Crossway, 1995), 155.

11. On February 17, 1826 Jefferson wrote to Madison: "You will recollect that before the revolution, Coke was the universal elementary book of law students." See also Daniel J. Boorstin, *Hidden History* (New York: Harper & Rowe, 1987), 103; and Evans, *The Theme is Freedom*, 85.

12. Sir Edward Coke, *The Reports of Sir Edward Coke, Kt., Late Lord Chief Justice of England.* (London: H. Twyford, 1680), Trin. 6, Jac. 1.7, 1.

13. Thomas Jefferson to Robert Skipwith, August 3, 1771; in *The Papers of Thomas Jefferson* (Princeton: Princeton University Press), I:374-81.

14. Sir William Blackstone, *Commentaries on the Laws of England*, 4 vols. (Oxford: Clarendon Press, 1765; reprinted Buntingford, England: Layton Press, 1966), I:39.

15. Ibid., introduction, section 2.

16. John Calvin, *Institutes of the Christian Religion*, 2 volumes, John T. McNeill, ed. (Philadelphia: Westminster, 1960), IV:XX:16.

17. For the connection between "just war and natural law," see Keith L. Griffin, *Revolution and Religion: American Revolutionary War and the Reformed Clergy* (New York: Paragon House, 1994), 18.

18. See Jonathan Clark, *The Language of Liberty* (Cambridge: Cambridge University Press, 1994), 5.

19. This is largely the language of the Virginia Constitution written by George Mason. The phrase "sacred and undeniable" is Jefferson's.

20. John Locke, *An Essay Concerning Human Understanding* (New York: Dover, 1959), IV:VII:2.

21. A small qualification needs to be added here: The people in question need to be functioning normally. People who are drunk or senile or mentally ill may fail to comprehend self-evident truths.

22. The Philadelphia printing house of John Dunlap produced the official broadside copy of the Declaration of Independence for the Continental Congress. That edition, now world-renowned, used the word "unalienable" rather than "inalienable."

23. Blackstone, *Commentaries*, bk. II, chs. 19-23.

24. Evans, *The Theme is Freedom*, 239.

25. In Julian P. Boyd, ed., *The Papers of Thomas Jefferson, 1760-1776* (Princeton: Princeton University Press, 1950), I:243-247.

26. Rutherford's phrase "born equally free" is the same language found in the New Hampshire and Pennsylvania constitutions.

27. Samuel Rutherford, *Lex Rex: or, The Law and the Prince* (Harrisonburg, Va.: Sprinkle Publications, 1982 [1644]), 162.

28. Ibid.

29. Ibid., 25.

30. Ibid., 51.

31. "Individual persons, in creating a magistrate, doth not properly surrender their right, which can be called a right." Ibid., 25.

32. "Where God hath not bound the conscience, men may not bind themselves, or the consciences of the[ir] posterity." Ibid., 44.

33. Ibid., 53.

34. Ibid., 51.

35. Ibid., 82.

36. Ibid.

37. Thomas Jefferson, A *Summary View of the Rights of British America* (1774), in Adler, *Annals*, II.

38. John Winthrop, A *Defence of an Order of Court Made in the Year 1637*, in Perry Miller, ed., *The Puritans* (New York: Harper & Rowe, 1938), 200.

39. Thomas Jefferson, Declaration of Independence, in Adler, *Annals*, II.

40. Winthrop Hudson, "John Locke: Heir of Puritan Political Theorists," in George L. Hunt, ed., *Calvinism and the Political Order* (Philadelphia: Westminster Press, 1965), 108-129.

41. See Evans, *The Theme is Freedom*, 167-203.

42. Ibid., 202.

43. Howard Mumford Jones mistakenly asserts the contrary. Cf. his *Revolution and Romanticism* (Cambridge, Mass.: Harvard University Press, 1974), 156.

44. Patrick Henry, March 23, 1775, in Adler, *Annals*, II:322.

45. Thomas Jefferson and John Dickinson, "The Necessity for Taking Up Arms," in Adler, *Annals*, II:340.

46. Joseph Warren, April 26, 1775, in Adler, *Annals*, II:326.

47. Joseph Warren, "Oration Delivered at Boston, March 5, 1772," in Adler, *Annals*, II:216.

48. John F. Berens, *Providence and Patriotism in Early America: 1640-1815.* (Charlottesville, Va.: University Press of Virginia, 1974), 84.

49. Gary Amos, *Defending the Declaration* (Charlottesville, Va.: Providence Foundation, 1989), 153ff; Berens, *Providence and Patriotism*, 84.

50. Robert S. Alley, ed., *James Madison on Religious Liberty* (Buffalo: Prometheus Books, 1985), 175ff.

51. John Eidsmoe, *Christianity and the Constitution: The Faith of our Founding Fathers* (Grand Rapids, Mich.: Baker, 1987), 94.

52. James H. Smylie, "Madison and Witherspoon: Theological Roots of American Political Thought," *American Presbyterians*, 1995, 73(3):155-163.

53. Alley, *James Madison*, 112.

54. Hamilton served during the war as a staff officer under George Washington. At the battle of Yorktown, Virginia, Hamilton pleaded with Washington to let him take part in the fighting against the British. In October 1781, Hamilton and his small squad of crack colonial soldiers stormed the last heavily defended British stronghold at Yorktown. They overran it in hand-to-hand combat and forced the surrender of Lord Cornwallis. The defeat of Cornwallis was a strategic disaster for England, leading ultimately to American victory in the revolution.

55. "Due process" is a fourteenth century natural law term. See Harold Berman, *Law and Revolution: The Formation of the Western Legal Tradition* (Cambridge, Mass.: Harvard University Press, 1983).

UNIT THREE / CHAPTER TEN

1. The Act of Toleration granted all Protestant groups freedom of worship on two conditions. First, dissenters had to swear an oath of allegiance to the Crown. Second, they had to swear an oath of "conformity" to the Thirty-Nine Articles of Faith of the Church of England, renouncing the authority of the pope, and rejecting the Catholic belief in transubstantiation, as well as certain Catholic beliefs about Mary, the saints, and the mass. See Reuben Edward Alley, *A History of Baptists in Virginia* (Richmond, Va.: Virginia Baptist General Board, 1973), 34n.

2. James H. Smylie, "Madison and Witherspoon: Theological Roots of American Political Thought," *American Presbyterians*, 1995, 73(3):155-163.

3. The bill actually proposed twelve amendments. The first two were not ratified at that time. The second was ratified in 1992 and is considered the twenty-seventh amendment.

4. Jefferson, for instance, was critical of Greek and Roman culture generally (to which Renaissance and Enlightenment thinkers often appealed), even though he praised the writings of a number of Greek philosophers who urged people to lead moral lives. In a syllabus and letter to Benjamin Rush on April 21, 1803, Jefferson pointed out that even at their best, the philosophers of Greece and Rome really went no farther than explaining the importance of discipline in one's own personal life. Their outlook was insufficient for guidance on how to build the right kind of nation and social order. Jefferson observed: "In developing our duties to others, *they were short and defective*." See Jefferson's letter and syllabus to Benjamin Rush, April 21, 1803, in Thomas Jefferson, *Life and Selected Writings of Thomas Jefferson*, Adrienne Koch and William Peden, eds. (New York: Random House, 1993), 521.

5. November 19, 1776, Resolutions of the House, in Charles F. James, *Documentary History of the Struggle for Religious Liberty in Virginia* (New York: DaCapo Press, 1971), 79.

6. Ibid.

7. See *Peter Kamper vs. Mary Hawkins*, General Court of Virginia, May 23, 1793, 69-73.

8. In his autobiography, written in 1821, Thomas Jefferson refers to the role played by Edmund Pendleton and Robert Carter Nicholas: "Our great opponents were Mr. Pendleton & Robert Carter Nicholas, honest men, but zealous churchmen. The petitions were referred to the committee of the whole house on the state of the country; and after desperate contests in that committee, almost daily from the 11th of Octob. to the 5th of December, we prevailed so far only as to repeal the laws which rendered criminal the maintenance of any religious opinions, the forbearance of repairing to church, or the exercise of any mode of worship: and further, to exempt dissenters from contributions to the support of the established church; and to suspend, only until the next session levies on the members of that church for the salaries of their own incumbents. For although the majority of our citizens were dissenters, as has been observed, a majority of the legislature were churchmen." Jefferson, *Life and Selected Writings*, 40.

9. Jefferson's original unedited 1779 draft can be found online through the ACA Center for Communication Law at http://www.uark.edu/depts/comminfo/www/tj.html.

10. Jefferson had been a member of the Anglican church in Albemarle County. His pastor, Rev. Charles Clay, was a patriot. Clay resigned from the Anglican church when independence was declared. In 1777, Jefferson assisted Rev. Clay in founding a new church in Charlottesville called the Calvinistical Reformed Church. Jefferson was one of the charter organizers of the new church, and provided funds for its creation.

11. See James, *Documentary History*, 107.

12. Ibid., 218ff. Compare Lewis Peyton Little, *Imprisoned Preachers and Religious Liberty in Virginia: A Narrative Drawn Largely from the Official Records of Virginia Counties, Unpublished Manuscripts, Letters, and Other Original Sources* (Lynchburg, Va.: J. P. Bell, 1938), 480-494.

13. Code of Virginia, Title 57, Religious and Charitable Matters, Section 57-1, *Act for Religious Freedom*, January 16, 1786.

14. Most likely, Jefferson had in mind the passage from Luke 9:52-56, routinely quoted by Baptists and other dissenters as support for the position that Jesus refused to use force to compel people to believe. See note 16 below.

15. If Jefferson was referring to Jesus of Nazareth in the preamble why did he not make a more direct reference to him than the words "the Holy Author of our religion"? Who was the "Holy Author" and what was the "our religion" to which the preamble referred? The religion clearly was Christianity. Up until this time the legislature had sought to enforce Christianity by state law. Many still thought that true Christianity required state involvement. The "Holy Author" in that case would be Jesus of Nazareth. Jesus, however, had refused to use coercion to promote his message.

We must remember that Jefferson's bill was written to embody a paradigm shift—a whole new way of understanding the relationship of Christianity and society. Traditional Anglicans and traditional Presbyterians still wanted to mention the name "Jesus Christ" directly in the text of the law. They also wanted to continue to use government's power to control religious belief. The challenge before Jefferson was to embody the right principles and arguments but to do so in familiar language. If the principle of liberty was universal, the language would have to be general and less explicit. Furthermore, in previous centuries, when laws had explicitly referred to Jesus, people assumed this meant that the government had the power to outlaw all religions except Christianity, and to outlaw minority sects who disagreed with the government's version of Christianity. Jefferson wanted to write the law in a way that would clearly embody Christian principles, without implying that other religions were not equally protected under the law.

In his 1821 autobiography, Jefferson explained how the issue was finally decided: "The bill for establishing religious freedom, the principles of which had, to a certain degree, been enacted before, I had drawn in all the latitude of reason & right. It still met with opposition; but, with some mutilations in the preamble, it was finally passed; and a singular proposition proved that it's protection of opinion was meant to be universal. Where the preamble declares that coercion is a departure from the plan of the holy author of our religion, an amendment was proposed, by inserting the word "Jesus Christ," so that it should read "a departure from the plan of Jesus Christ, the holy author of our religion." The insertion was rejected by a great majority, in proof that they meant to comprehend, within the mantle of it's protection, the Jew and the Gentile, the Christian and Mahometan, the Hindoo, and infidel of every denomination." In Thomas Jefferson, *Autobiography 1743–1790*, January 6, 1821. Jefferson, *Life and Selected Writings*, 45-46.

16. Luke 9:52-56 (KJV): "And they went, and entered into a village of the Samaritans, to make ready for him. And they did not receive him.... And when his disciples James and John saw this, they said, Lord, wilt thou that we command fire to come down from heaven, and consume them, even as Elias did? But he turned, and rebuked them, and said, Ye know not what manner of spirit ye are of. For the Son of man is not come to destroy men's lives, but to save them."

202

17. "That the impious presumption of legislators and rulers, civil as well as ecclesiastical, who, being themselves by fallible and uninspired men, have assumed dominion over the faith of others, setting up their own opinions and modes of thinking as the only true and infallible." *Act for Religious Freedom*, see note 13.

18. "That to compel a man to furnish contributions of money for the propagation of opinions which he disbelieves, is sinful and tyrannical." Ibid.

19. Ibid.

20. See Madison's letter to James Monroe, November 27, 1784, in James, *Documentary History*, 129.

21. For an account of the origin of the Baptist movement in England see A. C. Underwood, *A History of the English Baptists* (London: Carey Kingsgate, 1961). The incident cited is described on page 32.

22. Underwood, *English Baptists*, 42.

23. Cited in Anne Devereaux Jordan and J. M. Stifle, *The Baptists* (Bryn Mawr, Pa.: Combined Books, 1990), 19-20.

24. Alley, *Baptists in Virginia*, 101.

25. Little, *Religious Liberty in Virginia*, 488.

26. Alley, *Baptists in Virginia*, 101.

27. In a letter and syllabus to Benjamin Rush on April 21, 1803, Jefferson pointed out that Jesus was crucified when he fell victim to "the jealousy & combination of the altar and the throne, at about 33." This choice of terminology demonstrates clearly, particularly in the context of discussing the crucifixion of Jesus, that Jefferson had a discerning appreciation for the creator-redeemer distinction, and that it provided the correct rationale for separating church (altar) and state (throne). See Jefferson, *Life and Selected Writings*, 521.

INDEX

204

Catholics, Roman, 5–6, 14–15, 17, 22, 32, 34–35, 50, 129

Cavaliers, 22

Charles I, 14, 17–18, 22–24, 26, 39, 68, 119

Charles II, 17, 28, 33, 35, 119

Charleston, 28, 119

Chauncey, Charles, 115

Church of England, 13, 15, 22, 24, 39, 67, 105, 113–114

Cicero, 78, 128

Civil War (see English Civil War)

Clark, Jonas, 120

Coke, Edward, 63, 67–68, 70–71, 129, 133

College of New Jersey, 32, 53, 55–56, 83–84, 155

College of William and Mary, 35, 70, 76, 80–81, 129

Columbia (King's College), 57, 82

Committees of Correspondence, 120

Common Law (see English Common Law)

commonwealth, 27, 44–46

compact, 37, 40, 113, 122, 127, 150

Congregationalist, 26

Connecticut, 26, 35, 40, 43–44, 81–82, 85, 90, 124, 156

Consent of the Governed, 40, 139

Continental Congress, 26, 55–56, 70, 84–85, 120–122, 129, 135, 141, 161

conviction, 65, 70, 104, 112, 157, 167

Copenhagen, 34

Copernicus, 31

Cornwallis, 85

Cotton, Josiah, 92

covenant, 24, 34, 40, 43, 57, 128, 143–146

covenant theology, 34, 128, 143

Cranmer, Archbishop of Canterbury, 15

creator-redeemer, 7–8, 12, 27–28, 43, 46, 48–49, 52, 57, 129, 159

Cromwell's Head, 124

Cromwell, Oliver, 17, 26–28, 121, 124

D

Danbury Baptist Association, 155

Daniel, 13, 107

Dartmouth, 57, 82

Davies, Samuel, 53, 56, 84

Declaration of Independence, 35, 56, 62, 70–71, 81, 83, 85, 109, 118, 120, 127–128, 134–136, 141, 155, 158

Delaware, 28, 85

Delaware River, 85

Descartes, René, 32

Dickinson, John, 136, 140

Dickinson, Jonathan, 82

Discourses Concerning Government, 34–35

Divine Providence, 133, 140–141

Divine Right of Kings, 16–17, 68

divorce, 15, 138–139

domestic abuse, 87, 90–91

Dominion of New England, 35

Duke of York (see James II)

E

Edinburgh, Scotland, 24

Edward VI, 15, 17

Elizabeth I, 15–16, 35–36

English Civil War, 21–22, 26–27, 34–35, 37, 121, 124

English Common Law, 18, 47, 61–63, 65, 67–71, 81, 90, 115, 123, 128–129, 135, 156, 159

Enlightenment, 31–33, 41, 55, 128–129, 133, 140, 147, 156

Essay on Human Understanding, 135

Evans, Medford Stanton, 41, 66, 128, 140

F

Federal Constitution, 62, 141–142, 144–145, 151, 173

Federalism, 144

Federalist Papers, 145–148

Filmer, Robert, 34

Finley, Samuel, 53

First Amendment, 25, 155–156, 173

fœdus, 143

Founders, 11, 29–30, 33–36, 44, 52, 57, 63, 65, 67–69, 71, 73–75, 77–78, 112–113, 134–135, 140–141, 144, 153, 156, 165, 173

founding, 3, 5, 7, 13, 21, 23, 37, 41, 48, 50, 57, 59, 61–62, 65, 78, 82–85, 127, 129, 140, 144, 155–156, 170, 173

Franklin, Benjamin, 11, 26, 33, 54–56, 61, 70, 84, 107

Freylinghuysen, Theodore, 53

Fundamental Orders of Connecticut, 44

G

Galileo, 31

Gambling, 63

Genesis, 47, 89

Geneva Bible, 15, 17, 104

Geneva, Switzerland, 11, 13, 15, 46–48

George II, 56, 64

George III, 14, 56, 67, 77, 82, 85, 121, 133, 137, 146

Gerry, Elbridge, 77

Glorious Revolution, 3, 17, 21, 35–37, 121, 124, 154

Goodman, Christopher, 14

Græco-Roman era, 5, 16, 68, 129

Great Awakening, 33, 52–53, 55–57, 83–84, 119

Gregory VII, 5

Griffin, Keith, 57

Grotius, Hugo, 11

H

Hale, Nathan, 83

Half-Way Covenant, 50

Halle, Germany, 53

Hamilton, Alexander, 11, 76, 85, 136, 145–146

Hampden, John, 35, 124

Hampden-Sydney College, 35

Hancock, John, 11, 77–78, 116–117, 120–121

Hanovers, 17, 114

Hartford, Connecticut, 44, 45

Harvard, 25, 32, 70, 76–78, 80–82, 84, 111, 113, 115–117, 119, 134

Harvey, William, 47

Hawthorne, Nathaniel, 107

Hebrew, 66, 75, 105–106, 143

Helwys, Thomas, 165

Henry VII (The Navigator), 14

Henry VIII, 14, 15, 17, 67

Henry, Patrick, 56, 70, 84, 119–120, 140, 142, 156

heresy, 47, 50, 82

Hodge, Charles, 59

Holy Club, 53

homosexuality, 48

Hooker, Thomas, 40, 43–44, 89

207

Presbyterianism, 22, 27, 121

Pretenders, 52

Princeton, 25–26, 32, 53, 57, 76, 81–85, 142, 155

Propaganda, 118

Prostitution, 63

protectorship, 124

Protestant Reformation, 5–7, 15, 24, 37, 39, 48, 74, 98, 104, 124, 129, 159, 162, 173

providence, 64, 141

Publius, 151

Pufendorf, Samuel, 11, 32, 111

Puritanism, 17, 27, 30, 40, 48, 77, 81, 104, 113

Puritans, 14–18, 22–24, 26–27, 34–35, 37, 39–44, 47–52, 61, 68, 73–74, 77, 83–84, 87–92, 104–106, 112–113, 119–121, 124, 128–129, 140, 143–144, 146–147, 154, 173

Q
Quaker(s), 47– 48, 154, 170

R
reason, 25, 31–33, 37, 70, 79–80, 88, 106, 122, 157, 161, 167

religion, 5, 14, 25, 27–31, 33, 46–49, 51, 53, 59, 63–64, 66, 81, 83, 113–114, 116, 122, 153–162, 164–171, 173

republicanism, 28

Resistance Theory, 13

Restoration, 17, 28

Revere, Paul, 11, 61, 118, 121

Revolution, American, 3, 14, 21, 25, 32, 34, 37, 56–57, 61, 67, 73, 76–78, 82, 84, 109, 111–112, 114–117, 121, 124, 146, 148, 168

Rhode Island, 35, 49, 164

Right of Magistrates (Beza), 13

Roanoke, 39

Robertson, Donald, 142

Roman Empire, 173

Romans, 37, 40, 130

Roundhead, 22, 24, 34–36, 124

Rousseau, 41

Runnymede, 83

Rush, Benjamin, 11, 56, 85

Rutgers, 57

Rutherford, Samuel, 11, 14, 21–24, 26, 30, 34, 36–37, 57, 113, 117, 134, 137–139

Rye House Plot, 35

S
Sabbath-Breaking, 63, 65

Salem, Massachusetts, 28, 43, 51–53, 111

salutary, 56

salutary neglect, 52

Samuel Blair, 53

Savage, James, 103

Scottish Presbyterians, 22, 23, 35

self-evident truths, 128, 134–135

separation of church and state, 49, 153–155, 158, 161–162, 165, 171, 173

Servetus, Michael, 47

Shaftesbury, 28

Sherman, Roger, 11

Sidney, Algernon, 11, 14, 33–36, 57, 70, 113, 124, 128, 134

slavery, 119, 134, 137–139, 143

Smith, Page, 3, 124

Smylie, James, 155

Smyth, John, 165

social contract theory, 13, 26, 34

Gary Amos—Co-author. Gary Amos is an Adjunct Professor in the Schools of Law and Government, Regent University; an attorney and businessman. He holds a Juris Doctor degree and a B.A. in history, pre-law, and theology. He is a member of the Bar of the Commonwealth of Virginia. In 1983 he was a charter faculty member and co-founder of the Regent University masters degree program in Public Policy. In 1985-86 he assisted in the establishment of the Regent University Law School. His publications include *Defending the Declaration* (Wolgemuth & Hyatt, 1989) and several course materials for courses in government, constitutional law and jurisprudence.

Richard Gardiner—Co-author. History Instructor, University Lake School, Hartland, Wisconsin, since 1995; Coauthor (with Donald Fuller) of "Reformed Theology at Princeton and Amsterdam in the Late Nineteenth Century," in Presbyterion, Fall 1995, 21(2):89-117; B.A. (Magna Cum Laude) University of Maryland—College Park; M.Div., Princeton Theological Seminary; History Teacher's Certification, Princeton University. While at Princeton Theological Seminary, Richard Gardiner edited *The Princeton Theological Review* and helped found the Charles Hodge Society.

212

Thomas G. West—Foreword. Thomas West is Professor of Politics at the University of Dallas and a Senior Fellow of The Claremont Institute. He is the author of *Vindicating the Founders: Race, Sex, Class, and Justice in the Origins of America* (Rowman & Littlefield, 1997). Professor West received his undergraduate training at Cornell University and holds a Ph.D. from the Claremont Graduate School. With his wife Grace Starry West, he has edited and translated *Four Texts on Socrates: Plato's Euthyphro, Apology, and Crito, and Aristophanes' Clouds* (Cornell University Press, 1984).

William A. Dembski—Academic Editor. Ph.D., Mathematics, University of Chicago; Ph.D., Philosophy, University of Illinois at Chicago; M.Div, Princeton Theological Seminary; writer, lecturer, author of *The Design Inference* (Cambridge University Press, 1998) and editor of *Mere Creation: Science, Faith, and Intelligent Design* (InverVarsity Press, 1998). Post-doctoral work at MIT, University of Chicago, Northwestern, Princeton, Cambridge, and Notre Dame. National Science Foundation doctoral and post-doctoral fellow. Publications range from mathematics (*Journal of Theoretical Probability*) to philosophy (*Nous*) to theology (*Scottish Journal of Theology*). Fellow of the Discovery Institute's Center for the Renewal of Science and Culture.

Front Cover: Union League of Philadelphia

Northwind Picture Archives: 6–7, 12, 15–16,
  22, 24–29, 32–33, 44–45, 49, 52–53,
  56–57, 62, 66–67, 70, 74–76, 80, 84, 88,
  90–92, 103, 105, 114–115, 117–120, 128,
  136–138, 144, 146–147, 155

Corbis-Bettman: 9, 14–16, 27, 34–36, 51–52,
  54–56, 58, 66, 77, 82–83, 85, 93, 98, 112,
  114, 117–118, 121, 134, 142,
  156, 158